D1564825

The Hope for American School Reform

THE HOPE FOR AMERICAN SCHOOL REFORM

THE COLD WAR PURSUIT OF INQUIRY LEARNING IN SOCIAL STUDIES

RONALD W. EVANS

palgrave
macmillan

EDUC
LB
1584
.E94
2011

THE HOPE FOR AMERICAN SCHOOL REFORM
Copyright © Ronald W. Evans, 2011.

Cover Photo:

San Francisco, Calif., April 1942. Children at the Weill Public School for the so-called international settlement, and including many Japanese-Americans, saluting the flag. They include evacuees of Japanese descent who will be housed in war relocation authority centers for the duration.

(Library of Congress, Flag_salute_3a19329u, Library of Congress Prints and Photographs Division)

First published in 2011 by
PALGRAVE MACMILLAN®
in the United States – a division of St. Martin's Press LLC,
175 Fifth Avenue, New York, NY 10010.

Where this book is distributed in the UK, Europe and the rest of the world, this is by Palgrave Macmillan, a division of Macmillan Publishers Limited, registered in England, company number 785998, of Houndmills, Basingstoke, Hampshire RG21 6XS.

Palgrave Macmillan is the global academic imprint of the above companies and has companies and representatives throughout the world.

Palgrave® and Macmillan® are registered trademarks in the United States, the United Kingdom, Europe and other countries.

ISBN: 978–0–230–10797–7

Library of Congress Cataloging-in-Publication Data

Evans, Ronald W.
    The hope for American school reform : the Cold War pursuit of inquiry learning in social studies / Ronald W. Evans.
        p. cm.
    ISBN 978–0–230–10797–7 (alk. paper)
    1. Social sciences—Study and teaching—United States—History—20th century.
2. Cold War—Influence.   3. Critical thinking.   4. Educational change—United States.   I. Title.
    LB1584.E94 2011
    300.71'073—dc22

                                                                                              2010027716

A catalogue record of the book is available from the British Library.

Design by MPS Limited, A Macmillan Company

First edition: January 2011

11 10 9 8 7 6 5 4 3 2 1

Printed in the United States of America.

This book is dedicated to Dan Selakovich, my earliest mentor, who introduced me to the new social studies and gave me my first opportunity to teach at a university

CONTENTS

GALLERY

ACKNOWLEDGMENTS

As I send this book to press, I would like to acknowledge all of the people who made contributions to this project. First, the work could not have been completed without the helpful assistance of many archivists and the access to materials they provided. I would like to express my deep gratitude to: Jennie Benford at Carnegie Mellon University Archives; Nora Murphy of the Massachusetts Institute of Technology Archives; David Ment at Milbank Memorial Library and Archives at Teachers College, Columbia University; Janice Goldblum at the National Academy of Sciences Archives; Sharon Kelly of the John F. Kennedy Presidential Library; Alan Walker at the National Archives in College Park, Maryland; and the reference staff at Harvard University Archives. I thank the many archivists and support staff at each of these institutions and elsewhere who endured my endless requests, helped locate materials, and offered many wise suggestions. I would particularly like to acknowledge the helpful assistance of Alan Walker at the National Archives Civilian Record Unit, who guided me to many helpful materials, and Peter Dow, who gave me full access to the Education Development Center (EDC) materials while they were in his care. Both were extremely helpful.

I would also like to acknowledge the assistance of several archivists who supplied photographs and permissions including Bryan Whitledge and William Maher of the University of Illinois Archives; Scott Prouty of the Emilio Segre Visual Archive of the American Institute of Physics; David A. Flagg of the National Science Foundation; Darryl Baker and Michael Mohl of Navsource.org; Susan F. Witzell of the Woods Hole Historical Museum; Diana Carey of the Schelsinger Library at Radcliffe Institute, Harvard University; Maureen O'Brien of Dedham Civic Pride; Jennie Benford of Carnegie-Mellon University Archives; Jill Anderson, News Officer of the Harvard Graduate School of Education and photographer Martha Stewart. Pauline Oliver of Lexington, Massachusetts; Fred M. Newmann of Madison, Wisconsin; and Joe Wrinn and Stephanie Mitchell of the Harvard Office of Public Affairs and Communication.

I would also like to thank Jerome Bruner, Peter Dow, and Ted Fenton for generously agreeing to interviews, and for their many helpful insights. As key leaders of in the new social studies, nothing could substitute for meeting them in person and hearing their stories and answers to my questions. I found each extremely generous with time, resources, memories, and perspectives. In each case, my visit was a memorable experience. I am very appreciative.

My colleagues at San Diego State University have been very supportive of my research for many years, and of this project as well. I received consistent and invaluable support in the form of research-assigned time, small grants to fund archival visits, and a sabbatical leave, which provided ample time for writing. I would especially like to thank David Strom and Nancy Farnan for their support and encouragement. I would also like to acknowledge the support I received from countless other colleagues and staff, and the steadfast assistance of John Rizzo, Marc Pastor, Jim Edwards, and Ricardo Fitipaldi at Instructional Technology Services.

Several colleagues provided thoughtful comments on various portions of this work, or offered helpful comments and resources. I would especially like to thank Geoff Scheurman, Barbara Slater-Stern, Gregg Jorgensen, Barry Franklin, Catherine Broom, Lynn Burlbaw, and Jared Stallones. The pathbreaking work of several other scholars contributed in laying a strong foundation for this work, notably books by Peter Dow and John Rudolph. I would like to thank Gene Maeroff, William Reese, and John Rudolph for their wise counsel as I negotiated the path to publication. I would also like to express my gratitude to my colleagues in the Issues-Centered Education Community of the National Council for the Social Studies for their friendship and support. I would especially like to thank Gregg Jorgensen for his help with the index. I would also like to thank Dave Spierman, Andrew Ferrier, Jack Goldberg, Jon Wreschinsky, Kevin Riley, and Michael Shaffran for their generous and careful help with proofreading. While many others contributed to the work, I take full responsibility for any errors or omissions.

I would also like to acknowledge the support of family and friends who put up with this preoccupation over many years and offered encouragement as well as supportive questions and comments. I would especially like to thank my wife Mika, and my children, Kathryn, Mira, and Kai who have patiently endured many rambling discussions of this project, with special thanks to Katie for help with several photos. I would also like to express my appreciation to my men's support group and the Men's Fellowship of the First Unitarian Universalist Church of San Diego for listening to me talk at length about this project and offering their generous and unflagging support.

The research project behind this book aimed to cover the entire era of social studies curriculum reform from its inception in the 1950s through its undoing in the late 1970s. Because the initial draft was quite lengthy, my editor at Palgrave Macmillan asked whether I had considered breaking the work into two volumes. This, the first volume, examines the origins and development of the reform, the projects, and reactions from academics through the early 1970s. The second volume, *The Tragedy of American School Reform: How Curriculum Politics and Entrenched Dilemmas Have Diverted Us from Democracy*, examines changes in the direction of reform from the late 1960s through the 1970s, and the academic freedom battles and entrenched dilemmas that brought the era of the new social studies to a close. I will be forever grateful to my editor at Palgrave, Burke Gerstenschlager, and editorial assistant Samantha Hasey, for the opportunity to publish my full treatment of the topic and for their efforts to help bring the project to completion.

Ronald W. Evans
San Diego, California

PERSISTENT DILEMMAS OF CURRICULUM IMPROVEMENT

IT WAS AN INTERESTING time. As a child of the fifties, my recollections of the 1950s, 1960s, and 1970s, and of the time I spent in schools remain strong. The drama and turmoil of the period remain vivid in my memory: the assassinations, the riots, the marches and civil rights actions, the war, and the antiwar movement, all viewed through the media but mediated by friends, family, location, and personal experience. However, the strands of social studies reform detailed in this volume were largely missing from my own schooling. We seldom studied or discussed the issues of the time. Nor did we examine disciplinary knowledge through the lens of "doing" what historians and social scientists did. Mostly, the classes I had in history and the social sciences were taught in a traditional manner, dominated by teacher and text. As we shall see, despite an unprecedented attempt to improve teaching and learning in social studies, most children of the period had an experience similar to my own. In part, I have written this volume in an attempt to understand what I missed, and why I missed it.

The school reforms of the 1960s were far from the first attempt to transform schools. The efforts of the progressive era, and subsequent sidetracks, had tried and largely failed in their quest to transform the school from an institution of traditional learning to a dynamic center of interest and growth for all children. For our story, the important note is that the progressive era reforms were created and funded largely from outside the matrix of government, and were directed primarily by scholars in schools of education along with school administrators and teachers. The story of efforts to reform the American school began to change and emerge into its present form during the 1950s and 1960s, driven by collaboration among big science, government, business, and prestigious universities, with little attention to the history or social context of schooling. Though the seeds of reform were present prior to the cold war era, it was during that period that fears over Soviet manpower development led our government, via the National Science Foundation and other agencies, to fund large-scale school reform efforts for the first time, motivated by the highest purposes of science and learning, but funded and driven largely by a perceived threat to our national security and the goal of maintaining technological superiority. This occurred, it is important to point out, during a period when the United States enjoyed unprecedented global prestige and respect: the United States was the world's first superpower and held a nuclear monopoly, then strategic dominance, during much of the era. So, the reforms were partially guided by a vision of omnipotence inspired by the period of U.S. nuclear and technological hegemony following World War II.[1]

Ironically, this effort at American education reform was beset by specific problems stemming, in part, from its origins. Though the reformers faced what were likely to be insurmountable obstacles, in their self-assurance and general ignorance of the history and social context of schooling, they largely ignored those obstacles and proceeded as if the schools would naturally welcome their efforts for change. Despite this flaw, the curricular materials created during the period remain among the most interesting and educational in existence, a treasure trove for teachers who are willing to mine it.[2]

The school reforms that emerged in math and science gradually broadened to include the social sciences, the humanities, and other areas. Though the reforms were well intended, their fate was determined partly by their origins in cold war conflict, by the seeds of their growth within the context of the military-industrial-academic complex, and by the general failure of the reformers to situate their initiatives within what had long been an effort among educators to develop a vision of school and society that would further the ends of democracy. Instead, education for democratic purposes was largely submerged in a reform initiated by insiders in science, government, and academia who sought to reform the schools in their own image, bereft of a compelling social vision. They focused on meeting a perceived threat without full consideration of alternative possibilities and purposes, and without due consideration of how the reforms they envisioned might best be institutionalized in schools. What resulted led to efforts to makeover the classroom into something like a minor league extension of the research university, much as more recent reform efforts have sought to transform schools into an extension of the business world.

THE PROBLEM

Observers of the social studies field have witnessed several major attempts at reform over the years. The central, long-term problem posed by the social studies curriculum is centered on the difficulty of reform or improvement. More than perhaps any other curricular area, the field of social studies is constrained by curriculum politics, seared by conflict. The rhetoric of the social studies arena is composed of multiple theories and interest groups, each vying to influence the future of the field. The major competing camps, as I describe them in a recent book, *The Social Studies Wars*, struggling at different times to either retain control of social studies or to influence its direction include traditional historians, who support history as the core of social studies; social scientists, advocates of social science inquiry as the main focus of student activity; social efficiency educators, who hope to create a smoothly controlled and more efficient society; social meliorists, Deweyan experimentalists who want to develop students' reflective thinking and contribute to social improvement; and social reconstructionists, who cast social studies in schools in a leading role in the transformation of American society. Finally, consensus and eclectic camps include advocates of a general approach in which the term "social studies" serves as an umbrella, that is, social studies is history and the social sciences simplified, integrated, and adapted for pedagogical purposes, as well as those who choose to meld major aspects of more than one tradition.[3] During the era of the new social studies in the 1960s and 1970s, social science inquiry received its greatest boost. Fast on its heels, during the period of the newer social studies, a new and revitalized progressivism emerged. By the mid-1970s and beyond, traditional history and social efficiency interest groups reasserted their dominance. Through it all, the field was limited by institutional and cultural obstacles to change, barriers that I will refer to as the grammar of social studies.

In an ideal world, the schools would serve as a church of reason, developing in students not only basic skills and knowledge, but a critical facility and broad understanding of the social world, its competing influences and interests, and entrée to a host of issues and questions. Walter Parker summarized this forward-looking notion and its implications in the introduction to a recent book:

> Social studies is at the center of a good school curriculum because it is where students learn to see and interpret the world—its peoples, places, cultures, systems, and problems; its dreams and calamities—now and long ago. In social studies lessons and units of study, students don't simply experience the world (they always do anyway, in school and out), but are helped systematically to understand it, to care for it, to think deeply and

critically about it, and to take their place on the public stage, standing on equal footing with others. This, at any rate, is the goal.

It matters, for without social understanding, there can be no wisdom. Good judgment has always relied on the long view—historical under-standing—involving long-term thinking and long-term responsibility alongside intimate knowledge of particulars. So it is with the other social literacies: without geographic understanding, there can be no cultural or environmental intelligence; without economic understanding, no sane use of resources; without political understanding, no "we the people"; and without these in combination, no inventive, collaborative work on building a just and sustainable society, both locally and globally.[4]

However, the world we live in is far from ideal. Instead of serving as a church of reason, schools function primarily as an institution of social authority, efficiency, and cultural transmission.

This history of the new social studies is a case study of an era, examining issues related to purposes and practices in education. As such, it raises several broad questions pertinent to our understanding of social studies and of schools as institutions:

- Who controls the schools? To what ends?
- Whose interests are served? Who benefits?
- To what extent is schooling an arm of the state? Controlled by government, science, business, or some other influence?
- To what extent do schools serve the people and the democratic impulse?
- How does social studies function in schools? To what ends?
- Can we reform social studies to enhance the level of meaningful learning?

From its origins, the new social studies was an establishment turn, driven by national security and manpower concerns, its essence rooted in cold war fears. Despite, and perhaps because of, its origins, the founders of the reform and the projects they directed contributed powerful, inquiry-oriented theories and materials that made a strong contribution. With the advent of the newer social studies in the late 1960s, addressed in the second volume of this work, the direction of reform took a progressive, even revolutionary turn, driven by conflict, hope, and the human potential movements of the period. In its aftermath, a counterrevolution emerged and both movements for reform were censured by a powerful coalition of neoconservatives, the new right, and ultraconservative evangelicals who wanted to turn back the clock on the people's revolutions of the 1960s. Meanwhile, as they played out in schools, these movements for reform were stifled by the grammar of social studies, the persistent patterns of classroom instruction and the institutional constraints that seem to deflect most efforts at reform.[5]

One paradox of this remarkable era, among many, is that it was driven by purposes linked to national security, cold war fears and propaganda, and run by scholars in various disciplines who often lacked knowledge of previous efforts at school reform, with little understanding of educational purposes and practices, and even less cognizance of the ways of schools as an institution. The reformers, scholars at Harvard, MIT, and other leading research universities, represented the elite educational wing of a vision of omnipotence inspired by an era of nuclear and technological dominance. The reform model they crafted was heavily top-down, and assumed that reformers knew what was best for schools. Most shared a disdain for "educationists" and chose to bypass the educational establishment, education professors, and certification agencies, in implementing the reform. The combination of heady self-assurance and a technological, systems approach to reform assumed that new and innovative materials for instruction would lead to a transformation in teaching practices. The reformers badly underestimated the grammar of social studies, the persistence of traditional practices, the focus on content coverage and control of students mandated by school authorities, and the cultural danger of exceeding local limitations on what kinds of questions schools could raise.

Ironically, despite its origins, its adherents developed some of the most remarkable social studies materials ever created. But the implementation of their ideas and materials were seriously compromised by their lack of knowledge of schools. Reformers applied the ideas and techniques of big science, which had served the nation so well in wartime applications, to educational reform. From a perch at the apex of the military-industrial-academic complex, they applied a technological systems approach to reforming schools that took too little account of the culture and history of schooling. Big business, its apparatus and propaganda machine, also made significant contributions in support of the discipline-based reforms of the period. Ironically, through its funding of conservative foundations and advocacy groups in the 1970s and later, business also played a major role in the conservative restoration, which took the field in yet another direction.

In the end, the new social studies was to have a notable lack of impact. Despite such a high level of research and development activity, there was little lasting change. And, unfortunately, the aftermath of the era, described in the second volume, led to a great deal of influence for forces that supported the reinstitution of more traditional forms of education. As this study demonstrates, schools are highly permeable institutions. Reforms are driven largely by forces outside the classroom and school; deflected, mediated, or partially incorporated into the ways schools operate. From studying the era of the new social studies in depth we can learn a great deal about a massive and unprecedented attempt at social studies reform that remains relevant to our current situation. Hopefully, this study can help lead to a better understanding of the essential contours of a remarkable era, offer a healthy counterpoint to current accountability measures, provide historical perspective on the possibilities and dilemmas of school reform, and contribute to the continuing effort to improve social studies instruction in schools.

PART I

THE COLD WAR ORIGINS OF CURRICULUM REFORM

CHAPTER 1

CULTURE WAR OVER THE SCHOOLS

THE NEW SOCIAL STUDIES CAME into being during the 1960s, but was, for the most part, a product of the 1950s' confluence of the cold war struggle against communism and mounting criticisms of progressive education. In this context, as we shall see, the new social studies was born of cold war manpower development concerns and as a carryover from developments in science and mathematics. At root, it grew from national security anxieties that were linked to schooling in the context of a cold war struggle for survival. Largely discipline-centered, the social studies projects of the era, which received unprecedented federal and private financial support, were a direct outgrowth of the criticism of progressive education and of progressive social studies that had been brewing for decades. In a very real sense, this was an extension of the war on social studies and a culmination of decades of criticism. Attacks on social studies had been building from at least the 1930s, with many of the same charges repeated again and again.

In a recent book, I argued that controversies over the social studies curriculum developed in a sequential pattern, becoming broader and more damaging to progressive social studies as the years went on. Three major episodes of controversy preceded the era of the new social studies. They were the Rugg textbook controversy, which spanned 1939–1942, the controversy over American history, 1942–1944, and the controversy over progressive education, 1947–1958. As I argued previously, these three controversies were instrumental in the eventual evolution of the era of the new social studies, and were a strong reflection of the historical context.[1] These controversies combined to stir the passions of educational critics of various stripes, but especially those who wanted a stronger focus on the disciplines and a traditional view of the American way. In the postwar era, the controversy would spread to encompass all of progressive education.

If World War II signaled the coming death throes of progressive social studies, the cold war completed the act. During the last half of the 1940s and through the 1950s social studies was one of the prime targets during a deluge of attacks on progressive education. The tone of the Rugg and Nevins controversies, along with many specific charges, were reiterated, and quite stridently. The postwar era was a time of conformity, of economic prosperity and expansion, and a time during which American power around the globe was rivaled only by that of the Soviet Union. That competition, the ideological struggle involving two industrial behemoths and their opposing worldviews, capitalism and communism, set a tone for the entire era. It was an atmosphere of confrontation, secrecy, and self-righteousness, which established a pattern of attacks on academic freedom and autonomy of speech and thought that impacted schools and society like never before. The red scares of the 1920s and 1930s had similar effect, though they wielded little influence over the direction of the curriculum. In the postwar era, a chill settled over discussion of controversial issues and, by the late 1950s, the pendulum in education had swung so that government set a course to insure an academic curriculum emphasizing disciplinary knowledge.

The work of educational historian Clarence Karier suggests that it is impossible to understand the curriculum changes of the mid-twentieth century without understanding the profound impact of the cold war. "More than any other single phenomenon," Karier argues, "it was the cold war which profoundly shaped America's political, economic, and educational institutions for the next four decades."[2]

Karier locates the end of progressivism in the combined impact of the atomic age and the holocaust. Both led to an era of innocence and hopefulness lost. The red scare and McCarthyism of the cold war era set the tone, and "the future of western civilization was now open to question." Faith in the "idea of progress, grounded in science, reason, education, and freedom . . . became seriously open to question in 1945," because of the horrors of the holocaust and the atomic bomb. "Men and women did not appear as rational as once thought, the state as a vehicle for social meliorism was . . . more problematic and public education was not proving to be the workable panacea" that had been hoped.[3] World War II was a "fundamental break." After the war, the United States passed into a "post" culture. This shift, away from the idea of progress, brought the death of a main source of inspiration for progressive social studies. It was a similar mentality that gave rise to the rootlessness and questioning of modernism by beat generation writers and poets such as

Allen Ginsberg and Jack Kerouac. Their themes provide an alternative window on the times.

CONTEXT OF REFORM

The United States emerged from World War II as an industrial giant and as the unquestioned world leader. During the cold war years its new leadership would be challenged by the USSR and its alternative ideology and political and economic systems. The curriculum reform movement that emerged was driven by fears of a perceived external threat. It was led by an elite, that is, leading figures in the military-industrial-academic complex whose positions inside powerful academic and governmental institutions seemingly encouraged them to develop a vision of omnipotence, a belief that their power over science and technology could seamlessly extend to the reform of education. After all, the schools were largely in the hands of incompetent "educationists;" or so many believed. The reform movement they would instigate in science and math soon would spread to social studies, promising a new and exciting approach to the field.

In a very real sense, the curriculum reform movement grew out of the alliance between "big science at the service of big government" to develop new military technology for winning World War II. Big science involved interdisciplinary teams of researchers who marshaled both scientific and engineering expertise on goal-directed projects of national political and social significance. That alliance resulted in the wartime development of a variety of new weapons and technologies that culminated in the use of atomic bombs on Hiroshima and Nagasaki. The cold war extended the partnership between the military and scientists into peacetime and became the epitome of what many radicals called "the permanent war economy." Driven by economic, political, and national security interests, the interests of empire, and backed by the establishment, money poured into the university.[4] Spurred by cold war and growth, the state became the major patron of the academy. Along with growth in the number of universities, students, and degrees awarded, the cold war era saw tremendous growth in federal funds devoted to research and development. All this was part of the postwar boom and linked to America's rise to global power.

There were other important trends as well. According to the Educational Press Association, the outstanding educational events of 1947 included new and increased funding appropriations to raise teacher salaries, recommendations for compulsory military training for youth, county-by-county law suits in Virginia challenging racial segregation, creation of the National Commission on Life Adjustment for Youth because "most of the secondary school courses [were] obsolete and [did] not serve the needs of present-day pupils," and absorption of 2,338,226 students into colleges and universities, the "largest flood of college students in the history of any nation." At about the same time, at least one observer noticed the trend toward "anonymity of the individual" brought by industrialization and the machine age. For most people, he wrote, cultural continuity had been broken," upset in the abrupt emergence of mechanization" so the individual felt that "he was a machine himself."[5]

This was a period of dramatic growth for the nation. In the years immediately following the end of World War II, returning GIs fueled a postwar boom that lasted through most of the era. The "baby boom" was a time of unprecedented growth for the nation and its schools. This brought increased public attention to the schools, and heightened scrutiny. Moreover, the nation had just begun to live with the presence of nuclear weapons, after the dropping of atomic bombs on Japan that brought the war to a close. Their very existence changed the way people thought about the future because the possibility of their use cast doubt upon continued survival. The deepening conflict with the Soviet Union highlighted the growing and very real possibility of thermonuclear conflagration and cast a shadow of anxiety across the land. Some of that anxiety undoubtedly found release in criticism and concern over schools.[6]

The conflict evolved into a period of provocative rhetoric, a war of words and deeds. In the spring of 1950, President Truman declared that "[t]he cause of freedom" was being challenged like never before by "forces of imperialistic communism." It was, he argued, a "struggle for the minds of men."[7] The cold war was, in its essence, a conflict between American democracy and its capitalist economy, and Soviet totalitarianism. It was a conflict between truth and propaganda in the eyes of many Americans, though as we shall see, both sides were prone to excess.

Amid this worldwide ideological battle, criticism of schooling, and the curriculum, opened the door to reform. The heightened ideological context created fertile ground for the redirection of material concerns over school buildings, overcrowding, and shortages brought by the baby boom, and led to a focus on perceived curricular and instructional failures. The cold war struggle led to calls for increased rigor to compete with the Soviet Union and to uphold and strengthen democracy and the free market capitalist economy. Critics found an easy target in Life-Adjustment Education (LAE) that was focused partly on socializing students and seemed faintly collectivist and somehow related to Soviet totalitarianism.

The crisis in schools grew out of a number of conditions. One of the most important was the fact of overwhelming numbers as returning

GIs began families and swelled the ranks of entering students. By the fall of 1953, first grade enrollment increased by 34 percent. During the boom, the educational infrastructure would be strained beyond capacity. A report that appeared in *U.S. News* stated that three-quarter of a million new classrooms were needed to meet the growing demand. In many suburbs, where the growth was most pronounced, students attended classes in tents and local churches, and frequently shared textbooks and supplies. The dramatic growth in numbers led to a teacher shortage during which districts often hired unqualified applicants. Horror stories circulated of children taught by busboys and cabdrivers, rather than qualified teachers. The *New York Times* ran a series of articles on education authored by Benjamin Fine, which became an annual fixture.[8]

The "crisis" and shortages led to a National Education Association (NEA) push for Federal assistance in the form of an aid bill in 1950 that died in the House Education and Labor Committee, after having passed the Senate. The bill was stopped over opposition to federal "infringement" on the system of "local control" of education. Opposition was especially strong in the South, where local control was sometimes a euphemism used to perpetuate racial segregation. Following defeat of the aid bill, local school districts raised taxes and passed bond measures to fund growth. Almost overnight, citizens' groups sprang up to oppose taxes, and their criticisms extended to other aspects of schooling, including the curriculum and teaching methods.[9] This helped spawn a period of unprecedented criticism of schooling.

Another important aspect of the period that would have a profound effect in shaping the direction of school reform was the fear of subversion wrought by ideological conflict and turmoil. American foreign policy operated on the assumption that the Soviets were expansionist and aimed to convert the world to communism through a monolithic conspiracy bent on global domination. International events provided evidence of communist expansionism (Czechoslovakia, 1948; Berlin, 1948; the 1949 Soviet detonation of an atomic bomb; the control of China by Mao and the Red Army). During 1950 there was continual media attention to communist uprisings, along with a questioning of American resolve to resist communist expansion. Combined with the end of the U.S. nuclear monopoly, there was a sense that the nation was losing control. These perceived "failures" and international setbacks led critics to look behind events to find the root cause of these new challenges to U.S. status and the vision of omnipotence it had spawned.

In retrospect, 1949 was a turning point, after which many Americans believed that the problem must lie within the United States. This looking within for answers was a reflection of fears spawned by a spiral of world events and perceived threats that made conflict with the Soviet Union seem inevitable. It led to a growing red scare that would have a profound effect on American life for years to come.

In perhaps its most public manifestation, the red scare led to charges of espionage and gave ready justification for purges of "communists" and communist sympathizers. In January 1950, the Alger Hiss case involved a former State Department employee convicted of passing government documents to the Soviets. The same year, Klaus Fuchs, a British scientist who had helped with the Manhattan project, was arrested in a similar case. And, in 1953, Julius and Ethel Rosenberg were executed for conspiracy to commit espionage, after being convicted on charges related to passing information about the atomic bomb to the Soviet Union. With the invasion of South Korea, the red scare had intensified, and the cold war penetrated deep into American culture as self-styled "patriots" went after their countrymen.[10]

Members of the academic community were far from united against the purge. While some fought hard against any restriction on freedom, others developed arguments against communists being allowed to teach in schools and colleges. Many sought political cover by identifying communist colleagues in the name of academic integrity and national security. The argument had two parts. First, the communist party was a conspiracy using unethical means to gain power. Membership meant strict adherence to the party line. This meant that faith in communism stood in the way of free inquiry. Sidney Hook, chair of the New York University Philosophy Department, was probably the most prominent apologist. His arguments explaining the incompatibility of scholarship and party membership provided scholarly justification for the expulsion of communist teachers and contributed an air of legitimacy to the witch hunt that was underway.[11]

As they had during the Rugg controversy, patriotic critics targeted textbooks, school materials, and school personnel. In a well publicized case in Pasadena, a group of citizens led a successful attack on a progressive school superintendent.[12] The American Legion revived its attack on progressive education, publishing an article in *The American Legion Magazine* titled "Your Child Is Their Target," reprising allegations made during the Rugg controversy and critiquing the educational establishment for indoctrinating children.[13] Though it is difficult to quantify the day-to-day effect of all this on schools, it undoubtedly cast a chill and limited free expression by many teachers, whose tendency toward self-censorship was heightened. Nonetheless, evidence on public attitudes toward the schools in two communities in the Chicago area suggested that despite all the sound and fury, only 2 percent of parents were dissatisfied with the schooling of their children.[14]

ATTACKS ON PROGRESSIVE EDUCATION

During the late 1940s and early 1950s a growing upsurge of attacks on progressive education materialized. To some extent, the attacks were a reflection of the baby boom and a growth spurt in school population. With growth and change, battles over what to teach might be expected, as a growing number of Americans had children in school.[15] The battles might also be viewed as a part of a culture war, an extension of earlier struggles, and a continuation of attacks on progressive education. The deluge of articles and books attacking progressive education began in 1949 and peaked in 1953. The attacks came in several strands, sometimes woven together. The first strand of attack was the intellectual, best symbolized by Arthur Bestor, a historian and leading critic of anti-intellectualism in education. The second strand, red-baiting attacks, grew from the ideological conflict of the era, from those who viewed progressive education as a socialist plot. The third strand attacked the public funding of mass education. Each of these was conditioned by and articulated against the urgent backdrop of cold war crisis. In social studies, and on education generally, the impact of these attacks was to impose a chill, an atmosphere of restraint, censorship, and self-censorship. The attacks also precipitated a trend toward conformity in the curriculum, toward discipline-based subjects, toward a denatured form of inquiry, and away from modern problems and anything in the curriculum that represented a critical attitude toward society.

The intellectual critique of progressive education came from university professors and journalists. Detractors alleged that the curriculum in schools was soft, anti-intellectual, and lacked rigor when compared with schools in Europe and the USSR. Among the most respected critics were Robert Hutchins, Mortimer Smith, Albert Lynd, Arthur Bestor, and Paul Woodring. For several years, beginning in the late 1940s, the number of books and articles addressing the "crisis" in education was on the rise. The first major book containing the core of the intellectual critique was *And Madly Teach*, published by Mortimer Smith in 1949. Smith, who was a former school board member, charged that the progressive philosophy of education was undemocratic and anti-intellectual because it failed to "adhere to any standards of knowledge" and abandoned the concept of enlightening every child with humanity's wisdom by embracing "utilitarian how-to courses." Furthermore, he wrote that the emphasis on adjusting the individual to society eroded individual freedom and embellished the power of bureaucratic control.[16]

Following publication of Smith's book, the pages of popular magazines filled with articles on the new "crisis" in education, with articles focused on "life-adjustment" and other "sins" of progressives. In 1953 no less than four noteworthy books were published critically appraising progressive education. These included Robert Hutchins' *The Conflict in Education in a Democratic Society*, Albert Lynd's *Quackery in the Public Schools*, Arthur Bestor's *Educational Wastelands*, and Paul Woodring's *Let's Talk Sense About Our Schools*. Among these, Bestor's assessment was by far the most widely read.

Albert Lynd, a former teacher and a businessman, made schools of education the bogey, and charged that professors of education, whom he characterized as "mental lightweights," had rigged a system to control the schools through pay raises for continued credits in education. Basing his analysis on course catalogues from Teachers College, Columbia University, and similar institutions, he charged the programs with "unbelievable inflation of repetitious trivia," and teachers with "filling the public schools with hocus-pocus."[17] In his book he traced the poor performance of "the new education" to the work of John Dewey. Paul Woodring, a professor of education at Western Washington University, was fundamentally critical of progressive education in *Let's Talk Sense About Our Schools*, yet he stated his criticisms in a more palatable tone. He took educators to task for failing to meet criticisms honestly, and speculated that education was moving past progressivism.

Arthur Bestor, who became the leading intellectual critic of education, argued that modern education had become anti-intellectual, a critique that was in general agreement with Lynd and much of the accumulated criticism. In his book, *Educational Wastelands: The Retreat from Learning in Our Public Schools*, Bestor made it clear that he wanted an old style progressive education marked by respect for the disciplines and the primacy of intellectual values. He charged that a conspiracy existed among "professional educationists," and saw an "interlocking directorate" of progressive leaders as an obstacle to reform. Their techniques, he argued, serve as "a narcotic to kill the pain of thinking." He also suggested that educators abolish the term "social studies."[18] For Bestor and many other critics of progressive education, their criticism was rooted in dissatisfaction with Prosser's life-adjustment movement and the perceived anti-intellectual stance of American educators, with which social studies was identified.

Bestor, a respected historian at the University of Illinois, charged in his books and articles that educators had "undermined public confidence in the schools" by concentrating on trivial purposes and by "deliberately divorcing the schools from the disciplines of science and scholarship." Bestor posited that the schools' chief purpose was to train "the power to think," and argued for reinstatement of "the ideal of liberal education."[19] Ironically, the power to think was the same general purpose held by Dewey and the moderate, mainstream progressives. Bestor argued that the decline of liberal education endangered the national security and the well-being of our democratic institutions. He made a strong case for the primacy of intellectual education in "the scholarly and scientific disciplines" that represented, he wrote, "the most effective methods men have been able to devise . . . for liberating and then organizing the powers of the human mind."[20] The test of an educational program was the extent to which "it trains a man to think for himself and at the same time to think painstakingly." He argued, "The disciplined mind is what education at every level should strive to produce."[21] In the interest of creating the disciplined mind, he made a case for the academic disciplines as the core of the curriculum, and for history as the core of social studies.

Bestor's solution for the failings of American education was firmly grounded in the tradition of liberal arts education, in traditional subject matter such as history, literature, and languages, taught to give students the "cultural values of a nation," rather than for any utilitarian or functional reasons. His most important argument centered on the role of disciplined inquiry. In Bestor's words, the disciplines "must be presented . . . as systematic ways of thinking, each with an organized structure and methodology of its own." He explained, "The liberal disciplines are not chunks of frozen fact. They are not facts at all . . . [but] the most effective methods which men have been able to devise, through millennia of sustained effort, for liberating and then organizing the powers of the human mind." This could be achieved, Bestor argued, by students learning "the inner structure and logic" of the disciplines.[22]

As a historian, Bestor had few kind words for social studies, and urged the elimination of the term and a return to history. Ignoring actual practice in schools, which was largely organized chronologically and favored history as the dominant discipline, Bestor argued for the "logical organization of knowledge," and stressed that for history, "the essential thing is to comprehend the forces that are at work through a long sequence of events, and to incorporate the perspective of time into one's day to day judgments."[23] As for the study of contemporary problems, he wrote, "The study of what is near at hand and familiar—the study of contemporary problems, for example—is an easy door. But it must be, not a door into a dull miscellany and lumber-room, but a door opening outward upon the universe of human endeavor and natural process."[24]

Bestor considered himself a liberal and favored the earlier form of progressive education that he had experienced as a student at the Lincoln School at Teachers College. His teachers, he wrote, brought "the teaching of the basic disciplines to the highest perfection possible in the light of modern pedagogy. They did so by emphasizing the relevance of knowledge and intellectual skill to the problems of practical life and citizenship." Yet, he was critical of at least one aspect of his progressive early education, and wrote:

> Alongside excellent instruction in history, a course in the "social studies" was introduced. Subsequent work of my own in several of the fields supposedly embraced within this course has merely confirmed the opinion which my classmates and I entertained at the time. I remember being struck at the outset by the inferiority of this hodgepodge to the straightforward treatment of great public issues that I had learned to expect from my instructors in history. The "social studies" purported to throw light on contemporary problems, but the course signally failed, for it offered no perspective on the issues it raised, no basis for careful analysis, no encouragement to ordered thinking. There was plenty of discussion, but it was hardly responsible discussion. Quick and superficial opinions, not balanced and critical judgment, were at a premium. Freedom to think was elbowed aside by freedom not to think, and undisguised indoctrination loomed ahead. I am surprised at how accurately we as students appraised the course. I cannot now improve on the nickname we gave it at the time: "social stew."[25]

Bestor went on to suggest that the creation of social studies and "the more destructive programs that ensued" marked a turning point. Progressive education became "regressive," he wrote, because it began to undermine the "great traditions of liberal education" and to substitute "lesser aims, confused aims, or no aims at all."[26]

Bestor also challenged the progressive tendency toward a differentiated education and ability grouping as undemocratic, the tendency to dilute and integrate the disciplines as unsound and anti-intellectual, and the disappearance of classical and modern foreign languages from the schools as a decline in standards. Though he agreed that courses in pedagogy were necessary, he offered a mean-spirited critique of teacher training colleges for trivial and anti-intellectual courses and blatant vocationalism. He also charged the university as a whole with excessive emphasis on vocationalism. Furthermore, he suggested that professors of education had no business tinkering with the school curriculum as sole arbiters, but argued that the curriculum was the proper domain of scholars in the disciplines and the "learned world as a whole." Perhaps his most devastating critiques were aimed at "life-adjustment," which he saw as a parody of education with a classist intent. He cited numerous examples of the trivialization of the curriculum such as the recommendation that students make studies "of how the last war affected the dating pattern in our culture."[27] As an example of the low standards held by many educators, Bestor frequently cited a quote from a local junior high school principal stating that "not every child has to read, figure, write and spell . . . many of them either cannot or will not master these chores."[28] Bestor's colleague, University of Illinois botanist Harry J. Fuller, held similar views and lamented the focus on the functional over the humanistic. He argued that biology courses had been reduced to "personal hygiene" and suggested that students needed to study "the basic, the impressive, the truly significant biological phenomena," rather than meeting trivial life-adjustment needs. Study of the sciences, he insisted, contributed to a deeper understanding of life on earth and the place of humanity in the web of existence.[29]

Bestor, and many other critics of the time, viewed life-adjustment as an extension of an already suspect progressive education. This was in error. The life-adjustment movement with its goal of "adjusting the individual to society" had its origins in the social efficiency aims borrowed from business and the ideas of Frederick Winslow Taylor, rather than in the philosophy of John Dewey.

Throughout his critique of progressive education, teacher-training colleges, and life-adjustment, Bestor took course descriptions and labels and state department questionnaires as sound evidence of educational practice. In each case, these documents were not strongly indicative of educational practice in schools, though they did suggest one direction in which schools and educational practice were headed. His criticisms of life-adjustment were on target regarding the rhetoric of the movement, but he made the mistake of assuming it was fully implemented.

Behind it all, he argued, was an "interlocking directorate of professional educationists" made up of three main groups: professors of education, school administrators and supervisors, and bureaucrats at the state and federal level that controlled schooling.[30] In his most inflammatory language, he compared the educationists' control to "an iron curtain which the professional educationists are busily fashioning. Behind it, in slave-labor camps, are the classroom teachers, whose only hope of rescue is from without. On the hither side lies the free world of science and learning, menaced but not yet conquered."[31]

Bestor's work did find critics. William Clark Trow, a professor of educational psychology, responded that Bestor had created a "badly distorted" picture of American education, and that Bestor's program for developing the "disciplined mind" would undermine the relevance of education. Following Bestor's plan, Trow argued, "no one would be ready to solve a problem until he is at least through college." Trow admitted that there were some weak spots, that some superior students were not receiving the proper attention, and that some teachers were not fully competent. However, on the whole he characterized Bestor's ideas as "dubious," and suggested, "we don't march backward."[32]

Bestor's critique of social studies was treated as one of the many attacks, but did receive a belated response, published in *Social Education* in 1958. Describing Bestor as the most "embattled opponent" of the term "social studies," Leo J. Alilunas charged that Bestor had lumped together life-adjustment and social studies and had little appreciation for the attempts at defining the field by such august groups as the Wesley Committee on American History and the National Council for the Social Studies (NCSS). He wrote, "Bestor insists that history as history is indispensable to education for intelligent citizenship. He deplores the establishment of the social studies movement . . . and regards it as the product of the conspiracy of professional educationists." Alilunas criticized Bestor for making no effort to understand the development of the social studies movement and for ignoring the attempts to adjust the demands of history and the other social sciences. Bestor, he suggested, hadn't done his homework. In essence, Alilunas found Bestor's work alienating and believed that it only served to widen the gap between scholars in history and the social sciences and professional educationists. He charged that Bestor's dogmatic assertions about "social studies" made little contribution to the need for "bridge-building" among those who should have a hand in the social studies curriculum.[33]

How accurate was Bestor's critique of American education? On a few aspects of schooling his criticisms were on the mark. Life-adjustment was an undemocratic trivialization, and there were many sloppy and not very thoughtful educational practices undertaken in the name of progressivism that deserved critique and revision. Bestor's major error, alluded to above, is that he mistook educational rhetoric for school practice. His critique was a polemical broadside rather than a reasoned analysis of the actual status of schooling and the impact of progressive ideas on practice. Many of his criticisms were overwrought and mean-spirited, and contributed to an unfortunate blanket condemnation of schools of education that he seemed to grudgingly admit were necessary. He also assumed that a thoughtful, progressive, and enlightened approach to teaching the disciplines would be prevalent if schools focused on an idealized "liberal education."

Bestor and many other critics assumed that life-adjustment education and progressive education were cut from the same cloth. Bestor assumed that a few curriculum guides from a few places were an accurate reflection of classroom practice, and that life-adjustment education was having a profound and extensive influence. In each case, these assumptions were problematic, and bore only the weakest connection to the facts.

Educational Wastelands was widely read, and made Arthur Bestor the leading spokesperson of his time on education. A good deal of his activity over the ensuing years was based on the book and the fame it conferred. The Council for Basic Education (CBE) was formed by Bestor and others to advance the intellectual and moral development of youth and to promote a reform agenda calling for a restoration of traditional academic approaches to schooling. A new consensus emerged, based on the primacy, sanctity, and integrity of the academic disciplines; the value of inquiry or discovery learning; the suitability of academic study for the high school; support for gifted education; production of change materials; development of curriculum reform projects; and proper in-service teacher training.[34] With 135 charter members, the Council had a strong contingent of well-respected historians and regularly roasted educationists in its *Bulletin*.

There were many other attacks on social studies. John Dixon in *The American Legion Magazine*, charged that the teaching of American history was being short-changed by "so-called social science," which was being substituted for straight history so that students "are not taught history." Dixon also charged that in colleges and universities in which future teachers were educated, "ideologies covertly hostile to the American way of life, the American system of government and American conceptions and ideals are permitted to flourish." He went on to charge that "academic freedom" served as a "cloak for the propagation of alien aims and isms," and the "subtle poison" they dispense. Reviving many of the arguments from the Rugg era and before, Dixon called for "a renaissance of patriotism" in America's history classrooms.[35] Another critic charged that history and literature were being combined with trivialities in the "core curriculum," in which current problems were "endlessly discussed" by young people lacking historical knowledge, while history itself was neglected.

Robert Keohane responded, as Erling M. Hunt had in the Nevins controversy, to the renewed charges that social studies had been substituted for history by citing convincing evidence that American history is usually the most important single component of "the federation of subjects" that make up social studies. Another critic, Verne P. Kaub, vice president of Allen Zoll's National Council for American Education, in an article published in *The Saturday Review of Literature*, asserted that textbooks did not present the American way of life impartially, and were guilty of "indoctrination with collectivist ideas." One example, he charged, was the *Building America* series that printed so many "ugly pictures of American life and glowing pictures of life in the USSR" that the National Society of the Sons of the American Revolution had launched a successful campaign to drive the books out of schools.[36]

RED-BAITING ATTACKS

Like the articles by Dixon and Kaub, many of the attacks on progressive social studies had ideological roots. These attacks had origins much earlier, in the red scare, in the work of Sidney Hook, and in the hearings conducted by the House Un-American Activities Committee in the 1930s and 1940s. By the early 1950s, the fear of having one's career destroyed by the House Committee was very real. This was the "silent generation" of the McCarthy era. Also, during the same period, the CIA developed books and reports, labeled "manpower studies," which held education as part of the solution to a cold war manpower shortage projected by Harvard president James B. Conant, vice admiral Hyman G. Rickover, and many other military, educational, and political leaders.[37]

Behind rising fears of communism were the realities of living in the atomic age. Stated most simply, people became less optimistic about the future of humanity. In the years immediately following the first use of atomic weaponry, the nation was seized by atom bomb hysteria. Numerous articles appeared in the popular press that captured the fears and hopes of many Americans. Several representative articles were included on a list that accompanied a letter in 1946 to Merrill Hartshorn, executive director of NCSS, and sent to others in the social sciences and education, from Daniel Melcher, director of the National Committee on Atomic Information, asking support for "world action" to avoid an atomic war. Among the titles were: "The Challenge of the Atomic Bomb," "Sovereignty in the Atomic Age," and "I'm a Frightened Man."[38]

The hysteria is especially well represented by an article that appeared in *Look* magazine in 1946 titled "Your Last Chance." In graphic drawings and detail the article described the alternative uses of this new power, including to "conquer the world," to "try to defend yourself," or to "put an end to war." The authors of the article then assert, "Sheer self-interest should make you work for a world without war . . . Your life will be unbearable in a world where atom bombs may fall at any hour."[39] Undoubtedly, this hysteria had an impact on schools and the curriculum. It certainly had an impact on *Social Education*, the official journal of NCSS. Items related to atomic fears appeared as early as 1946, in an article titled "Education or Annihilation," and in 1954, in an article titled "Sanity."[40] At the very least, atomic fears served to heighten cold war tensions and strengthen anticommunist sentiment.

Long before the rise of cold war fears and atomic bomb hysteria, critics of progressive education had frequently asserted that it was subversive and had made numerous efforts to save the schools by routing progressive educators and "left-wing" textbooks, notably during the Rugg controversy. In the late 1940s and early 1950s, criticism reached a new level of intensity. The thesis of the political critique of progressive social studies in the postwar era was stated clearly in an article by John T. Flynn published in *Reader's Digest* in 1951. Flynn charged that a group of progressive educators "set out to introduce into the social science courses of our high schools a seductive form of propaganda for collectivism—chiefly of that type we call socialism." Flynn wrote that the "propaganda" put forth in schools, largely by the Rugg textbook series, taught that the "American system of free enterprise is a failure," that our "republic of limited powers is a mistake," and that "our way of life must give way to a collectivist society."[41] He cited numerous quotes from the writings of Counts and Rugg to support his argument. However, Flynn failed to note that the Rugg textbook series had been discontinued and was no longer used extensively in the nation's schools.

Other red-baiting critics included Kitty Jones and Robert Olivier in *Progressive Education is REDucation*, and Mary Allen in *Education or Indoctrination*, both appearing in 1956. These books echoed many of Flynn's charges and went even further. Jones and Olivier charged that progressive educators were at work "making little socialists," and criticized the plan of "frontier thinkers . . . to indoctrinate this and future generations with their view," and to have the entire nation "participate in solving problems . . . total collectivism by consensus." The book also condemned the "scrambling" of history, geography, and government into the "social studies," and bemoaned the "anti-intellectualism" of educationists, all well-known themes by this time. The authors also made the spurious charge that progressive education was linked to communism.[42]

In her book *Education or Indoctrination* Mary L. Allen reviewed much of the literature disapproving of progressive education. She criticized Dewey's pragmatism, traced linkages between progressive educators and socialist organizations, and disparaged the social reconstructionist agenda of the frontier thinkers. She also alleged that communism had attached itself to progressive education, that the "aims of the communists and the social planners are parallel," and that the "danger of progressive education lies in its proximity to socialistic and communistic theories" and the subsequent threat of "communist infiltration in our schools." In sum, she cautioned, "there is overwhelming evidence to indicate that there is a well-organized, well-financed plan to impose a new social order on the people of America whether they like it or not."[43]

A number of right-wing groups contributed to the general ferment against the communists and socialists who were purportedly undermining American education. The most well-known of these was Allen Zoll's National Council for American Education that supplied speakers and pamphlets to community groups, published a periodical, disseminated critiques of "un-American" textbooks, and circulated lists of the communist-front affiliations of professors at leading universities. Though attacks were ostensibly local in origin, the usual pattern of organized attack erupted from local malcontents and critics supported by self-constituted organizations with official sounding names created to replicate legitimate, long-standing and respected organizations. All the while the attacks were supported by national organizations that supplied local affiliates with ammunition and strategy.[44]

The attacks were reinforced by support from politically potent groups like the American Legion, the Sons and Daughters of the American Revolution, and the Minute Women. Attackers sought out the schools not because they were rife with subversion but primarily because they were ubiquitous and accessible. Purging controversial books and teachers was an attempt to do something about the communist threat, a "crusade to purify American education of its political and ideological errors."[45] Though instances of ousted teachers were rare, manipulation of the communist issue put teachers, textbooks, and the curriculum at the mercy of right-wing pressure groups and imposed serious limitations on academic freedom.

Perhaps the most well-known school controversy resulting from such action occurred in Pasadena, California, where Willard Goslin, a progressive school superintendent, was asked to resign following attacks by a community group that complained that progressive education was weakening and subverting schools. The local organization behind the ouster, the School Development Council of Pasadena, was apparently acting under the influence of Allen Zoll.[46] Also in California, the Tenney Committee had been formed in 1941 as a fact-finding committee on un-American activities charged with finding teachers who advocated philosophies opposed to democracy. In 1946, two Problems of Democracy teachers in Canoga Park, California, were charged with espousing left-wing tendencies and one was believed to be a member of a "communist front" educational center. Tenney Committee hearings later led to the removal from schools of the *Building America* series, the brainchild of Paul Hanna.[47] The field of social studies was often singled out partly because social studies drew content from the social sciences and revisionist history, which were under attack in the 1950s as inherently subversive. Thus, social studies was frequently "charged with meddling in matters that threatened the social order."[48]

At the same time as the attacks on progressive education emerged, historians were shifting their focus from progressive history, of which social studies was a part, toward the new "consensus" history. Consonant with the times, consensus history was a major shift among historians. It represented a revolt against Charles Beard and other social activist historians, in favor of conservation of the status quo and a more modest approach to change. The new conception of the historian was historian as scientific observer, not activist. Consensus historians emphasized the continuities and agreements in history rather than conflict. It was, in many ways, a "life-adjustment" approach to history.[49]

In conclusion, attacks on progressive education focused on several charges. As summarized by one progressive observer, these included:

1. The schools are neglecting the fundamentals.
2. The schools have abandoned drill and recitation and substituted inefficient and easy methods.
3. Work has been taken out of school.
4. Schools have abandoned discipline.
5. There are too many "fads and frills."
6. The schools are wasting time on inconsequential subjects, especially in social studies.
7. The schools are dealing with controversial issues and leading the young toward "socialism."
8. The schools are not doing a good job of preparing young people for college.
9. Young people who attempt to enter the business world cannot hold a job because they cannot read, write, spell, or do arithmetic.[50]

What was behind the attacks? As in the Rugg controversy and earlier, attacks on education often seemed to have local origins among concerned citizens, but were frequently orchestrated, supported by national pressure groups linking unofficial "coalitions" with "interlocking directorates." Dean Ernest Melby, remarking on the results of a study by the Defense Commission of the National Education Association in which more than 15,000 questionnaires had been sent to school systems, stated:

> And so throughout the country. Always there is evidence of the interlocking directorates working to fight the schools. The same evasiveness, the same materials or failure to prove charges in public debate, the same failure to

criticize constructively. In many distant points appears the bubbling up of reaction—almost always with the symptoms of a central source.[51]

All of this was taking place within the context of a national crisis over communism, a critical fact to bear in mind. The social milieu of the cold war era is especially pertinent to a deeper understanding of the origins of the new social studies. With the dropping of atomic bombs on Japan, and the subsequent development of the nuclear arms race, the world had entered the nuclear age, and the threat of global holocaust was very real. Competition with the Soviet Union, growing national security concerns, the development of McCarthyism, and the deluge of intellectual and red-baiting attacks on progressive education were all conditioned by this context.

Fear of subversion and loyalty programs were on the rise, accompanied by sensational spy trials and congressional hearings. Two national committees, the Senate Internal Security Subcommittee and the House Committee on Un-American Activities were investigating educators on a national stage. In this context, right wing extremists found a ready audience for their allegations. Loyalty oaths and legislation providing for the ouster of disloyal teachers were passed in an increasing number of states. And, in several high-profile cases, university professors were fired either as a result of government led anticommunist crusades or refusal to sign loyalty oaths. The public schools were not immune to such pressures. In a number of instances teachers were dismissed for refusing to testify or for perjury. In New York the Feinberg law, which required certification of the loyalty of every teacher, was upheld by the U.S. Supreme Court.

In short, the atmosphere in the schools was heavily influenced by the anticommunist crusade. While university professors differed over the question of whether communists should be allowed to teach, 90 percent of the public believed that communists should be fired. It appears that the typical citizen did not have a problem with the witch hunts. Unfortunately, charges of subversion were difficult to disprove, and tended to damage and sometimes put an end to careers. At the very least, they spread an ambience of fear and suspicion, and resulted in the closing of many minds.[52] The notion that progressive educators, especially in social studies, were subversive, socialist, or linked to communism, gained increasing prevalence during the cold war era and undoubtedly harmed the cause of progressive, meliorist, and reconstructionist-oriented social studies.

THE RESPONSE

Educators responded to the attacks by writing books and articles examining, explaining, and contradicting them. The journals *Progressive*

Education and *Phi Delta Kappan* ran special issues dedicated to analysis of critics and aimed at helping teachers, administrators, and professors answer attacks from local groups.[53] At least one published work provided a compilation of writing covering "the great debate" on education, as it was frequently named. In *Public Education Under Criticism* (1954), C. Winfield Scott and Clyde M. Hill presented excerpts from critics comprised of sections on general and philosophical matters, progressive education, the fundamentals, religion, social studies, and teacher education. The volume also contained sections defending education, supplying analysis and assessment of the criticisms, and a concluding segment on "How to Handle Criticisms."[54] The noteworthy fact that social studies was the only specific subject field given its own section is a sign that social studies was one of the main targets. The book was reviewed in *Social Education* by a high school teacher from Colorado who mourned the frightening hostility and caustic quality of the attacks. These comprised "the explosive situation in Pasadena, Senator McCarthy's feinting skirmishes, and Allen Zoll's overt attacks." The reviewer identified each of these as "flagrant and disturbing symptoms" of a dangerous period in American education. In closing, he recommended the book to assist educators and laymen as they coped with critics.[55]

Most of the commentaries printed as rejoinders to the wave of criticism admitted that schools could be doing a better job, but also offered opposing analysis and evidence on the matter. One scholar in particular, Archibald W. Anderson, a professor of education at the University of Illinois, made a meticulous review of evidence related to nearly all of the critiques. Regarding the accusation that schools were neglecting the fundamentals, he wrote that while it was true that schools are devoting a considerable amount of time to subjects other than the 3 R's, the conclusion that "this means a neglect of the fundamentals is incorrect." He found substantial research evidence to counter the allegation, and argued that fundamental skills were usually included in newer subjects and activities. In response to the charge that modern methods were inefficient, a waste of time, he found considerable research evidence pointing to "one inevitable conclusion: Schools using modern and progressive methods of teaching and a modern curriculum are doing a good job, and in most instances a better job of teaching the fundamentals as traditional schools." And, he found evidence that progressive schools were doing a good job of preparing students for college, that wasting time on fads and frills had not materialized in schools. Moreover, he argued that attention to "educational activities designed to develop competence in dealing with social problems" was a necessity in a democratic society and in keeping with the American tradition. Despite offering a convincing case that schools were, on the whole, "doing a better job than formerly in teaching the basic intellectual skills," and in preparing young people for college, Anderson did not investigate the extent to which life-adjustment education was actually being implemented in schools, a critical omission.[56]

Most of the responses to the detractors were not as systematic as Anderson's, nor were they printed in periodicals that would reach the general public. Once again, aggressive assaults and startling claims garnered greater public awareness than the rational and well-documented responses of educators. In the social studies arena, the response seemed especially feeble and deferred. There was no Erling M. Hunt offering a point-by-point rebuttal to the frequently scurrilous and unsupported charges of the critics. It seemed that the opponents of progressive education had the upper hand and the nation's ear.

Perhaps many of the commentators' arguments were not taken seriously. Similar criticisms had been voiced earlier, and were seemingly repeated yet again. Despite mounting disparagement, it seemed that most progressive educators continued doing business as usual, and that schools were mostly functioning much as they had for years, in quite conventional ways. Near the climax of the debate, in 1955, the Progressive Education Association ceased business operations, and two years later, the magazine *Progressive Education* terminated publication. Progressive education had gone from its zenith in the 1930s during which it seemed the bulk of educators claimed the label of progressivism, to a new time during which progressives were held responsible for all the ills of schools. In retrospect, their reaction seems subdued. However, given the suspicious tenor of the times, such a response was probably reasonable.

NCSS RESPONDS TO CRITICS

There were several critical responses from social studies educators to the debate on education including a number of articles, books, and special issues of journals.[57] Yet, despite a good deal of discussion of and resistance to criticisms of social studies during the postwar era, by the late 1950s it appears that NCSS had largely given in to critics and followed their recommendations for a curriculum built around the disciplines.

Karier argues that progressive leaders fell short of an adequate response to the assaults on progressive education "in large part because they were retired or about to retire from Teachers College."[58] In a praiseworthy effort, from 1953–1955, in collaboration with other clusters of educators, NCSS prepared and disseminated kits titled "Attacks on Education" that were intended to help teachers and school administrators repel attacks. Mostly, however, social studies educators recoiled under the weight of the attacks, and even elected a critic of the field, with views similar to Bestor, to the position of president of NCSS. In his presidential address to the organization in 1957, William H. Cartwright decried a "drift from scholarship" in social studies that is "all too evident" and can be seen in:

> the scornful use of the word "traditional"; in the dogmatic rather than questioning condemnation of separate subjects; . . . in great curricular "experiments" conducted without reference to academic scholars in the fields of knowledge involved; and in what John Haefner referred to in his presidential message to this Council a few years ago as the "creeping curriculum," in which as he said so eloquently, "never have so many learned so little about so much."

Cartwright went on to argue, "The most crying need in education today is that the gap between schools and scholars must be bridged and, eventually, filled," and called for new spirit of cooperation among educators and "their natural allies, the academic scholars."[59]

Three volumes circulated by NCSS in the late 1950s and early 1960s exemplify the extent of the trend. In 1958, NCSS published a yearbook edited by Roy A. Price titled *New Viewpoints in the Social Sciences* in which the social science disciplines were represented in essays by scholars from a variety of fields. The volume largely overlooked educators and schools. Then in 1961, NCSS published a book by Cartwright and Watson entitled *Interpreting and Teaching American History*. The volume included chronologically sequenced essays reviewing the latest scholarship on American history, an essay by Arthur Bestor, and some commentary on educational practice. Another endeavor, begun in 1958 as a collaboration between NCSS and the American Council of Learned Societies (ACLS), resulted in release of *The Social Sciences and the Social Studies* in 1963. Each of these volumes emphasized an academic and disciplines-oriented approach in correspondence with the nature of the criticism.

Of course, there were other trends in evidence as well. NCSS continued to publish articles on a variety of ideas and perspectives in its journal and supported bulletins on a range of topics. Possibly the trend toward more disciplines-oriented work was merely a reflection of the times. In any event, the criticisms of social studies in the early postwar period had evidently borne fruit.

If the victors in the struggle for social studies were the disciplines, the losers were the proponents of reflective or issues-centered approaches. Yet, these traditions continued to develop, though their impact on schools may have been curtailed. The crusade against communism sent a chill through schools, and could not have been healthy, either for teacher freedom or for the continuing growth of reflective teaching. One factor that probably had some impact was a change in key leadership positions within NCSS. Merrill Hartshorn, a fervent anticommunist, replaced Wilbur Murra as executive secretary in 1943, and Lewis Paul Todd replaced Erling M. Hunt as editor of *Social Education*. Murra and Hunt were among the long-time progressive leaders who had helped give birth to social studies. Many other progressive educators had retired or were nearing the usual age. It appears, looking backward, that the younger generation of progressive educators was not up to the challenge brought by criticisms. Perhaps they simply had little choice aside from letting the national crisis pass.

THE ANTICOMMUNIST CRUSADE

In trying to comprehend the NCSS cave-in to attacks on social studies, the almost total disappearance of social reconstructionism and the fading of the social problems approach and Problems of Democracy course, it is imperative to bear in mind the context of the cold war. The development of an anticommunist perspective and emphasis on the academic disciplines were both parts of a long-term trend toward educational retrenchment, as the evidence presented below will remind us. The major ideological focus of the cold war era revolved around the menace of communism.[60] As we have seen, many of the attacks came from red-baiters and were clearly ideological. Some other critics put the red scare into the background, and focused on education as part of manpower development in scientific and technological competition with the Russians. Others, such as Bestor, were critics of both life-adjustment and progressivism and favored a more academic education. Yet, even among intellectual critics, the cold war backdrop lent an urgency to their concerns.

There was a certain mentality present in rhetoric regarding communism. For the most part, communism was viewed as a danger to democracy. It was perceived as a form of totalitarian fascism, monolithic in nature, and teaching about communism was regarded as necessary in order to defeat it. Ample evidence on the impact of anticommunism on the social studies literature may be found in the journal *Social Education,* as articles related to the threat of communism appeared throughout the cold war era.[61]

Moreover, communism, when it was given attention in schools, was portrayed as a threat to democracy. From 1947 until the early 1970s, the threat of communism was a major focal point of the curriculum. This focus represented an attempted ideological purification of the American citizenry through the schools. As a focal point in many social studies courses, anticommunism became a topical vehicle for the enactment of education for social efficiency, and for the direct inculcation of mainstream American values via the discrediting of ideas that were seen as un-American.

Direct anticommunism materialized in a number of educational settings during the postwar era: in school textbooks and supplemental materials, in the professional literature of the time, and among school leaders. Moreover, anticommunist sentiment was one of the driving forces in the major curricular developments of the times. However, I do not mean to suggest that the anticommunist stance was, on the whole, "bad." It was plainly a fact. A number of leading progressive educators came to hold an anticommunist perspective.[62] Of more relevant concern are the consequences of anticommunism and the cold war conflict for social studies education. In its excesses, anticommunism created a precarious climate for the expression of dissent, thus profoundly influencing schools and society. Much of the anticommunist crusade in schools illustrated the subtle hazards of citizenship transmission and the prospective limitations it may place on free expression and free thought, creating a one-dimensional curriculum that might, potentially, deter alternatives.

Evidence of staunch anticommunist thinking may be found among certain prominent social studies leaders. Archival sources suggest that one key manager, Merrill Hartshorn, longtime executive director of NCSS, 1943–1974, was an ardent anticommunist, with links to the power elite in Washington, D.C., and membership or board service on a number of strongly anticommunist organizations including the Zeal for Democracy Program created under the auspices of the U.S. Office of Education; the American Heritage Foundation; the American Legion; American Viewpoint; and the Committee on American Education and Communism, which was allied with FRASCO, or The Foundation for Religious Action in the Social and Civil Order. Each of these organizations had a tendency to view communism as a "unified system," or a monolith, "a totalitarian empire which holds in its iron grip one-third of the world."[63]

Ironically, given Hartshorn's orientation, NCSS was among a number of educational and philanthropic organizations that were investigated by the Reece Commission, also known as the House Committee to Investigate Tax Exempt Foundations, beginning in 1954. The Committee was authorized to investigate these organizations "to determine whether the resources of such foundations [were] being improperly or subversively used."[64]

Hartshorn's interest in anticommunism and his involvement with anticommunist organizations both preceded and coincided with a flurry of activity on the topic in social studies publications including articles and a special issue of *Social Education* and other journals, a bulletin sponsored by NCSS, a number of books, and textbooks. The depth of cold war fears is highlighted by the fact that the special issue devoted to communism, titled "The Communist Challenge," in 1958, was one of the first special issues ever developed in the journal.

THE BRAINWASHING CONTROVERSY

The cold war context of the 1950s, which was behind the "crisis" over schools, would be felt in a number of other arenas as well. The "brainwashing" controversy over American prisoners of war (POWs) being held in Korea is one especially interesting, and frequently cited, episode, which also served as an opportunity for increased concerns over the social studies curriculum. Several POWs were converted to communism by the North Koreans, after being questioned about American social problems, thus raising concerns over the "inadequacy of citizenship training which has been received by our youth." A POW code was passed in 1955 and adopted by the Defense Department. The code aimed at instructing POWs to resist "brainwashing," and the Department of Health, Education, and Welfare was instructed to "provide contact and liaison with educational groups and organizations" in an effort to strengthen citizenship education in schools.

Apparently, the role of NCSS in this controversy was to send a representative, Hartshorn, to a conference held at the Pentagon on October 25, 1955.[65] A paper, addressing the matter, "The Prisoner of War Problem—A Challenge to U.S. Educators," written by Hugh Milton, assistant secretary of the Army, was presented at the conference. Milton argued that public school should play a stronger role in preparing soldiers to resist political indoctrination by potential communist captors. He wrote that the real challenge was to make citizens more adept at applying their knowledge of American democracy "to combat the precepts of theoretical Marxism."[66] He went on to call for giving young men a "dedication to our American way of life and strength of moral character," and for those qualities to be "inculcated during early years in the home, church and school." Finally, he called for knowledge to be supplemented "by faith so strong as to obviate the necessity to reason logical answers to all our social problems."[67]

LOYALTY OATHS

Also linked to the cold war culture of fear and ideological repression were battles over academic freedom and the use of loyalty oaths in schools and colleges. In most cases, an employee would be asked to sign a statement testifying to the fact that he or she did not and had not previously belonged to any communist organization. Undoubtedly, this was a restriction on American's freedoms and reflected an aversion to asking deep questions. An article by Morris Mitchell, "Fever Spots in American Education," appearing in *The Nation* in 1951, cited growing imposition of loyalty oaths and called for citizen action to counter the threat to free education from four groups: real-estate conservatives, super-patriots, dogma peddlers, and race haters.[68]

Soviet and American relations had soured and issues of loyalty and internal security became major preoccupations in American politics. These sentiments resulted in witch hunts, blacklists, and the imposition of loyalty oaths. In California, for example, professors at the University of California were required to swear to an oath that read "I am not a member of the Communist Party, or under any oath, or a party to any agreement, or under any commitment that is in conflict with any obligations under this oath."

Several important questions related to communism were being decided during the period. Among these were: (1) Should communists be permitted to teach in public schools? (2) Should controversial material including communism be taught in the schools? (3) Are loyalty oaths appropriate for teachers?[69] One of the most famous deliberations over whether communists should be permitted to teach appeared in a pair of *New York Times Magazine* articles under the title "Should Communists Be Allowed to Teach?," published in 1949. In the first article, Sidney Hook argued that Communist Party members should not teach because they are restricted in the search for the truth. He argued, "According to the Communist party itself politics is bound up, through the class struggle, with every field of knowledge . . . A party line is laid down for every area of thought from art to zoology. No person who is known to hold a view incompatible with the party line is accepted as a member." Furthermore, he wrote, "Once he joins and remains a member, he is not a free mind." Hook argued that a college professor's academic liberty included the responsibility to maintain an open mind.

In a response to Hook, Alexander Meiklejohn argued that communists should be allowed to teach, and that their ideas should be considered along with others. He suggested that democracy would triumph in the "competition of ideas," and condemned the "probationary" status deriving from academic freedom cases in which tenured professors could lose their positions. Meiklejohn described the cases of several "dismissed" professors and argued that their removal illustrated an administration "misled by the hatreds and fears of the cold war," and embodied an overly zealous interpretation of the "control" of Communist Party members by Moscow. He argued that such scholars became members of the Party because "they accept Communist beliefs," and are of like mind, as could be said for members of any political party.[70] Like other trends, debate on whether communists should be permitted to teach contributed to a climate of oppression that gripped the nation and limited teacher freedom.

CONCLUSION

As we have seen in this chapter, the school reform movement that would eventually launch the new social studies had its roots in a continuing series of controversies over education writ large, and in the cold war context, which was instrumental in generating a climate of hope amid paralyzing fears. Attacks on education, both the intellectual and red-baiting variety, were deeply linked to the social milieu of the cold war era. Academic critics such as Arthur Bestor argued that schools were failing to prepare students intellectually. Simultaneously, axe-grinders such as John Flynn and Allen Zoll along with a host of "patriotic" groups attacked schools and social studies for their ideological sins. Given the rhetoric of the times, and what was at stake, the responses of educators seem rather anemic. For its part, NCSS more or less endorsed the trend to the disciplines as a replacement for progressive social studies. In sum, all of this contributed to an escalation of cold war rhetoric and increasing skepticism toward both progressive education broadly and social studies in particular, and fed the growing movement for curriculum reform. As we shall see in the next chapter, the evolving drive for curricular reform owed much of its potency to cold war fears centered on concerns over manpower development. Over the next few years, those concerns would prove a powerful force behind the germination of a broad curriculum reform and its extension to social studies.

CHAPTER 2

THE ULTIMATE WEAPON

DURING THE 1950S, the growing interest in curriculum reform was driven by the cultural context, a landscape dominated by cold war fears and anticommunist rhetoric and activity. The broader curriculum reform movement that gave rise to the new social studies grew, in part, out of cold war manpower concerns and studies conducted by the Central Intelligence Agency (CIA). Though there were other factors, concerns over Soviet manpower development would create pressure for improving the outcomes of American schooling, and for upgrading instruction in science and mathematics. Manpower worries were raised beginning in the late 1940s and early 1950s and were partly behind creation of the National Science Foundation (NSF). Established by Congress in 1950 with the aim of promoting basic research and education in the sciences, the NSF initially had little to do with the lower schools, though it did begin to sponsor science fairs and summer institutes for teachers in science and mathematics.

MANPOWER DEVELOPMENT

Manpower concerns were heightened by a series of confidential CIA reports on developments in the Soviet Union. The first of these reports provided evidence that the Soviets were training "new cadres" of scientists, engineers, and technical manpower at a rapid rate, and employing the "Stakhanov" movement, or "socialist competition," to spur productivity gains. From 1947 the Soviets began giving monetary awards for innovation and "Stalin Prizes" and "Hero of Socialist Labor" awards to recognize achievement. As described in the CIA report, Soviet manpower planning and the focus on education was part of a series of five-year plans under

Stalin, with control vested in a highly centralized governmental authority. The fifth five-year plan, for example, provided for a 15 percent increase in workers and employees by 1955 over 1950, pouring manpower into the technical and industrial workforce. In short, the report suggested that the Soviet Union was an awakening industrial and technological giant.[1] The rapid increase in numbers and the reorientation of the Soviet education system to focus on producing more scientists and engineers heightened concerns that the United States might lose its edge of superiority. A later report confirmed the earlier findings and indicated that the Soviets were devoting "large sums to education, especially in the fields of science and engineering," and that in many fields, "Soviet technology equals or even exceeds that of the west."[2] By 1963, a report classified as "secret" found that Soviet productivity was "second only to the U.S.," and that the Soviets had made especially rapid progress in "development of engineering and other professional and technical manpower," with a 237 percent increase in engineers from 1939 to 1959.[3]

Among U.S. policymakers, the CIA manpower reports were cause for alarm at the highest levels and led to a manpower report from the Office of Defense Mobilization (ODM) commissioned by President Dwight D. Eisenhower in 1953.[4] The ODM study reported on the "availability of manpower simultaneously to operate a military training program, to supply military personnel for active service, and to meet the needs of the civilian economy." In essence, civilian scientific and technical manpower was viewed as an adjunct to military power and as an essential part of national security.[5] The report stated that manpower resources, especially "our supply of highly trained and skilled workers," were not keeping abreast of the current and potential requirements of the rapidly expanding technology" on which the nation's "growth and security depend." The authors of the report cast manpower as a key ingredient for "success on the diplomatic front."[6] By the fall of 1954 national security and manpower concerns had become the subject of alarming media coverage. An interview with NSF director Alan T. Waterman published in *Nation's Business*, organ of the U.S. Chamber of Commerce, was titled "Russian Science Threatens the West," and a *New York Times* article reported, "Russia Is Overtaking U.S. in Training of Technicians."[7] Manpower concerns continued to loom large throughout the cold war era and stood behind government and business-led efforts to develop more scientific and technical personnel, and better trained citizens.

It is important to note that concerns over the manpower "shortage" arose during a time in which the role of science was changing significantly. The role of science had grown dramatically during World War II, a time in which technological advances played a prominent role in the allied victory. These successes contributed to the "mutual embrace" of science and the military and created the origins of a technocratic political organization in the United States in which the nation fully embraced the "institutionalization of technological change for state purposes."[8] Indeed, military patronage was the driving force behind technological development. The nation's defense strategy during the Truman administration rested on evolving military technology. The outbreak of the Korean War led to an intensification of government research efforts and the establishment of the Science Advisory Committee (SAC) within the ODM to advise the director and the president. Leaders from the scientific research and development community including Massachusetts Institute of Technology (MIT) president James R. Killian, Robert Oppenheimer, Waterman, and physicist Jerrold R. Zacharias became "key players in postwar national security policy making."[9] They were involved at the highest levels of discussion on policy matters related to weapons systems and the threat of nuclear warfare. In 1949, shortly after the Soviet detonation of a nuclear device, Killian circulated a survey among the nation's scientific elite, asking their opinions on such questions as "Which of the following conditions in your opinion would justify atomic war? . . . If you faced an ultimate choice between Russian occupation and atomic war, would you . . . If atomic war activity seems imminent, would you prefer . . . ?"[10] The specter of nuclear annihilation loomed large in their thoughts along with the secrecy and seriousness of the cold war context.

The NSF, as an independent funding and coordinating agency for scientific research, was organized along lines first outlined by Vannevar Bush in a 1945 report titled *Science: The Endless Frontier*. In that report Bush proposed an agency that would support basic research and education without immediate practical ends, and be governed by the community of scientists. The eventual shape and form of the NSF was a "victory of elitism" as the elite members of the scientific community assumed leadership of the NSF, which shaped the role of science in the postwar era. Most were physicists with experience in wartime military science labs under the direction of the Office of Scientific Research and Development at places like the Rad Lab at the MIT and the Manhattan Project in Los Alamos.[11]

Several other factors contributed to the scientists' engagement with curricular reform. Security restrictions imposed during the McCarthy era disrupted scientists' freedom of movement, access to classified information, and social interactions. Loyalty investigations seemed arbitrary and capricious charges were made against reputable scientists on the basis of hearsay and unsubstantiated evidence. There was the Oppenheimer case, in which Robert Oppenheimer, former director of the Manhattan Project was identified as a security risk by the Atomic Energy Commission

(AEC), apparently due to his affiliations with communist and left wing organizations during the 1930s. Hearings held in the spring of 1954, in which Zacharias testified, resulted in the revocation of Oppenheimer's security clearance. That case, in particular, damaged relations between government and the scientific community. Vannevar Bush, in an article that appeared in the *New York Times Magazine*, "If We Alienate Our Scientists," outlined the threat to science and to national security. Seemingly a harassed profession, in a defensive position, scientists sought to rebuild and redefine their public image. They argued for a vision of science as a means to "rational understanding" that would ultimately help to improve many social and political problems. As the cold war threat grew, scientists argued that the further dissemination of scientific thinking was a good way to promote democracy, both as an antidote to communism and as a means to counter the excesses of McCarthyism. So, education reform was viewed as a means to continue the growth of science and, simultaneously, to promote democracy.[12]

Though academic freedom concerns were important, the main factors leading to the growth of science education reform were related to the manpower shortage in science and engineering and the climate of cold war conflict. Although it had been simmering for some time, the manpower crisis seemingly burst upon the scene with the outbreak of the Korean War. Demographic factors apparently contributed to the crisis. One factor behind the shortage of scientific and technical manpower was the "baby bust" of the depression era when fewer children were being born. However, many scientists thought the demographic factors would even out over the long run and erase the shortage. Nonetheless, demographic concerns and the manpower shortage were the focus of a special issue of *Scientific American* in September 1951. Interest was so strong that the magazine sold out immediately, and ran three printings to meet demand.[13]

Early efforts to address the "manpower shortage" focused on graduate fellowships provided by the NSF for advanced training in science and engineering. Businesses, including General Electric and Westinghouse, had previously invested in training programs for high school science teachers, and the National Manpower Council was established at Columbia University in 1951, while Eisenhower served as University president. During the early 1950s a teacher shortage was a chronic problem. In a 1953 report, the National Manpower Council linked a teacher shortage in science and math to the issue of manpower production.[14]

Once he was inaugurated as president, Eisenhower initiated a review of government policies seeking to coordinate all foreign and domestic policy to succeed in the cold war struggle with communism. In October 1953, information from the CIA report on Soviet manpower development led to discussion of manpower training at a meeting of the National Security Council and at a subsequent cabinet meeting held in April 1954. President Eisenhower expressed concern in both meetings that the United States might lose its edge in technical and military superiority. As the meeting went on, the cabinet discussed ways to encourage efforts to improve science education over the long term. At the end of the meeting, Eisenhower charged Arthur Fleming, head of the ODM, with establishment of an informal committee to look into the matter. The committee, which was titled the Special Interdepartmental Committee on the Training of Scientists and Engineers (SICTSE) would have representatives from the NSF, the AEC, and the Department of Defense, as well as the Departments of Labor and Health, Education, and Welfare (HEW). This marked an official beginning, of sorts, for what would become the nation's effort to improve the schools. The fact that the ODM led the initial push for federal involvement in science education reform reflected deep-seated concerns about national security. An internal memo stated, "If this were merely a temporary lag, the matter would be of no more than general concern to the federal government . . . however, the security of the nation is at stake. The danger lies in our possible inability to maintain the present substantial margin of superiority in scientific and technological development which we have over our potential enemies."[15] And so, with the seeds planted for federal involvement, science education reform became another weapon in the nation's cold war arsenal.

Though many scientists had long been concerned about the quality of science education in the schools, it gradually moved from the realm of a nebulous general concern, to become a major plank in the nation's efforts to strengthen national security in what appeared headed toward a protracted struggle. In comments published in the *New York Times*, Eisenhower predicted that it might be a 40-year struggle. Long-term preparations to enhance the nation's security seemed warranted. Several factors influenced concerns about the supply and demand of science teachers, as well as the quality of science teaching. Teachers received low pay and low prestige. In fact, in the early 1950s, nearly 65,000 teachers were working with emergency credentials. And, there was the perception, fortified with some factual evidence, that schools of education attracted lower quality students than many other subject areas, that some were lazy and looking for an easy major, and that most were of lower innate ability. The poor quality of teacher education made the problem even worse. Many observers believed that schools of education lacked "depth and intellectual rigor" and that emphasis on pedagogy came at the expense of a solid grounding in subject matter. Most scientists and other academics believed that the professional education "directorate" was part of the problem. So, scientists at ODM, NSF, and on the SICTSE focused attention on improving the quality of science teaching in classrooms and bypassed the education establishment to aim directly at teachers.[16]

During the mid-1950s, the NSF and science establishment sought to muster support for reform. NSF director Alan Waterman made a pitch for increased funds for science education reform before a congressional committee in February 1955. One congressman's response summed up the feelings of others, and was indicative of the general attitude toward a federal role in schools. Representative Albert Thomas of Texas argued, the "charge may arise that NSF is trying to take over in this country." Waterman responded, "We are not planning to mastermind the educational pattern from Washington . . . We are trying to determine what it is *the scientists* feel should be done." The subcommittee recommended no increase in funds for the education program and cut the overall NSF budget request from $20 million to $12 million for fiscal 1956.[17] The episode suggests the difficulty of obtaining funds for science and for any education reform directed from the federal level. This attitude was prevalent despite a growing and concerted effort by the administration and the press to convince Americans that the manpower shortage was real.

The battle to convince Americans that the Soviet manpower threat should be taken seriously had been waged on many fronts, and by a number of "soldiers," over several years. Concerns heightened at the outbreak of hostilities in Korea in 1950 led to an increase in spending for military research and development. However, once a truce was signed, it seemed that support was somewhat in doubt. In August 1953, President Eisenhower authorized Dr. Arthur Fleming and the ODM to form the Committee on Manpower Resources for National Security to examine the situation.[18] The Committee issued a report on December 18, 1953 expressing concern about a shortage in engineering and the need for personnel in the scientific specialties, arguing that demand was "greatly increased by the defense program," and finding that "manpower requirements in the sciences as a whole will probably have a continuing upward trend."[19]

During the next year, a number of experts and government insiders weighed in on the matter. In April, Henry H. Armsby, chief for Engineering Education of the Division of Higher Education, United States Office of Education (USOE), reported on the "problems" growing out of "the current and impending national shortages of scientific and professional manpower, describing it as a "vital need . . . especially in a period of mobilization which can lead to an all-out war economy."[20] In September, M. H. Trytten, director of the Office of Scientific Personnel, National Research Council (NRC), who was later cited in many news articles, reported to a conference of mechanical engineers that the Soviets had "never failed" to consciously understand "the role of technology and of technological education as the basis of economic and military power."[21] His speech included comparative data on the number of engineers produced by Russian and American universities, showing that with over 50,000 graduates compared to the 20,000 produced in the United States, the Soviets had effectively caught up, and would soon reach superiority. Later that fall, Trytten issued data on engineering graduates in Russia and the United States showing a sharp increase in Soviet engineering graduates for 1953 and 1954 while the numbers for the United States declined. After outlining the Soviet education system and its gains in developing scientists and engineers, Trytten argued for "improving the teaching of science at the high school level [and] expanding the training of scientists and engineers." His implication was that the United States, like Russia, should develop a "realistic policy of considering scientific and technical personnel as merely another but most important factor in the total national military potential."[22]

In the interview published in *Nations Business* in September 1954, "Russian Science Threatens the West," Waterman cited evidence that the Soviets were steadily enlarging their stockpile of scientific manpower and suggested that they may have surpassed the United States in training engineers. Moreover, a document in Waterman's files titled "Educational Factors Basic to Economic Growth" illustrates the connection of the manpower problem to the nation's business interests. The paper noted evidence of "shortages in the professions: engineering, medical, scientific, teaching," as a "prime obstacle to the realization of our full economic development" and cited the 1951 special issue of *Scientific American* and more recent reports from a variety of government agencies. Along with a broad list of needed improvements to the education system, the paper called for "an effective educational program and for the guidance into professional and scientific careers of those citizens who have the native abilities and interests to be successful in such work."[23] The impact of the "shortage" on business and industry was a major topic of discussion for SICTSE. An annotated agenda for a 1954 meeting confirmed that "supply [was] well below demand for engineers." It warned that enrollments of high school students in chemistry and physics had decreased, and noted the difficulty in "building up a solid core of competent, inspiring teachers" in science and math. Finally, it noted a "continual increase" in scientists and engineers called to business and industrial posts, underscoring the need to address the shortage at all levels of the education system.[24]

A slew of articles appeared on the topic in the popular press from 1953 to 1955. In 1955, the *New York Times* index contained a new category titled "training and supply of scientists and engineers" with more than 120 entries, and *Times* education reporter Benjamin Fine authored a series of articles on the manpower situation, all conveying a tone of alarm. In one front-page story, appearing on November 7, 1954, under the head-line "Russia is Overtaking U.S. in Training of Technicians" he warned, "[W]hile the democracies of the world . . . are looking the other way, the Soviet Union and its satellites are training scientists and engineers at an almost feverish pace." He went on to blame schools and the life-adjust-ment curriculum for a lack of attention to math and science education. In later articles, he highlighted a "critical shortage of technically trained Americans," and echoed industry's cry for "more engineers."[25]

An article appearing in *Business Week* reported on a conference of top-flight businessmen and educators conducted by the Edison Foundation (sponsored by the Engineering Manpower Commission of the Engineers Joint Council and the Scientific Manpower Commission), which echoed many of the same concerns and underlined the crucial role of science teachers in the elementary and secondary schools in addressing the need for development of more scientists, engineers, and technicians. Only by "training" young people to "maintain America's high level of technologi-cal development" could the need be met, combined with "more and bet-ter guidance" from schoolteachers by encouraging scientific careers.[26]

An article in *Newsweek* titled "The Red Challenger" stated the matter even more bluntly. The article began with the line, "Trained brains are the basic fuel of a technological society," and went on to detail the pending crisis, citing data from Trytten of the NRC indicating Soviet gains and showing that Soviet "output of graduate engineers this year . . . exceeds the number of American engineers graduated by a ratio of 2 ½ to 1." The article also cited evidence that Russia's total engineering force was close to the U.S. total of 500,000, and would soon be larger. The article described the improvement of science teaching as an urgent need, and argued that if the "traditional local control of education" is to be main-tained in the hands of local and state officials, then it is these people who have "the power to develop the real ultimate weapon in the deadly race for technological progress—tomorrow's scientists and engineers." The article described a concerted effort by scientific manpower experts, school officials, a government task force, and groups from business and industry, including the National Association of Manufacturers (NAM), to support the campaign for manpower development by improvements in education. In New York City, a committee of the NAM was busy drawing up plans for renewed cooperation between local industry and the science teacher.[27] And so, big media and big business joined big science and big government in the push to enlist science education reform in the cold war conflict.

Apparently the campaign by media and government to publicize the shortage was beginning to have the desired effect. Early in 1955, a group of Austin, Texas, businessmen formed a nonprofit educational organization to lobby for a renewal of U.S. scientific and technological leadership. The Grass Roots Educational League of Texas, as it was called, was determined to do something about the "output" of scientists and engineers, which had "steadily declined," the "critically meager" number of available teachers in physics, chemistry, and math, and the "steady decline" in the number of students in science education. Their concern was motivated by the "necessity of maintaining our scientific leadership in a push button cold war or hot war."[28]

Scientists opened a second front in their efforts with publication of an NSF-sponsored book in the summer of 1955 titled *Soviet Professional Manpower* by Nicholas DeWitt. The book offered a complete and well documented portrayal of the Soviet education system and served as an eye-opener to many in Congress, who had assumed that scientists and other experts were exaggerating the threat posed by the growing levels of Soviet development. DeWitt's book provided evidence that the Soviet's bottom line was trained manpower in science and engineering and that Soviet training was very effective. It portrayed secondary schools focused on science instruction and a nation directing education toward national security goals.[29]

These government efforts led to a White House Conference on Education, held in the fall of 1955, intended as a forum for the administration to address the nation and convey the seriousness of the manpower and education issue. Citizen delegates numbering 1,800 were called to the nation's capitol, formed into roundtable discussion groups, and asked to reach consensus on six questions ranging from curriculum to school finance. MIT president James R. Killian, who chaired the curriculum discussion group, consulted Waterman in advance of the meeting, then circulated a document that outlined two competing goals for public schooling, mirroring public debate over schools, with one position focusing on "adjustment" for happy lives, and the other emphasizing an intellectual focus with high educational standards for all. The document was even circulated to Bestor and Fuller. Despite this plain attempt to influence the outcome, conference attendees expressed more concern with more mundane needs of school construction, and support for a life-adjustment style curriculum.[30]

In November 1955, after the Soviets successfully detonated a militarily deliverable hydrogen bomb, a shift in attitude occurred on Capitol Hill. Concerns over federal control over education seemed to evaporate and the NSF budget for nonfellowship education programs was increased nearly eightfold to $10.9 million. Congressman Albert Thomas, who had earlier raised objections, cited the DeWitt book that had "completely reversed" his thinking.[31]

Throughout the period, the primary goals of the scientists at NSF continued to center on science as a handmaiden to maintaining U.S. "technological superiority." This goal was highlighted in a confidential memo detailing a presentation made by Waterman at a meeting of the National Security Council on May 31, 1956. The NSF director began with a statement on the role of basic research as the linchpin for maintaining superiority, and linked that to a call for development of the needed scientific manpower. Support for basic research was essential, he argued, "for future advances . . . and development in weapons, atomic energy, medicine . . . agriculture and industrial technology." It was also "essential," he noted, that the number of high school graduates of "superior ability" who choose to go to college be increased.[32]

QUESTIONS?

Despite continuous expressions of concern from the nation's scientific, political, and business elite, there is some question whether the manpower threat was real, whether the various descriptions of Soviet gains were overstated, and whether there really was any serious "breakdown" in the U.S. education system. James Killian, who was later appointed the special assistant to the president for Science and Technology, wrote in his memoir:

> It had been charged repeatedly during the 1950s that the Russians were out-producing the United States in the education of engineers. A lot of figures were bandied about, and we became caught up in an academic numbers game. It was difficult to make statistical comparisons, particularly since it was not always clear that the Russians defined "engineer" in the same way that we do in the United States. It was not clear that their engineering graduates enjoyed the same broad professional training . . . [Yet, the thinking was] sooner or later the Russian pool of engineering skills would surpass our own. But I did not see any such outcome.

> As far as comparative accomplishment in science was concerned, the fear that Russia was about to surpass the United States or had already done so was patent nonsense . . . [It] was no secret to the scientists themselves . . . that the United States had become during the postwar years immeasurably the home of the most impressive scientific efforts in the world.[33]

Killian's memoir comments questioning the truth of the "shortage" were supported by another important source during the 1950s. It seems that in 1953, in an attempt to obtain "better information" on the demand for and supply of scientists and engineers, the NSF commissioned a study conducted by the National Bureau of Economic Research whose findings also questioned the existence of shortages. A book reporting their findings, *The Demand and Supply of Scientific Personnel*, released in 1957, received media attention in a syndicated column by Sylvia Porter, attention that concerned Killian and Waterman.[34] Waterman believed the book's findings were based on a theoretical model and provided insufficient evidence to substantiate its claims. However, based on a flurry of letters from Waterman to other players in the bureaucracy, he worried that the book's appearance would undercut the basis for the reform.[35]

Though several factors explain the growing focus on educational reform, the cold war context and the perceived threat posed by Soviet manpower development was most pressing. Among other influential factors was the desire to channel broader aid to schools and to somehow get around objections to federal invasion of local control. A focus on science education reform was less controversial and more palatable, now that the national security case had been made. Moreover, science was portrayed as the "objective" pursuit of truth, in keeping with the aim of furthering democracy. Having received a boost in confidence and funding from Congress, the Foundation wasted little time in consolidating its leadership of the reform effort. Its aim was to enlist leading scientists to improve science education. Because of their prestige, this led other groups (ODM, SICTSE) to defer to what NSF thought best. While leaders in the science education profession, part of Bestor's "interlocking directorate," expressed interest in participating, and even lobbied for inclusion, NSF officials clearly weren't interested in fostering substantive cooperation with the science education establishment. As one staffer wrote, science educators were "definitely more education than science oriented . . . Care should be taken to prevent their dominating any of the Committee projects."[36]

EARLY YEARS OF THE CURRICULUM
REFORM MOVEMENT

The curriculum reform movement that would eventually result in creation of the new social studies also had its seeds in the curriculum materials reform movement, which began, almost unnoticed, at two universities in the 1950s. The University of Illinois Committee on School Mathematics (UICSM) was formed in 1951 out of concerns over the math deficiencies of entering freshmen at the University of Illinois. On the basis of similar concerns in science, Jerrold Zacharias at MIT proposed a project for the improvement of physics, which led to the creation of what was called the Physical Science Study Committee (PSSC), which received NSF funding. In each case, the rationale for the development of the curriculum improvement projects was rooted in manpower concerns that surfaced earlier, and which continued to be aired, in one form or another, throughout the period. Each of these committees also began with concerns over college teaching, but quickly focused on the precollegiate level, concentrating on college prep students and courses in the secondary schools.

UICSM emphasized the "structure of mathematics" and learning mathematics principles "through discovery, consistency, and precise terminology." These guidelines grew out of UICSM leader Max Beberman's analysis of the math deficiencies of entering freshmen. The rationale for curriculum development for a *new* math education was stated as follows:

> Structure, proof, generalization, and abstraction were seen as the essence of modern mathematics . . . In teaching mathematics, then, these four essentials should be evident to the learner . . . To make mathematics applicable the problem solver must perceive the structures inherent in both the application and in the mathematics to be used. From this viewpoint the first essential in applying mathematics is the perception of a mathematical structure or system that has abstract properties corresponding to the physical system's properties.[37]

The rationale went on to suggest that an understanding of mathematical structures and theory were required to solve a problem situation, and that students well prepared in mathematical theory "should be able to apply mathematics to completely novel situations."[38]

Once a rationale had been clearly established, the UICSM began the task of developing a new mathematics program for grades ninth–twelfth. Seven years elapsed from the creation of UICSM to the availability of textbooks for purchase in 1958, an indication that more was involved than simply writing new textbooks, but that a new curriculum, new pedagogies, and classroom experimentation were required as well. The scope of the UICSM project also demanded substantial funding. The project received grant monies from the Carnegie Corporation of New York and later from both the USOE and the NSF.

Illinois Math, as the project was commonly known, involved faculty from education, engineering, liberal arts, and sciences but focused on collaboration between schoolteachers and university professors. Its essence was the education of high school students with the methods, materials, and approaches of the university mathematician. Beberman, who taught at the University of Illinois lab school, sought "to bring the mind of the adolescent some of the ideas and modes of thinking which are basic in the work of the contemporary mathematician."[39] Illinois Math set the pattern that would be followed by most of the curriculum reform projects that followed. It sidestepped the math education establishment to work directly with teachers. It disregarded common assumptions about what the child could learn, and what it should learn, instead taking concepts from the university research lab to high school mathematics, with the clearly stated aim of helping students learn to think like a mathematician. This meant less focus on the computational skills traditionally taught in math classes (i.e., the multiplication tables) and more time on the conceptual structure of math. To think mathematically meant to use inductive reasoning via materials and activities, which were aimed at helping students "discover" the underlying principles of mathematics, such as theorems and algorithms. The materials tended to delay verbalization and to encourage students to understand an idea fully before attempting to express it verbally.

Beberman argued that this approach, while time consuming, led to long-range memory and deeper understanding, rather than immediate recall on tests. The aim, put most nobly, was to build a love of math as a way of using the mind, as a form of thinking. The aim is captured most succinctly by the following quote: "The discovery method of teaching is practiced by those who believe that mathematics is more than a tool to be used in solving the 'real-life' problems of mankind . . . [it] develops interest in mathematics, and power in mathematical thinking."[40]

The NSF also funded the PSSC project to revise the high school physics curriculum, the pioneer pilot curriculum development project for the foundation. Prior to its funding of the MIT Committee, the NSF had supported in-service teacher institutes but not the development of curriculum materials. Jerrold Zacharias' decision to propose development of a high school physics curriculum was motivated by critics of schools like Arthur Bestor, who had railed against the weakening of the disciplines as they were presented in schools, and by the fact that Zacharias was appalled at the outdated content of high school physics textbooks. Similar to Beberman at Illinois, he wanted to bring the physicist's world from the research lab to the high school classroom. Zacharias, at the MIT, wrote a memorandum in March 1956 to James Killian, MIT president, titled "Movie Aids for Teaching Physics in High School" in which he proposed a project for the improvement of physics teaching by creating 90 20-minute films as the heart of the curriculum, each with a "real physicist."[41] Killian's response was enthusiastic, and he suggested that Zacharias gather a group of first-rate scientists to plan the project, because they knew the field best. Then, during one of his trips to Washington that summer, Zacharias showed the memorandum to Alan Waterman, director of the NSF. The two knew each other well from Waterman's time as chief scientist at the Office of Naval Research (ONR). The proposal interested Waterman immediately, and he asked Harry C. Kelly, assistant director for scientific personnel and education at NSF, to arrange a meeting that very evening at the Cosmos Club in Washington, a favorite hangout for the nation's scientific elite, with Waterman, Kelly, Zacharias, Lee DuBridge, and several others present. In an interview some years later Kelly remembered that "they were all enthusiastic about this [education] thing." The scientists at NSF were charged, from their initial founding in 1950, with helping to improve not only basic research, but also science education. As Kelly remembered, they were "looking for some way of attacking the course content thing, and we were kind of lost . . . and it just happened that Zach was interested in the same thing. So we just jumped on it, like that. A physicist from MIT, respected guy, boy, you're our man."[42] And so, Zacharias walked away from the meeting with promises of start-up funding of between $200,000 and $300,000.

Back at MIT, at Killian's urging, Zacharias formed a steering committee including many scientists with strong national reputations.[43] The first meeting of a small steering committee was held on a Saturday in early September, and included Francis Friedman, an MIT theoretical physicist, I. I. Rabi, who had been part of the Manhattan Project, and Edwin Land, inventor of the Polaroid process. Others who would join within the next few months included Vannevar Bush, chairman of the MIT Corporation, film producer Frank Capra, and Henry Chauncey, president of Educational Testing Services. The Committee developed a statement of purpose and the project received the promised NSF funding. Zacharias and colleague Francis Friedman later formed a nonprofit corporation to give the project a home, converted an abandoned movie theater into a film studio, hired a film director, and began work. Over the next five years the project produced 56 films, a textbook, lab experiments with inexpensive apparatus and became the best selling physics program in the nation's history. Collaborators included leading physicists, media specialists, science writers and editors, and high school teachers of physics. Ultimately, the physics project of the PSSC became the prototype for curriculum reform projects in the sciences, mathematics, and other areas of the curriculum such as the social sciences. And, like Illinois Math before it, in an effort to make a difference in the curriculum, the project detoured the science education establishment to work directly with teachers.

And so, Jerrold Zacharias became the chief architect of the curriculum reform movement. Zacharias was a Columbia University–educated physicist who joined the staff of MIT's Radiation Laboratory in 1940 as head of the division on radar transmitter components, the lab that developed radar for use in World War II. He served as one of the four directors of the Manhattan Project in 1945. After the war he returned to MIT to serve as professor of physics and director of the Laboratory for Nuclear Science (LNS). He also served as director of a number of summer studies and projects important to national defense including Project Lexington (1948, nuclear powered flight); Project Hartwell (1950, undersea warfare); Project Charles (1951, air defense); Project Lamp Light (1954, continental defense); and the Summer Study Program of 1952 in which the DEW Line was conceived (distant early warning).[44] Zacharias' style of leading the summer study was also important. Rather than a narrowly defined, security-restricted project with only technical aims (i.e., produce a weapon), he preferred a more flexible approach in which the free exchange of ideas would lead to a new framing of the problem. As he stated, "You've got to allow people to argue the general issues, not just look at technological ones."[45] He was also a member of the President's Science Advisory Committee (PSAC) for a total of nine years between 1952 and 1964.

In 1955, Zacharias ended his involvement in summer studies and stepped down as director of the LNS at MIT, looking for a new direction. Exploratory physics was moving beyond his area of expertise. For the first time he questioned whether he could keep up with younger people in the field, and whether he wanted to invest the personal energy it would take. It is difficult to pin down exact reasons for his interest in educational reform. His service on SAC-ODM provided one stimulus: "The American military would come in [to meetings] and complain that the Russians were getting ahead of us, that we had to do something about education, about teaching—getting more engineers, more scientists—this mind you, all before Sputnik." Concerns over education were widely shared during the early 1950s, with the attacks on progressive education and life-adjustment, and the publication of Bestor's *Educational Wastelands*. Zacharias' own teaching experience raised similar concerns about the quality of schooling. His teaching of undergraduates brought awareness that they had little appreciation of physics as an experimental science, not just theory: "Theory is important ... but only a piece of what goes on ... An experiment, people say that's what you do with your hands; the truth is, you do it with your head."[46] Zacharias, who believed that he could see what was wrong with the standard textbook-driven approach in schools, would become an apostle of a "hands-on" approach to science. So, an awareness of the "out-moded methods of teaching physics" in secondary schools led him to form the PSSC in 1956. In that project, and in subsequent work in curriculum reform, he would employ the processes and modes of operation that had served so well in military research projects.

He believed that the problem under consideration must be understood fully, and given the widest interpretation and discussion. Zacharias and his colleagues applied a systems engineering approach, thoroughly analyzing the problem, its context, and possible solutions, to the PSSC project and subsequent curriculum reform efforts. Also, it must be noted once again, they generally chose not to include members of the education establishment, such as professors of education, in their projects.

Zacharias' proposal for a physics curriculum reform project came at a good time. Concerns over science and engineering manpower led to pressure on NSF to take action, and Zacharias' proposal came from a prestigious physicist whom the leaders at NSF had known for many years.

REFORMER'S AIMS AND MOTIVATIONS

Despite its origins in cold war manpower concerns, the overarching aim of the PSSC and of the curriculum reform work of Zacharias and other physicists was to develop the "rational man" through exposure to and participation in an empirical process of observation and inductive reasoning. The PSSC project drew on a new physics syllabus developed in New York State, which focused attention on the process of science. For Zacharias and other scientists at the time, the "scientific method" as it was described in textbooks was woefully inadequate and came nowhere near explaining or even describing what scientists actually did. They saw the process given to teachers based on John Dewey's description in *How We Think* as a gross oversimplification that would do more harm than good. Such "Deweyite simplicity" was part of what they believed was wrong with education schools, and with the curriculum in high schools when such formulae were applied. Science, as they experienced it, was a far cry from the lock-step process described in most discussions of rational thought. Though Dewey clearly stated that the process was not a linear one, for the most part, when the "thinking process" or "problems approach" made it into schools at all, it was in just the kind of simplified version that the scientists objected to. Instead of such a wooden caricature, they wanted students to get an unvarnished and close-up sense of the scientific spirit that "leaves no stone unturned" in the search for truth, through use of films, labs, and other new materials.[47]

The reformers were also motivated by a number of other factors, not the least of which was their concern over the teaching of science in schools and their desire to improve the process. Many had also experienced, and were negatively affected by encounters with anti-intellectualism and red-baiting. As Zacharias later commented, in his mind the reform was undertaken for "deep political reasons" related to the McCarthy era, and in the hope that education could play a stronger role in fostering logical thought. The positivistic spirit of the reform is captured in a "white paper" drafted by the PSAC in 1959. *Education for the Age of Science* offered a complete articulation of the rationale for the new reform, which was aimed at overcoming "public misunderstanding of science." Understanding included appreciation, respect, and some level of deference. Appreciation also included some knowledge of and experience with the process of rational thought. Their experience with McCarthyism and concern about the general level of anti-intellectualism in the nation also played a role. Zacharias, reflecting on this some time later, said:

> Having lived through World War II, Hitler, Stalin, Joe McCarthy . . . it was perfectly clear that you had to get used to the notion that you have to understand why you believe what you believe . . . where's the evidence? Show me . . .
>
> The reason I was willing to do it [PSSC] was not because I wanted more physics or more physicists or more science; it was because I believed then, and I believe now, that in order to get people to be decent in this world, they have to have some kind of intellectual training that involves knowing [about] Observation, Evidence, the Basis for Belief.[48]

Though the scientists were clearly devoted to the lofty ideals behind the reform, status anxiety also played a role, as they observed, with some envy, the lofty prestige bestowed upon scientists in the USSR.[49] One member of the Education Panel of PSAC commented that a society that "puts Jane Mansfield's breasts or Dietrich's legs above the value of an Oppenheimer" was in serious need of more education. Behind such broad concerns for the future of rationalism was a cold war justification for the proposed new curricular system. As they wrote in their 1959 report, the reform presented a way that "our education can be strengthened so that it will more fully meet the requirement of this age of science, and best serve the nation at a time when the security of the Free World and the defense of human freedom are inescapable responsibilities of the United States."[50] Moreover, the report reiterated the central rationale for the reform when it projected "a permanent shortage" of scientists and engineers.[51] The scientists hoped that the new curriculum would extend greater understanding of modern science and support for the technocratic society run by experts that had emerged from World War II. Beyond this, and in the loftiest terms, they hoped to educate the top 25 percent of the high school population, the future "lawyers, businessmen, statesmen, and other professionals" who would assume positions of power, to support a rational approach to public policy. As Zacharias later recalled, "We had to establish a first-class collection of stuff for the intellectual elite of the country, no question."[52] The fact that the reform was aimed at a hierarchically selected segment of the school population was of apparently little concern, though it was ironic, given that the reform was partly rooted in Bestor's notion of an intellectual education for all. As Jerome Bruner would later comment, "We were very struck by the Soviet selection system" and even "envied" it, but it "ran counter to the egalitarian ideal."[53]

The early programs established initial patterns for the funding of national curriculum development projects that would largely continue for the next 15 to 20 years. One pattern, represented by the University of Illinois Committee, was initial funding by private foundations (often Carnegie or Ford) followed by support from the NSF or the USOE. A second pattern, represented by the MIT Committee, was long-term funding by the NSF or USOE from start-up to publication. By the late 1950s, six national projects were established and funded in science and math, five of which aimed at curriculum reform. By this time, it was apparent that several broad assumptions or guidelines were shared by virtually all of these endeavors, and included the need to change the content, materials, and methods of instruction; a focus on the textbook or learning materials; directors of projects drawn from the academic disciplines; a focus on courses for the academically talented and gifted because it was seen as more critical to the national interest; overriding concern about the integrity of the academic disciplines and their "structures"; learning by discovery and inquiry; and a focus on the cognitive over affective, personal, or social action dimensions. Another shared assumption, if the problem with schools was the shoddy stuff they taught, the solution was to bypass the teacher by creating new and innovative materials under the direction of some of the leading minds in each discipline.[54]

By the end of the decade, projects proliferated, made possible by increased funding from the NSF and the USOE following passage of the National Defense Education Act (NDEA) in 1958. Gradually, the directors of funded projects became the new "leadership" in American education. With the backing of the national government, these new reforms represented a sort of "official" direction for the creation and transmission of knowledge in the nation's schools, one that was built around the academic disciplines and the cold war aim of manpower development.

WARTIME RESEARCH MODEL

Virtually all of the later curriculum development projects involved an application of the same innovative model of research and development embodied in the initial projects. Reformers, most of whom had little previous experience with educational reform efforts, imported methods of research and development from military research programs to the field of education. In effect, the projects owed much of their form to the military-industrial-research complex as it evolved during and after World War II. As illustrated by the work of curriculum historian John Rudolph, the reforms of the era were "designed and implemented by a small cadre of scientists," led by Jerrold Zacharias of MIT, who transferred techniques "almost seamlessly" from military weapons research and development programs of the postwar period to the field of education. Though the push for a more rigorous and academic education originated in critiques of progressivism and cold war manpower concerns, the trend was enhanced and given its "fundamental operational characteristics," along with its conception of the essential "problem of education, and the means of its solution," by the newer research and development techniques drawn from wartime weapons research. The particular "intellectual skills and technical methods" involved had proven their worth during World War II.[55] This interpretation is confirmed by a "Privileged" document drafted by the PSAC on October 4, 1960, three years after the launch of Sputnik, which stated:

> In the United States, large-scale government investment in science and technology is primarily an outgrowth of World War II. The extraordinary contribution of science and technology to the war effort initially sold "science" to the nation, and has led to the present situation in which about 1% of the Federal budget is allocated to science (basic and applied research) and about 10% to technology (development or engineering).
>
> The organizational patterns for the conduct and support of research and development by the Government are mainly adaptations based on World War II experience. In the past 15 years these patterns have matured and generally proved effective.[56]

In the eyes of scientists and policymakers during the cold war era, there seemed no limit to the power of these techniques to solve virtually any problem. Partly due to its origins in wartime research and development, the reform strategy took little account of the culture, history, mores, or social and economic context of the school. If its reform implementation strategies were flawed, an oversimplification that failed to understand the complexities of schools and teaching, few inside the growing reform juggernaut were aware of its limitations. Buoyed by their lofty status and prestige during the cold war years, and their role as advisors to presidents during the height of the cold war, they simply made an assumption that the systems engineering approach that worked so well with radar, missiles, and warfare could be applied to the education of children. The essence of that attitude, and the direction of the reform, was captured in a paper written by Killian in 1963 titled "The Return to Learning: The Curse of Obsolescence in the Schools Can Be Mitigated by the Scholars in the Universities." Indeed, through the myopic vantage point of many participants in the reform, the possibilities seemed limitless. In a later work recounting and reflecting on the reform, Jerome Bruner would write:

> Zack, along with other reformers was convinced that the trouble with schools was the shoddy stuff they taught. The cure was to narrow the gap between knowledge locked up in the university library or the scholar's mind and the fare being taught in schools. If, as in physics, an untrained teacher stood between the knowledge and the student, then bypass the teacher. Put physics on film instead . . . Never mind the oversimplification. It was extraordinarily energizing, and its generous view of educational possibilities seemed "revolutionary" to all of us who were involved.[57]

SPUTNIK AND THE NATIONAL DEFENSE EDUCATION ACT

The ideological backdrop for the NDEA developed over many years of red-baiting and criticism of progressive social studies from academic critics. The stage was set, and the launching of Sputnik, the Soviet satellite, on October 4, 1957, affirmed the criticism and unleashed massive funding for educational reform. Sputnik served as a clarion call for education in science and math, and in studies that would strengthen U.S. brainpower for the cold war. That call was answered by the NDEA, passed in 1958, which provided unprecedented categorical aid in the hundreds of millions of dollars for the improvement of mathematics, science, and foreign language instruction. The NDEA was supported by two main arguments: that national security required the "fullest development of the mental resources and technical skills" of American youth, and that the national interest required federal "assistance to education for programs which are important to our national defense."[58]

The launch of Sputnik was perhaps the key event of the era. It came at an opportune time for Jerrold Zacharias and the physicists in positions of power at NSF and on the administration's Science Advisory Committee. The furor and controversy surrounding Sputnik meant that the Foundation would have to give more attention to curriculum improvement studies on a broadened basis, beyond physics and math and into biology, chemistry, and additional subject areas. The prestige given to physicists and their placement in key positions of power in both NSF and the Science Advisory Committee led to a commanding influence for Zacharias and other key players on the PSSC Steering Committee, and they directly shaped the reform projects that followed. For his part, Zacharias worried that the Sputnik "crisis" would serve "to draw more crap into the vacuum" of reform. The problem, as he saw it, was to create reform projects in biology and chemistry at a level "comparable to the MIT program in physics." This was, partly, a personnel matter, a question of finding brilliant and dynamic leaders, the "leading scholars in each field."[59]

Despite its small size and light weight (under two feet in diameter and made of aluminum), and despite the fact that the United States planned to launch its own satellite in 1958, Sputnik exerted a profound influence on the nation, and on the curriculum reform movement. To James R. Killian, who would be appointed as the president's first science advisor three days later, the launch of Sputnik came as something of a shock, as he recalled his comments to a *Boston Globe* reporter on October 4, 1957:

> That the Russians had accomplished the feat of placing a satellite in orbit suggested to me that this country had grievously underestimated the technological capacity of our adversaries. We were faced with the irreducible fact that both our countries had set out . . . to place a satellite in orbit, and that the Russians had succeeded before we did.[60]

To most Americans it meant that the threat of Soviet technological development that could eclipse American superiority was very real. It also suggested, quite strongly, that if we were to meet that threat, we would have to give more attention to improving education, especially in the sciences. Of course, the origins of the reform extend back into the 1940s, with the previous "crisis" in education, and the emphasis on ideological threats from without and within raised during the McCarthy era. Sputnik, in the context of other recent Soviet actions such as the move into Hungary and the explosion of a new and more powerful nuclear device, led to a gradual shift in public opinion toward the perceived threat of Soviet technological and military strength. The threat of thermonuclear war seemed somehow more real. This shift in public attention gave added legitimacy and a sense of urgency to scientists' calls for curriculum reform, and enhanced the gravitas of their perspective on what specific kind of reform was needed. It spawned a crisis atmosphere, and scientists were called upon to meet the challenge.

THE BLAME

A new flurry of articles and books blamed public schools for the perceived American failure. *Life* magazine ran a five-part series, suggesting that the

Soviet "victory" was the result of a soft curriculum. The gist of the media attention amounted to a new and more urgent assault on life-adjustment education, and its perceived parent, progressive education. The essence of the critique suggested that manpower development concerns had connected to the seemingly perpetual crisis in schooling in a new and more powerful way.

Following Sputnik, national magazines stoked the fires of a renewed "crisis" in education, this time with a more certain focus on national security and a direct linkage to schooling. Though much of this attention was over-zealous, it did serve to help marshal public support for reforming schools. Critics such as Vice Admiral Hyman G. Rickover, known as the father of the nuclear submarine, blamed the schools for our nation falling behind the Russians in science, math, and engineering, endangering the national secu-rity, and called for a renewed emphasis on those subjects. Rickover planted some of the seeds for this interpretation of the Soviet success in a series of speeches he gave beginning around 1956, which were later published in a book titled *Education and Freedom*. In his criticisms of American education he called attention to Soviet advances, and described the superiority of the Soviet and European educational systems. He criticized life-adjustment and asserted that John Dewey and a mistaken and misapplied notion of equality had led to the decline of American schools and neglect of the nation's most talented students. He argued, with force and impact, that development of intellect was the key to winning the cold war.[61] Admiral Rickover expressed what many Americans were thinking when he wrote: "We are engaged in a grim duel. We are beginning to recognize the threat to American technical supremacy which could materialize if Russia succeeds in her ambitious pro-gram of achieving world scientific and engineering supremacy by turning out vast numbers of well-trained scientists and engineers."[62]

An English professor dedicated to rooting out communist and "un-American" influences, E. Merrill Root authored a critique of textbooks that exemplified the anticommunist tenor of the times, and contributed to the crisis mentality. In *Brainwashing in the High Schools*, published in 1958, Root sought to show that "the United States is losing the cold war" because of what is said or left unsaid in senior high school American history textbooks. Root charged that "one third of all the American soldiers made prisoner in Korea succumbed to brainwashing," becoming communist "sympathizers or collaborators." According to Root, these young men yielded because of the failings of their education, because they had never been taught to understand "American politics, American economics, American history, and American ideals."

Using incomplete quotes taken out of context, reasoning from false premises, and other dubious tricks, Root supported his thesis with evidence from the 11 textbooks he cited. He described the books as "critical of free enterprise" and an "anti-capitalistic warping of truth." He also described them as "belittling authentic patriotism" and preaching "class war." He charged that the textbooks attacked Congress, corruption, big business, and the Republican Party, and favored the Populists, the Progressives, and the muckrakers. In addition, he charged that the texts gave the reader "no warning against the sly infiltration of the alien conspiracy called Communism."[63] Root was appointed as a member of the Textbook Evaluation Committee of Operation Textbook, sponsored by America's Future, Inc. "Operation Textbook" was described in a promotional pamphlet as: "A major project designed to report misleading propaganda in high school textbooks in a proper, constructive manner by providing an objective, professional, documented evaluation of each book and by informing school officials, parents, and the general public of the findings."[64]

Shortly after Sputnik, another book appeared that seemed to sum up many of the criticisms of education spawned by cold war competition. *Second Rate Brains* contained a compendium of thought on Soviet schools and scientists, described the achievements and long-range goals of the Soviet "educational machine," offered critiques of "mediocrity" in American schools, and included articles by Rickover and Bestor. The volume concluded with an assessment of the education crisis and suggestions on how to meet it, with the goal of developing "First Rate Brains." The entire volume was published as a Doubleday News Book and edited by Kermit Lansner, general editor of *Newsweek*.[65] The cumulative effect of these persistent and strident attacks on education led to a shift in direction, toward a renewed emphasis on academic study. The attacks led social studies away from its progressive roots and toward the social science disciplines.

Even President Eisenhower urged parents to demand that schools change course, away from the "educational path . . . they have been following as a result of John Dewey's teachings."[66] In a series of speeches he sought to reassure the public that their safety and security were in good hands and that the United States had a long-term commitment to maintain superiority in its science and military prowess.

Eisenhower also took action. He created a new office in the administration by appointing Killian as special assistant to the president for Science and Technology. Perhaps more importantly for the curriculum reform program, he recommended stronger support for education and singled out the science education reform effort in an article that he wrote for *Scientific American*. Shortly after the launch of Sputnik, on October 15, 1957, Eisenhower met with the newly reconstituted PSAC, which included Killian, Waterman, Zacharias, and other insiders. Following the meeting, Eisenhower was quoted in the *New York Times* as saying that the crisis was "awakening the United States to the importance and indeed the absolute necessity of increasing our scientific output of our colleges and universities," and expressed his faith in whatever plans the scientists might develop. A short time later, Waterman sent Eisenhower a first draft of the PSSC textbook along with a note, which read, in part, that "it may well set a pattern for other sciences to follow."[67]

Eisenhower planned to ask for $1 billion to improve science education. Amid bipartisan support, Congress pushed for more, no longer so concerned over large-scale federal involvement in education. While much of the funding would be distributed via the USOE to address a wide range of needs, it was clear that the scientists were at the intellectual helm, steering the general direction of reform. With the support of the president and Congress, it appeared that the fledgling curriculum reform movement was heading for lift off.

Eisenhower gave strong support to the PSSC and the growing movement for curriculum reform. Indeed, his unflagging support was one of the major factors behind its success. In addition to money, he provided much of the necessary rhetoric linking science education to the survival issue of national security. In a speech titled "Our Future Security" delivered in Oklahoma City in November 1957, Eisenhower gave voice to the need for improvements in science education. He framed his argument with a discussion of the dangers posed by Soviet military strength, and recent "dramatic evidence" of Soviet material achievements, and said:

> When such competence in things material is at the service of leaders who have so little regard for things human, and who command the power of an empire, there is danger ahead for free men everywhere. That, my friends, is why the American people have been so aroused about the earth satellites . . . Now, once again, we hear an expansionist regime declaring, "We will bury you."

These were inflammatory words, quoting one of Soviet leader Nikita Khrushchev's more well-known comments. In outlining the nation's defense preparation, Eisenhower cited, "a strong nuclear retaliatory power," to which we are "adding long-range missiles," and other elements. Later in the speech, he discussed long-term problems:

> Time is a big factor in two longer-term problems: strengthening our scientific education and our basic research. The Soviet Union now has—in the combined category of scientists and engineers—a greater number than

the United States. And it is producing graduates in these fields at a much faster rate [which] can no longer be considered offset by lack of quality. This trend is disturbing. Indeed, according to my scientific advisers, this is for the American people the most critical problem of all. My scientific advisers place this problem above all other immediate tasks of producing missiles, of developing new techniques in the Armed Services. We need scientists in the ten years ahead. They say we need them by thousands more than we are presently planning to have.

We should, among other things, have a system of nation-wide testing of high school students; a system of incentives for high-aptitude students to pursue scientific or professional studies; a program to stimulate good quality teaching of mathematics and science.[68]

And so, in keeping with the tenor of the times, and the tone of earlier developments, the science education reform, though fledgling, had support from the nation's highest office, and was laden with the urgency attached to national security in a dangerous time.

A press release from late December 1957 provides a preview of the government's overall plan for improving science education, including programs of the USOE and the NSF. The effort was to include continuation of summer training institutes, programs to interest students in science careers, and programs aimed at improving the teaching of sciences. NSF appropriations for educational undertakings amounted to $14.5 million for 1958, a little more than one-third of the agency's budget. For fiscal 1959, the president would request a substantial increase in the NSF budget, with more than half, or about $79 million, programmed for science education activities. The justification for the increases reflected the national security rationale that was consistently behind the reform, framing it with some "plain truths":

First, education is now more crucially important to long-term national security than ever before.
    Second, there are deficiencies in education which, if allowed to continue, could seriously weaken our national security effort . . . [and]
    The teaching of science and mathematics is one of the foundations for the survival of our free society in the modern world.[69]

The document concluded with a statement indicating that HEW's programs would "complement, not duplicate" the NSF program for education. Finally, it reported that proposed appropriations for both would total about $225 million in the first year, and the aggregate for the four-year period would probably total about $1 billion.

In the months that followed, American interest in science education reform increased dramatically, mainly as a reflection of genuine concern stoked by statements from government and scientific leaders. Evidence of grassroots interest in science education reform may be seen in several initiatives that appeared across the land including a conference on the Educational Implications of Sputnik, called by Idaho governor Robert E. Smylie. The conference, held in Boise, Idaho, on January 20, 1958, involved discussion of "Our Present Sputnik Anxieties" and noted that "the pride of the United States has been wounded and its complacency has been shattered," along with a "growing awareness of the need for the United States to catch up to Russia in scientific achievement." The program described "an emergency because of the Atomic age," and called on the nation as a whole to meet the challenge.[70]

The New York State University Board of Regents also went into action, based on concerns expressed by President Eisenhower and others in November 1957, and developed a 17-point statement on the crisis. The statement called on each school and institution of higher learning to "examine its curriculum, equipment standards, and methods of teaching in science and mathematics and take necessary steps to strengthen and adapt them for the stern requirements of the day." It called on leaders in government, industry, agriculture, and labor to give support to improving the educational program. Officials and teachers in the Huron, Ohio, school system developed an innovative new science program so that students would be "better able to cope with science and math and to take their place in the 'space age.'" The new program, which drew praise from President Eisenhower, had been in development for some time, and involved joint action by the school board, industry, and private citizens.[71]

Officials from NSF continued a lobbying campaign on behalf of what they believed was necessary. A paper drafted by Waterman in July 1958, endorsed by the National Science Board, and published later that year, clearly outlined the need, and reiterated the central justification for the reforms. After describing Soviet efforts to achieve world leadership in science and technology "without need of military domination," Waterman wrote:

We can only insure the possibility of full protection of national security by giving every encouragement to scientific research (as contrasted with development and production). It is only in this way that we can achieve the ideas and the breakthroughs which promise clear superiority.[72]

Thus, as in the early to mid-1950s, the government aim was to maintain "clear superiority" in science and technology. This would only be possible over the long term, it was believed, by improvements in science and mathematics education, duplicating and exceeding the Soviet effort.

The NDEA, the nation's first comprehensive education bill, passed in September 1958, was a direct outgrowth of Sputnik and the cold war, and represented a major shift in the level of federal involvement in public education. While the change in the federal role in education corresponded to a profound long-term broadening and deepening of the federal role in a number of spheres, both the change and the circumstances were no less remarkable. Public Law 85-864, as it was officially known, allocated $1 billion over four years to the Department of HEW for educational improvement and reforms ranging from new school buildings to new experimental curricula.[73] Passage of the NDEA provided a funding base from which even larger programs would be launched in the 1960s, and continued into the 1970s.[74] Funding for the NSF nearly tripled in its budget for 1959 with additional money for its fellowship and teacher institute programs and for the Course Content Improvement Program. For curriculum improvement, PSSC became the prototype. Zacharias' curriculum work was featured in the *Life* magazine series on education, and made headlines in the *New York Times* and *Time* magazine.

With the increase in funding and attention, new curriculum reform projects were established in chemistry, math, earth science, and biology. Although the amount of money allocated to HEW was much larger than what NSF received, a seven to one ratio, the intellectual direction of the reform was still held by NSF and centered in the PSAC. Arthur Fleming, who had served as director of ODM, was appointed to serve as the new secretary of HEW. The modus operandi of the science reforms begun by Zacharias, PSSC, and NSF was embraced by officials at the USOE and eventually applied to nonscience subjects. In the end, the Sputnik "threat," whether real or perceived, raised the status of science even higher, and Zacharias and others at the NSF and on the PSAC grew more confident in their ability to solve nearly any problem, including those in education. As a physicist and veteran of the Rad Lab, Project Hartwell, and a participant in the PSSC, Edward Purcell remembered in an interview some time later, "We were at that time pretty much imbued with the idea that we could do anything if we started from scratch and did it in a rational way, and applied all our technology to it and so on. It was, of course, a time of almost euphoria in that respect, because wartime successes of high technology and physics applied to new problems were still fresh on our minds."[75]

Social studies educators were aware of the trend. Just prior to the launch of Sputnik, a committee appointed by the board of directors of NCSS made its report on "ways and means of strengthening the social studies." A resolution addressing our national "preoccupation with science and math" read, in part: "science and math themselves, important as they are, cannot provide solutions to many of the grave problems that we face today. The most serious issues of our time lie within the field of human affairs. For the solutions to these problems, we must look to the social sciences and the humanities."[76] Notwithstanding the efforts of social studies educators, the first two versions of the NDEA, in 1958 and 1961 did not include funds specifically for social studies. Only in the 1964 version, following NSF and USOE allocations to social studies projects, did the NDEA authorize allocation of funds to improve the teaching of history, geography, and civics.[77]

ALTERNATIVE VOICES

Despite the overwhelming momentum for science education reform as an appendage of cold war politics, there were several thoughtful voices raising questions about the direction in which schools were headed. In the months after Sputnik, critics derided the narrow emphasis of curricular reform on science education. Karl Shapiro, the Pulitzer Prize winning poet, argued in an article titled "Why Out-Russia Russia" that the government had gone too far in adopting a plan for science education reform, and lamented the failure to give equal attention to the humanities. Other writers charged that the United States was attempting to emulate the school system of a totalitarian Soviet state, and suggested that it would ultimately lead to a decline in democratic freedom.[78]

An article by Thomas N. Bonner, which appeared in *The Journal of Higher Education,* declared that science and education had become "the main battleground of the cold war." Arguing that Sputnik has "equally devastating implications for humanities and social-science teaching and for our whole educational enterprise from top to bottom," he called for a "new climate of values in our schools" in which all areas of learning are undertaken seriously, with an understanding of "the real thrill, the excitement, and the enthusiasm of a life devoted to scholarship." Bonner also called for an end to the "childish war in the universities between the academicians and the educators over teacher training."[79]

Perhaps the most widely read critique came with publication of John Hershey's fictional bestseller *The Child Buyer* published in the fall of 1960, about a company that contracted with the federal government to conduct top-secret research crucial to national security and which scoured the nation in search of the best brains, seeking to purchase a child prodigy. "I buy brains," a leading character stated, "that have not been spoiled by . . . what passes for education." The child's development would then be enhanced through a highly technological training process with the power to increase the IQ of its students nearly tenfold by a focus on cognition processes and by avoiding the distracting and often fruitless search "for meaning, for values, for the significance of life." The book was written as a cautionary tale in the wake of the cold war rush to develop stronger math and science education after Sputnik, and what Hershey saw as a misguided and government-supported system to identify and develop the most intellectually gifted students, all driven by concerns over national security.[80] Reviewers described the book's most important contribution as a "frightening demonstration of the possibility of a monstrous misuse of education," one that would stifle "the free will and ranging spirit of the liberal mind."[81] Hershey's book was a thoughtful caricature of the "brain race," paralleling the arms race and the space race.[82]

A BROADENED AGENDA

Following the launch of Sputnik and the new frenzy of criticism and concern over the schools, discussions among educational leaders and policymakers took a new turn, and reached a higher level of intensity. Several key groups held a series of meetings at which the framework for the new reform continued to develop. These groups included the Board of the National Academy of Sciences (NAS), the PSSC, the PSAC, the Education Panel of the NSF and others.

With passage of the NDEA, the growth of research and development for curriculum improvement that began in the technical fields of math and science, was gradually broadened to include the humanities and social sciences. Two important meetings took place in April 1958, six months after the launch of Sputnik, and before passage of the NDEA, which would have an important influence on the direction of curriculum reform. The first of these was a conference on Psychological Research in Education aimed at investigating better approaches to teaching science and math "than are now being utilized."[83] The second was a meeting held at the NAS at which virtually all of the major decisionmakers in funding the growing curriculum reform movement were present. At that meeting it was decided to broaden the PSSC curriculum reform model to other science areas. That decision would open the door to curriculum reform in social studies. At the same meeting, it was agreed that the PSSC would form a small corporation known as Educational Services Incorporated or ESI.[84]

The furor and flurry of interest in education that followed Sputnik provided an invaluable assist to those who wanted schools to raise academic standards and give more attention to gifted students. At the NSF, the "crisis" in education and the intense interest following Sputnik dramatically increased the Foundation's role in secondary school reform. Projects proliferated, made possible by increased funding following passage of the NDEA in 1958, and inspired by Sputnik. At the heart of the curriculum reform movement was Jerrold Zacharias. As Jerome Bruner later recalled, "I think it was Zach, more than anybody else, who converted the Sputnik shock into the curriculum reform movement that it became rather than taking some other form."[85] Though Sputnik "shock" may have served as catalyst for both curriculum reform and for a new and much larger federal role in schools, archival evidence indicates that a broader reform was on the mind of at least one key figure from the earliest period. From at least January 1957, Zacharias projected a larger curriculum reform movement going far beyond the sciences and encompassing "Science, Literature, History, Art, Law, etc.," virtually the entire curriculum. He envisioned a broad reform of the federal role in education, encompassing all levels of the system from grade school through postdoctoral research. The objectives of the reform, as outlined in a January 1957 memo included:

a. Bridge or remove two gaps
   (1) between intellectuals and nonintellectuals;
   (2) between humanitarians and scientists.
b. Reduce age of students when specialized.
c. Generate an age of outstanding intellectuals without so much dependence on the vanishing western European supply.
d. Generate an understanding of the power of reasoning on ordinary matters such as management and public relations.[86]

The reform would involve "a half million teachers in total," a "hundred thousand science teachers" and "ten thousand physics teachers." It would encompass "cross-breeding of the subjects," along with preparation, production, and distribution of learning and teaching aids, essentially reproducing the PSSC model across the entire system. And, while improving education for all, it would clearly focus on developing "the best and brightest" from an early age.[87]

Gradually, as the reform took hold, the directors of funded projects became the new "leadership" in American education. With the backing of the national government, these new reforms represented a sort of "official" direction for the creation and transmission of knowledge in the nation's schools, one that was built around the academic disciplines and the cold war aim of manpower development, even if only a few of those involved seemed to explicitly acknowledge it at the time.

CONCLUSION

Schools and the curriculum have frequently served as an ideological battleground and as a site for the attempted purification of American ideology. Debate over education is inexorably linked to questions of purpose. Whom shall the schools serve? Whose purposes shall receive priority? Schools have served many functions over the years that go far beyond their professed curricular aim of teaching the subject matter and developing student knowledge, skills, and attitudes. They have been cast in the institutional role of preparing workers for business, sorting the child into prearranged life roles, and educating for democratic citizenship, among other possible uses. Debate over the school and what it taught encapsulated many of the nation's deepest concerns, a projection of hopes and fears on the screen of curriculum reform. During the postwar period, rhetoric in education passed from the progressive "life-adjustment" manpower planner of the late 1940s to the cold war manpower planner of the 1950s. Cold war conflict and related fears dominated educational discourse, influenced practice in social studies classrooms, and served as catalyst to a major effort to reform and improve the nation's schools. Cold war fears combined with the critique of progressive social studies ensured that a new reform, the new social studies movement, would take an academic and largely discipline-based approach to the field.

The "death" of progressive education and the launch of Sputnik opened the door to a new reform. Renewal of schooling with emphasis on an academic orientation was conditioned by several factors: long simmering criticisms of life-adjustment and progressive education; concerns over manpower developments in the Soviet Union; and fears that we were falling behind. Thus, schools, and the effort to develop students' minds, were cast as the ultimate weapon, another tool in the nation's arsenal. The reform focused on developing an education second to none, led by an elite, framed by the best and brightest scholars in privileged positions at the nation's leading research universities. It would bring scientists, and later social scientists, into the classroom in an effort to upgrade the nation's education system. Though scientists had high expectations for reforming schools, their hopes were kindled by a vision of omnipotence and an arrogance linked to their lofty status at the apex of the nation's military-industrial-academic complex. Key leaders of the reform were prestigious physicists many of whom had participated in wartime military research in the Manhattan Project and subsequent endeavors. Though handicapped by their own lack of knowledge and understanding of the social, political, and historical context of schooling, they chose to circumvent the education establishment, in hindsight a tragic strategic miss-step. All of this was occurring, of course, within the context of the nuclear age, with the threat of annihilation looming just around the bend and creating an atmosphere of extreme urgency.

PART II

FROM WOODS HOLE TO PROJECT SOCIAL STUDIES: EMERGENCE OF A REFORM

CHAPTER 3

GREAT MINDS AT WOODS HOLE

By THE LATE 1950s, the curriculum reform movement spawned by the cold war was well underway, with work of the Physical Science Study Committee (PSSC) beginning to bear fruit, and new projects underway in chemistry and biology. Though the reform had begun to spread to other hard sciences, it had yet to make much headway toward the original blueprint sketched out by Jerrold Zacharias in 1957 for a broader reform that reached across the curriculum and up and down the grades, from the earliest years to graduate school. Given his success with summer studies, and perhaps because he was less comfortable with the social sciences and humanities and wanted to gather the best minds, Zacharias organized several conferences that played an instrumental role in the broadening of the reform. The most well-known of these, the Woods Hole Conference in 1959, led to a seminal book that would largely define the era of educational reform, at least its early years. Another conference, held in 1962, would give shape to the emerging social science reforms that would come to be known as the new social studies, and would play a key part in the drive toward broader reform of the curriculum. While the curriculum reform movement was gathering steam, the cold war was generating heat. Soviet missiles would be placed in Cuba, leading to one major cold war confrontation, and American military advisors would be sent to Vietnam, leading to another. Meanwhile, the civil rights movement, the free speech movement, and a growing spirit of resistance to the demands of the military-industrial complex would continue to emerge. All of these would eventually come together into what would later become known as the counter-culture movement, with serious implications for the curriculum. By the late 1950s, the early steps of the curriculum reform were beginning to shift into high gear, becoming a movement that would, at least for several years, have significant influence on schools.

THE EASTON CONFERENCE

Seldom mentioned in histories of the period, the Easton Conference was, in a sense, a preliminary test-run for Woods Hole. Initially known as the "Exploratory Conference on Psychological Research in Education," sponsorship of the conference reflected the National Academy's Advisory Board on Education's (ABE) observation that "relatively little direct attention was being given to the fundamental processes in education by professional research psychologists," and their desire to do something about it.[1]

The conference proposal for the Easton meeting mailed to prospective participants included a list of five questions related to the contributions of and new directions for psychological research on teaching, beginning with: "Are there now available better educational procedures, techniques, and devices for the teaching of scientific and mathematical subjects than are now being utilized?" The aim of the conference was to assess the present status of research and recommend new research and actions that the Academy and its National Research Council (NRC) could take to promote "effective psychological research having a potential value for education." Invited participants included many of the leading psychologists of the time, including Jerome Bruner, B. F. Skinner, Robert M. Gagne, and several others who would later be at Woods Hole.[2] Though Bruner did not attend, Skinner, Gagne, Max Beberman, Paul Woodring, Kenneth Spence, John Carroll, C. R. Carpenter, and Randall M. Whaley were present and served on various conference panels, each of which produced a report. The main work of the conference was done in three panels that separately considered the following topics: (a) fundamental learning processes in education, including the status of relevant research and promising directions of future research; (b) problems of communication in education, with special reference to research in the preparation and programming of instructional materials; and (c) the research methodology of educational evaluation.

The conference, held in Easton, Maryland, from April 24–26, 1958, began with an overview by Whaley of the activities of the Academy's ABE and its objectives in sponsoring the conference. C. R. Carpenter reviewed the implications of pending federal legislation (NDEA), and in an evening session, William A. Hunt described Northwestern University's cooperative project involving the School of Education and the Department of Psychology. Another evening session involved Max Beberman discussing the Illinois Mathematics project. The three panel reports raised several of the key issues that would later be addressed in greater depth at Woods Hole the following year. The report of the first panel discussed possible "laws of learning," the need for research on "learned motives," and on "creativity" and "decision-making." It also asked about the "optimal times for introducing certain subjects, and asked whether there were "history readiness ages," or "algebra readiness ages," or "reading readiness ages." It closed with a statement suggesting, "[T]he panel believes that a technology of learning can be developed so that maximum efficiency— where efficiency is viewed broadly—can be obtained."[3] The report of the second panel at the Easton conference focused on communication in education, and discussed objectives, attitudes, and "transfer of training," the "sequencing" and "programming" of instructional materials, and the "problem of motivating learning." The panel also called for more research and investigation on various aspects of both the "*content* of educational experience and the methods by which the content is presented."[4] Though its findings were preliminary, many of the conference topics, themes, and tentative conclusions strongly foreshadowed Woods Hole. And, though there was not as much discussion of the "systems" theme, the model was strikingly similar.

THE WOODS HOLE CONFERENCE

The Woods Hole Conference, held in September 1959, at Woods Hole on Cape Cod, Massachusetts, brought together leaders in the new reforms in science and math for a ten-day conference, and led to a concise and well-crafted formulation of the principles of curriculum development shared in the new movement. The meeting began with the steering committee getting together on September 8, the eve of the conference.[5] As conference director Jerome Bruner later recalled, "September on Cape Cod can be a glory of late summer: crisp, cool, brilliant. And 1959 was one such year."[6] Officially known as the "Study Group on Fundamental Processes in Education," the aim of the gathering was to "take stock of" the reform movement, and to broaden participation, branching out beyond the hard sciences to include psychologists, historians, linguists, and others. Among the 34 participants were the curriculum makers—biologists, mathematicians, physicists—a large number of psychologists, and a few professional educators. Participants included luminaries such as Jerome Bruner, a cognitive psychologist at Harvard; psychologist Richard Alpert of Harvard; mathematician Edward Begle of Yale; Lee Cronbach, a psychologist from the University of Illinois; John H. Fischer, dean of Teachers College; psychologist Robert M. Gagne of Princeton; biologist

H. Bentley Glass of Johns Hopkins; psychologist Barbel Inhelder from Geneva, Switzerland; mathematician David Page of Illinois; and Jerrold Zacharias of Massachusetts Institute of Technology (MIT). Also included among the attendees were two historians, John Blum of Harvard, and Donald Cole of the Phillips Exeter Academy.[7] This was the first time that psychologists were brought together with leading scientists to discuss the teaching of the various disciplines. The psychologists were representative of a wide spectrum of orientations including behaviorist, Gestalt, psychometric, and developmental. The group was "leavened" with a few professional educators, two historians, and a classicist. As Bruner later wrote, the conference planners had decided it would be "unwise to limit ourselves exclusively to the teaching of science, that the eventual problem would be more general than that, and that it would be in the interest of perspective to compare the issues involved in teaching science with those in a more humanistic field, such as history."[8]

The meeting was conducted under the auspices of the National Academy of Sciences (NAS), and instigated by Randall M. Whaley, chair of the Academy's ABE, who had also been instrumental in sponsoring the Easton Conference on psychology and education held the year before. The National Academy of Sciences—NRC is a private, nonprofit organization of scientists. The Academy, founded in 1863 under a charter granted by President Lincoln, is dedicated to the furtherance of science and its use for the general welfare. Its charter empowered it to provide for all activities appropriate to academies of science, and it was required to act as scientific adviser to the federal government. The NAS receives funds from both public and private sources; works to stimulate research and its application; and promotes effective utilization of scientific and technical resources.[9]

Funding for the Woods Hole Conference came from the National Science Foundation (NSF) and United States Office of Education (USOE), under the Cooperative Research Program and Title VIIB of the NDEA of 1958, but also from several other prestigious agencies including the NAS/NRC, the American Association for the Advancement of Science, the Carnegie Corporation of New York, the United States Air Force Research and Development Command, and the Rand Corporation. All funding sources were "establishment" organizations and key components of the military-industrial-academic complex.

Harvard psychologist Jerome Bruner was chosen to chair the conference. To the scientists arranging the meeting, and supporting the reform, he seemed a good choice.[10] Bruner had "inside knowledge" of both the reform and the national security structure of the nation. An "establishment man" as he recalled much later, "Oppenheimer was my friend."[11]

As one of the leading cognitive psychologists in the world, Bruner was well versed in learning theory. The thinking was that perhaps he, along with other psychologists in attendance, could help make sense of the reform, reframing it by developing a stronger theory, especially important as the reform was broadened beyond the hard sciences. In a preconference memo, Bruner drew a parallel between the work of the conference and "the experience of psychologists working in the armed forces at the beginning of World War II. Both with respect to training devices being used and in the design of instruments to be used in combat and support operations, it turned out to be the case that a great deal of useful work could be done without the support of new research . . . I rather suspect that at the outset there will be a parallel in work on the curricula."[12] Bruner had served in the Psychological Warfare division of the Office of War Intelligence during World War II and was a veteran of Project Troy as were Morison, Friedman, and Zacharias. Specific objectives described in the initial proposal for the conference included (1 improvement of communication of knowledge of subject matter [and] (2) improvement of use of technological devices and systems for education.[13]

Instructional technologies were prominent on the agenda. There were presentations from several early projects, films from the projects were screened in the evenings, and afternoon sessions were held on teaching machines and audio-visual aids.

In a sense, what was emerging was a manufactured consensus, paid for by stakeholders with an interest in education conducted on behalf of national security. It was a direct outgrowth of the cold war, and of the persistent attacks on progressive education. As such, it represented the United States of America, or at least a significant selection of its national intellectual leadership, in concerted action against progressive education, and later, against progressive versions of social studies. By the 1950s and 1960s, the thinking of disciplinarians had come a long way from the American Social Science Association's nineteenth century notion of a general and redemptive social science, aimed at social welfare. Now, the aim of cold, disinterested social science, and teaching that carried the same approach, was in vogue. It represented positivism, structuralism, and the logic of the educational machine run to its coherent conclusion.

THEORETICAL FOUNDATIONS

The aim of the new social studies movement was to transform students into "junior" social scientists and "little league" historians. The developments of the 1960s rested, in part, on a small, influential book,

The Process of Education, written by conference director Jerome Bruner, reporting on the proceedings of the Woods Hole Conference.

The Woods Hole Conference was held at the secluded Whitney Estate in Woods Hole, Massachusetts, from September 9 to 18, 1959, and aimed at improving precollegiate science education. The Whitney Estate, summer headquarters of the Academy, had previously hosted defense studies sponsored by the Air Force, and was a big, rambling house that could easily hold the meetings. The Woods Hole Conference was, in part, a direct reaction to Sputnik and the complaints of critics such as Vice Admiral Hyman Rickover. The conference, dominated by scientists from Harvard and MIT, brought together scientists, scholars, and educators, all but one of them men, with the purpose of discussing how science education in schools might be improved. Though the ten-day meeting aimed to examine "fundamental processes involved in imparting to young students a sense of the substance and method of science," in actuality, the conference went beyond the teaching of science to comparison of the problems of teaching science with the problems of teaching more humanistic fields such as history.

Participants were divided into study groups that met throughout the conference; each prepared a report to be presented at the end of the ten days. The first three days of the meeting were devoted largely to presentations on curriculum reform work being done in biology, history, mathematics, and physics, along with demonstrations of teaching devices such as the teaching machine and films. This early portion of the conference would also include a teaching demonstration by a young mathematician, David Page, who rounded up some local schoolchildren to demonstrate his approach to teaching mathematics from the Illinois Math project.[14]

One study group, on the apparatus of teaching, lamented the lack of modern technology in education and believed that application of "systems development principles" held great promise for educational improvement because it would "further the application of modern technology to improve education." The group, strongly influenced by Zacharias, put forth a template for curriculum design drawn on the systems development approach: (1) define course goals; (2) determine the functions to be performed; and (3) assign functions to men and machines to optimize the effectiveness of the entire system.[15] The model was borrowed directly from wartime research projects such as Hartwell and Troy.

One month prior to the conference on education, there had been an Air Force study on education at Woods Hole, and their report, which applied a weapons system analysis to education (i.e., "human functions and tasks . . . can be exactly and objectively specified . . . as in the Atlas

Weapons system"), was circulated among conference attendees.[16] In the minds of the reformers, it was a powerful model to be emulated. Moreover, as John Rudolph has pointed out, several techniques were borrowed from a defense "systems engineering" perspective, including the use of the summer study; a fast-paced and loosely structured working environment; and an emphasis on engineering the whole system.

Zacharias and at least a few other participants were well aware that they were applying this model. In a later interview, Zacharias described his primary contribution to school reform as "bringing a systems engineering approach to the problems of education."[17] While on the surface it appears logical and imminently useful to apply such a powerful and successful model to education, in the application of any model one must proceed with caution. Based on an analogy to a weapons system, the application breaks down in use. Weapons are used for military purposes: to defend, to destroy, to kill, and to conquer. Institutionalized education, on the other hand, has the central aim of helping students learn about and understand a complex world. Application of a defense systems analysis approach to the problems of education gave the reformers, and their supporters, an arrogance that contributed to their decision to largely ignore the history of previous educational reform, and to consciously bypass much of the educational establishment.

Despite an inauspicious beginning, the conferees at Woods Hole came up with some interesting ideas. In *The Process of Education*, Bruner summarized his own "sense of the meeting" based on the reports of the five working groups formed at the conference. Moreover, in writing his report Bruner set out to develop what he later called "universal statements."[18] In his introductory chapter, Bruner briefly described the work of a few of the curriculum development projects in science and mathematics, and asserted:

> The main objective of this work has been to present subject matter effectively—that is, with due regard not only for coverage but also for structure . . . emphasizing the structure of a subject, be it mathematics or history—emphasizing it in a way that seeks to give a student as quickly as possible a sense of the fundamental ideas of a discipline.[19]

The conference took the "structure of the disciplines" as its central theme and overriding assumption, and examined in some depth "the role of structure in learning and how it may be made central in teaching." Further, conferees assumed the goal of "giving students an understanding of the fundamental structure of whatever subjects we choose to teach," and the "teaching and learning of structure" rather than simply the "mastery of facts and techniques."[20] In a restatement of one of the main premises of the emerging curriculum reform, Bruner argued that design of the curriculum required a fundamental understanding of the subject, and could not be carried out effectively "without the active participation of the ablest scholars and scientists."[21]

In a chapter on the importance of structure, Bruner asserted, "The first object of any act of learning . . . is that it should serve us in the future" through "specific transfer of training" to similar tasks and "non-specific transfer . . . [which] consists of learning initially not a skill but a general idea, which can then be used as a basis for recognizing subsequent problems as special cases of the idea originally mastered." Transfer of ideas and principles, Bruner asserted, "is dependent upon mastery of the structure of the subject matter."[22] Moreover, Bruner went on, "Mastery of the fundamental ideas of a field involves not only the grasping of general principles, but also the development of an attitude toward learning and inquiry, toward guessing and hunches, toward the possibility of solving problems on one's own . . . To instill such attitudes by teaching . . . it would seem that an important ingredient is a sense of excitement about discovery."[23]

Bruner reported that various people who had worked on curriculum development in science and math had urged, "[I]t is possible to present the fundamental structure of a discipline in such a way as to preserve some of the exciting sequences that lead a student to discover for himself." He cited the Illinois Math project and reported, "They have been active in devising methods that permit a student to discover for himself the generalization that lies behind a particular mathematical operation." He also cited an example from social studies carried out with a sixth grade class in which students were asked to locate the major cities of an area on a map of physical features and natural resources, but with no place names. The ensuing class discussion "rapidly produced a variety of plausible theories concerning the requirements of a city."[24] Bruner summarized the chapter on structure with four general principles: that it makes the subject more comprehensible, that students will be better able to remember the main ideas or principles, that it would lead to greater transfer, and that it would narrow the gap between advanced knowledge and elementary knowledge.

The second theme of the conference had to do with readiness for learning and the common assumption that many subjects must be postponed on the grounds that they are too difficult. The chapter devoted to this theme built upon its memorable opening sentence: "We begin with the hypothesis that any subject can be taught effectively in some intellectually honest form to any child at any stage of development." The hypothesis was premised on the judgment "that any idea can be represented honestly and usefully in the thought forms of children of school age, and that these first representations can later be made more powerful and precise more easily by virtue of this early learning."[25] This notion, when combined with the focus on the structure of the disciplines, was at the heart of the reform, and was captured succinctly in Bruner's opening sentence. It directly challenged the conventional wisdom of the adult world about how children learn, and led to new and exciting possibilities for curriculum reform. At the same time, it was, perhaps, understood only dimly by many who read it, and was not to be accepted without qualification. After describing Piaget's stage theory (from trial and error, to concrete mental operations, to the hypothetical) Bruner asserted that the intellectual development of the child is "no clockwork sequence of events," that it is influenced by the environment, and could be influenced by "the school environment."[26]

Barb Inhelder, when asked to address "ways in which the child could be moved along faster through the various stages of intellectual development," wrote, in a memorandum prepared for the conference, that "basic notions" in math and science "are perfectly accessible to children of seven to ten years of age, *provided that they are divorced from their mathematical expression and studied through materials that the child can handle himself.*" She gave examples from mathematics and physics, and argued that "systematic instruction" at a younger age can "lay a groundwork in the fundamentals that can be used later and with great profit at the secondary level."[27] In a passage making a case for the "spiral curriculum," and directly relevant to social studies, Bruner wrote, "If the hypothesis with which this section was introduced is true—that any subject can be taught to any child in some honest form—then it should follow that a curriculum ought to be built around the great issues, principles, and values that a society deems worthy of the continual concern of its members."[28] Thus, relatively sophisticated concepts in any field, including history and the social sciences, could be introduced in simpler form in the early years and revisited later as the curriculum spirals through and revisits important topics, themes, and issues.

A third theme involved the nature of intuition and the training of hunches. "Unfortunately," Bruner wrote, "the formalism of school learning has somehow devalued intuition." Those involved in developing math and science curricula believe that "much more work is needed to discover how we may develop the intuitive gifts for our students, from the earliest grades onward . . . The shrewd guess, the fertile hypothesis," Bruner asserted, "is a much-neglected and essential feature of productive thinking."[29]

These three themes, Bruner wrote, were all premised on a central conviction:

> That intellectual activity anywhere is the same, whether at the frontier of knowledge or in a third-grade classroom . . . The difference is in degree, not in kind. The schoolboy learning physics *is* a physicist, and it is easier for him to learn physics behaving like a physicist than doing something else. The 'something else' usually involves the task of mastering . . . classroom discussions and textbooks that talk about the conclusions in a field of intellectual inquiry rather than centering upon the inquiry itself. Approached in that way, high school physics often looks very little like physics, social studies are removed from the issues of life and society as usually discussed, and school mathematics too often has lost contact with what is at the heart of the subject, the idea of order.[30]

At Woods Hole, the "something else" Bruner referred to was called "a middle language," and it seemed to members of the conference that its use was at the heart of the problem with the schools. That is, most teaching focused on the conclusions of research, on facts and stories encapsulated in textbooks, and regurgitation of material on tests, rather than emphasizing inquiry or deep understanding.

A fourth theme centered on how to stimulate student motivation through interest in the material. In discussing motivation, Bruner suggested that there was, in America, "a new emphasis upon the pursuit of excellence." Admitting that there will always be a range of motivations for learning at work among schoolchildren, such as "parents and teachers to be pleased, one's contemporaries to be dealt with, one's sense of mastery to be developed," there was a growing focus, he suggested, on "increasing the inherent interest of materials taught" along with developing in the child "an appropriate set of attitudes and values about intellectual activity." Bruner captured the essence of the aim of motivating students in another often cited passage:

> Somewhere between apathy and wild excitement, there is an optimum level of aroused attention that is ideal for classroom activity. What is that level? Frenzied activity fostered by the competitive project may leave no pause for reflection, for evaluation, for generalization, while excessive orderliness, with each student waiting passively for his turn, produces boredom and ultimate apathy. There is a day-to-day problem here of great significance.[31]

He warned of the dangers of excessive emphasis on math and science, which could lead to the "devaluation of humanistic learning," and of the consequences of too much competition, in an age during which it seemed the schools and society were absorbed in an ever-intensifying focus upon competitiveness. One of the dangers, he pointed out, with an overemphasis on competition, was its impact on schools and society by creating a sorting mechanism by which students may be categorized and ranked at too early an age, based on hard-to-change variables.

> A meritocracy, however, implies a system of competition in which students are moved ahead and given further opportunities on the base of their achievement, with position in later life increasingly and irreversibly determined by earlier school records. Not only later educational opportunities but subsequent job opportunities become increasingly fixed by earlier school performance. The late bloomer, the early rebel, the child from an educationally indifferent home—all of them, in a full-scale meritocracy, become victims of an often senseless irreversibility of decision.[32]

By writing these passages, Bruner acknowledged "several undesirable effects [of meritocracy] on the climate in which education occurs," and demonstrated an awareness of the social, economic, and political context of schooling. However, in a manner befitting the tenor of the reform, the arrogance of the reformers, and their confidence in systems analysis, he rather hopefully suggested, "with advance planning we may be able to control them."[33]

In a memo to the panel on motivation, Bruner suggested that it might be "worthwhile to have a fresh look at the culture of the American school," and wrote, "There is some evidence now available to indicate that the overachiever tends to be a conformist to the patterns of thinking required by the schools—often these are patterns of thought that are inimical to good analytical thinking, stressing the requirement of storing available information for the regurgitation of this material on examinations."

"If the situation is changed," he wondered, "so that analytic skills are honored by the teacher, will we still have the same overachievers or will a new group emerge? . . . Indeed, classrooms might even be called 'mimicry factories,' in contrast to the atmosphere that a Dave Page creates or that is created by emphasis upon discovery by the Illinois Mathematics group."[34]

In the final chapter, Bruner discussed the findings of the Panel on the Apparatus of Teaching, and the uses of audio-visual aids, which he described as "devices for vicarious experience." Much of his discussion focused on systems analysis with the aim of integrating the various devices (film, teaching machine, textbook, etc.) so that they could be used in concert to optimum effect.

Not everyone involved at Woods Hole supported all of Bruner's ideas. Some feared that the approach could lead to a superficial memorization of main ideas or principles, with little knowledge and even less real understanding. Others were skeptical about the assertions on readiness, and wanted to pin down the age at which children were really ready to grasp the major concepts of a discipline. Zacharias, who had collaborated in planning the conference, was particularly critical of the notion of "structure," and recalled in an interview: "Structure gives me the pip when you apply it to education. Jerry makes such a point that the way to remember something is to understand its structure; that's the way Jerry remembers, but that may not capture the interests of the kid." In an unpublished paper Zacharias pointed out that scientific principles like Newton's laws of motion and gravity are not what science is all about at "the cutting edge." Instead, for Zacharias, science was more about intuitive thinking, the kind of thinking that scientists use when examining unexplored terrain, or as Zacharias put it, "rummaging around in the intellectual attic."[35] Analytic thinking involves the use of logic and deductive reasoning and tends to proceed in a step-by-step fashion, while intuitive thinking is less organized and may proceed somewhat haphazardly. Intuitive thought is often represented by the creative flash of insight or the leap to a bold hypothesis, while the proof or verification process is more analytic. Most of the curriculum reformers at Woods Hole sought to cultivate a wide spectrum of thinking styles, ranging from logic and rationalism to intuition and creativity.

Not all of these ideas were new. In fact, few of them were. In social studies the concept of inquiry or discovery-oriented teaching had been around at least since the days of the scientific historians in the nineteenth century, and was increasingly championed by many progressive educators. Motivation through student interest was also an old song. Parts of the new curriculum movement were a recapitulation of common ideas in the rhetoric of education. The focus on the "structures" of the disciplines was a reformulation, though what it actually meant in terms of classroom practice remained somewhat unclear.

OMISSIONS

At least two important ideas from the conference were left out of Bruner's description in *The Process of Education*. The report from the panel on Apparatus of Teaching contained a great deal of commentary on, theorizing about, and explicit discussion of, the systems analysis approach and its application to the curriculum. The panel clearly thought of "teaching-communicating-learning operations" as "*systems of activities* which manage or regulate content and media for the purpose of instigating defined changes in understanding and actions of students." It discussed its hope that "the adoption and exploitation of a *systems approach* to educational design" would improve education through the "technical integrations of men and machines in the form of systems." The panel went on, "While perhaps the most spectacular examples of system design are to be found in complex military situations, increasing application is being made" in business and industry, banking, marketing, production, distribution, and transportation. It argued that the education system was "the kind of complex organismic enterprise the improvement of which can aptly be planned according to system development principles." It advocated creation of an "analog model" for educational improvement, and cited the ongoing curriculum reform efforts in physics, mathematics, and biology as "excellent examples of the kind of thoroughgoing planning operations implied by a system model." They were "subsystems" which could be easily integrated into the "total system" in an effort to "optimize the effectiveness of the whole system."[36] The report went on to lay out a full argument for applying a systems approach to education, which would include analysis of major functions, a conceptual framework, identification of strengths and weaknesses in resources, the proper phasing of actions, use of advances in technology, and limiting factors, which could be addressed by making adjustments. It called for research via adoption of "a teaching-learning systems approach," and framed the entire process as "a matter of national survival."[37] Though Zacharias was not an official member of the panel, it is clear that he had made his mark on its thinking.

A second panel report that also contained a good deal of interesting material ultimately left out of Bruner's final report in *The Process of Education* was from the Panel on Sequence and its discussion of the very real constraints that often serve as impediments to reform. That panel, in a section titled "Considerations of Practice and Policy" included several passages that reformers would do well to consider seriously. They wrote:

> The construction of curricula proceeds, of course, in a real world where changing social, cultural and political conditions continually alter the surrounds and the goals of the school . . . The society . . . imposes constraints upon curriculum and sequence planning . . . American school systems, school boards and superintendents, PTA's and the like constitute a network of institutions that have developed patterns of behavior and of resistance that invariably impinge upon the pace and direction of change.

They went on to cite the fact that some topics, such as "the word evolution," were taboo, and would be rejected by many schools, while many teachers would have "strong genteel predilections" against discussing eggs and sperm with children of a "tender" age.

Furthermore, they argued:

> Such constraints are real. Some are bound to exist for a long time. A few may impose clumsy limitations upon all kinds of improvements . . . a school board might reject a curriculum plan which seemed to endanger local autonomy . . . Some school boards and parents tend to regard their own last experience in the class room as the best of all possible experiences . . . The old school tie continues to impede circulation above its knot.[38]

They also suggested that while it is important to recognize social constraints on the curriculum, it is more important "to proceed in planning curricula on the assumption that intelligent cooperation can overcome them. Indeed, many school boards, parents, and teachers are eager for cooperation and need only to be shown a good product in order to be persuaded to adopt it."[39] So while recognizing constraints on curriculum reform, the panel seemed to imply that it was not so serious as to stand in the way of good materials. It could be "overcome." The presence of this discussion of constraints suggests that many members of the conference were aware of the cultural and institutional factors that could derail reform. However, the panel's upbeat attitude toward them, and the fact that Bruner made little mention of constraints in his book, served to assure that ways of dealing effectively with the possible obstacles to reform were given little serious attention.

The fact that Bruner left this discussion out of his book is especially ironic, given the eventual crisis over the Man: A Course of Study (MACOS) project that would bring the period of reform to a close. Perhaps it reflects a lack of experience with schooling, a lack of knowledge of the long history of controversy over the curriculum, or both. In a letter to Harvard president James B. Conant, who had expressed concerns about the nature of the reform, Bruner argued that the reformers were "mindful" of the difficulties involved in any attempt to reform the curriculum, and stated, "We are convinced that a few years of intense work can take us a long way in getting across those difficulties."[40] In any event, the virtual omission of the topic from *The Process of Education* suggests a rather high level of naiveté.

These ideas, relating the reform to the context of schools and society, hints strongly at what Peter Dow has referred to as "the missing issue." In *Schoolhouse Politics* Dow writes, "What is strikingly absent from the

Woods Hole discussions is an examination of the social and political implications of the proposed reforms." Though Bruner did make some effort to relate *Process* to the aims of education in a meritocratic society and raised several troubling issues such as the potential impact of a tendency "to push the brighter students ahead" to later schooling and jobs, that discussion was largely lost in the emphasis on what he perceived as a new and revolutionary "cutting edge" theory of pedagogy.[41] To at least a few others, notably former Harvard president James B. Conant, it seemed that Bruner, Zacharias, and the other reformers were behaving presumptuously. Even Bruner had some doubts about plans for the reform of elementary school science, and lamented the "opposition of Mr. Conant, who I think has the impression that a few of us are setting ourselves up as self-styled arbiters of elementary education and science," going against a long tradition of community control over education.[42]

It was an approach to education that favored the elite, explicitly focused on the top 25 percent, and that sought to develop a product, especially for science and technology, fashioned in the image of the reformers. That the emerging reform had such a focus is partially understandable, given the driving wheel of cold war politics and the perceived manpower shortage that framed education as an essential component of competition for survival. However, in hindsight, the reform appears deeply flawed, focused on the child's cognitive and intellectual development at the expense of other areas. Moreover, the reformers not only lacked deep and contextualized knowledge of the schools, their positions of power and the critiques of education which they appeared to purchase led them to ignore logical sources of such knowledge that might have helped build a stronger, deeply grounded and more well-rounded effort at reform.

At least some of this was rooted in arrogance and an antieducation attitude. Zacharias was well-known for his arrogance.[43] As for Bruner, in a late 1950s exchange he admitted: "Of course I am *arrogant*. Is there an alternative?"[44] Later, an exchange of postcards between Bruner and educational psychologist Lee Cronbach, a participant at Woods Hole and a reviewer of Bruner's final draft, sharply delineated opposing attitudes on education following release of *The Process of Education*. Cronbach wrote to Bruner with sarcastic humor:

> You, sir, are one hell of a politician. Diplomat—pfa!
> I quote: Lee Cronbach, Psychology
>   Gilbert Finlay, Physics
>   Barb Inhelder, Psychology
>   David Page, Math

Everyone of these holds a title in education!
You *are* a Rickover at heart.

Lee

To which Bruner responded:

Dear Lee,

I have just ordered a salted crow to eat along with a canned humble pie.
I now understand why Dag Hammarskjold is so highly valued!
    I remain, sir, your most loyal and obedient servant.

J. B.[45]

In correspondence a few weeks later, Bruner revisited similar concerns, and revealed perhaps even greater complexity:

We are a funny society. After generations of neglecting the sphere of education, we expect to wake up and find it peopled with some sort of mixture of geniuses and angels. Come now, they are not all stinkers you know and I think the proper thing to do is to find the good ones among them and given [*sic*] them some aid and comfort while trying to find some replacements.[46]

Reflecting on his experiences many years later, Peter Dow, who would become a leading figure in the reform, recalled that reformers were "very skeptical" of Colleges of Education and those who taught there, but did not have the same attitude toward teachers. "Zacharias was very contemptuous" of education schools. He started looking at the way physics was taught, thus leading to his involvement. "Colleges of Education were a ghetto on the university campus . . . I shared that view myself."[47]

Schools of education have long been held in low esteem.[48] Moreover, we must recall, the reform was rooted in the antieducation rhetoric of the 1950s. Reformers' condescending attitudes were linked to the movement's origins in the deluge of postwar criticism. That attitudes of overconfidence, superiority, and self-importance should influence the reform comes as no surprise. However, in the mythology of American society, and to a lesser extent in reality, schooling has historically been linked to notions of democracy and equality. Any school reform, despite the rhetoric of the reformers, is inevitably entwined with questions of value, endorsing a particular set of values and either minimizing or ignoring a competing set. In the morality play represented by struggles over the American curriculum, reforms that are more likely to stand the test of time are those that have deep roots in American traditions.

Despite these rather serious limitations, the reaction to *The Process of Education* took Bruner "completely by surprise." *Fortune* magazine called it "a centerpiece in the debate on education in America." The book made Bruner the most famous educator in the nation, at least for a time, and led to a keynote address before the National Education Association and a call from John F. Kennedy during his presidential campaign to discuss ideas for legislation. It would sell more than 400,000 copies within a few years. Its success would make Bruner a recognizable figure to educators and many others, worldwide. Yet, Bruner later confessed skepticism about the "easy acceptance" of the positions he had taken. "Rationalist, structuralist, and intuitionist, I was quite off the main line of American educational theory," which had favored facts and experience over reason and structure. Instead of being repositories of knowledge, he conceived of the great disciplines more as methods for use of the mind, providing a structure that helped make sense of the details. In Bruner's thinking, the object of education was "to get as swiftly as possible to that structure—to penetrate a subject, not cover it. You did this by 'spiraling' into it; a first pass to get the intuitive sense of it, later passes over the same domain to go into it more deeply and more formally." That, after all, is what scholars do. Most of all, it seemed, the book "served as a manifesto for those out to improve the intellectual quality of our schools."[49] Bruner stated his thoughts on the book's success in a later autobiographical work:

I think the book's "success" grew from a worldwide need to reassess the functions of education in the light of the knowledge explosion and the new, postindustrial technology. Its attention was on the knower and knowing. Its ideas spring from epistemology and the sciences of knowing, rather than from ethics or Freud, as in the round before. It reflected the intellectual ferment of its times, and if there were echoes of Chomsky and Levi-Strauss as well as Piaget, that was no surprise. For all of us were, I think, responding to the same "epistemic" malaise, the doubts about the nature of knowing that had come first out of the revolution in physics and then been formalized and amplified by philosophy. Eventually, it pervaded the "postindustrial" society. And so finally it came to education. I think that is why the book was such a "success" and why it hit a nerve wherever it was translated.[50]

In many ways, the book, and the curriculum reform movement it represented, might best be characterized as a counterreformation, one in search of theoretical moorings. Born of the confluence of critiques of progressive education and the cold war manpower crisis, it was a logical progression toward a more "intellectual" and academic approach to schooling. Perhaps what is most interesting, when one reads over the reports of the various conference panels and the ideas that then appear in *The Process of Education*, is the extent to which the ideas are consistent.[51] Pared down a bit, as noted above, but consistent with the general notion of centering school reform among university academics and the intellectual disciplines they had created. At the time, it seemed, it gave reformers, both within and outside of the military-industrial-academic complex, more or less what they had called for: a plan for the schools that was more intellectual in orientation, more objective, less focused on the needs and interests of children, and less attentive to the social and political context of schooling and its general improvement.

The book and its support for inquiry or "discovery" learning was also built on an important insight that Bruner recalled much later, and that is the notion that "the world is not a given" but is instead "a creation." It emphasized imparting to children the notion that "[y]ou produce the realities" and they are "subject to change."[52]

Prior to 1960 there were only a few hints that social studies would be added to the mix of curriculum reform. The conferees at Woods Hole included two historians and Bruner mentioned history and geography in theory and example. Moreover, during the late 1950s, a National Council for the Social Studies (NCSS) committee had begun to demand that social studies be included as a priority subject, along with mathematics and science, and the organization passed a resolution recommending that social studies receive funding under the National Defense Education Act (NDEA).[53] And, as we have seen, Zacharias and other leaders envisioned a broader reform.

COLD WAR CONNECTIONS

Though there was little explicit acknowledgment of the cold war backdrop to which the conferees at Woods Hole owed their existence, Bruner, a cold war liberal in politics, did refer somewhat obliquely in his introduction to *The Process of Education* to the social milieu. He wrote: "If all students are helped to the full utilization of their intellectual powers, we will have a better chance of surviving as a democracy in an age of enormous technological and social complexity."[54] A part of that "complexity" was no doubt entangled in the cold war struggle with communism in the minds of Bruner and his colleagues. Moreover, Bruner later referred to the cold war manpower shortage, and to national security concerns, in a direct manner in a few passages of *Process*, notably in the chapter discussing motives for learning. In a passage discussing the renewal of interest in education, he wrote, "Unquestionably, there has also been a surge of awareness born of our sense of imperiled national security. The Soviet Union's conquests in space, its capability of producing not only powerful weapons but also an effective industrial society, have shaken American complacency . . . [and so] there will be an increasing demand for the teaching of science, technology, and supporting subjects" as needed to meet the demands of the community and the shortages in science and engineering.[55]

In his role as director, Bruner wrote memos during the conference to each of five working groups on: the apparatus of teaching, the sequence of the curriculum, the motivation of learning, the role of intuition, and cognitive processes. One of the most telling comments was contained in Bruner's memo to the work group on the apparatus of teaching. "Perhaps rather unfortunately," the memo began, "we introduced this subject for discussion today by suggesting the analogy to a weapon system— proposing that the teacher, the book, the laboratory, the teaching machine, the film, and the organization of the craft might serve together to form a balanced teaching system."[56] It was a revealing comment. It alluded to the cold war backdrop, through which the entire program of curriculum reform might be seen as both a weapons system and an outgrowth of national security concerns, and it made an implicit connection to the earlier involvement of Bruner, Zacharias, and others in the development of weapons systems. It also alluded to the process of systems analysis that was at the heart of the reformer's approach to education. Bruner's initial direct involvement with the wartime research model apparently came with his work on Project Troy, a highly classified summer study invited by the State Department and ostensibly created to find a way to overcome Soviet jamming of Radio Free Europe, but with the broader aim of getting "the truth behind the Iron Curtain" by bringing together some of the "best brains in the country" to work on the problem and to counter the Soviet propaganda program.[57] Bruner had also served in the Office of War Intelligence (OWI) during World War II and had many other contacts and involvements with wartime research.

As we have seen, Jerrold Zacharias was also deeply involved in similar wartime government projects and had been for some time, with key leadership roles in the MIT Radiation Lab and the Manhattan Project, as a consultant on Project Troy, and notably, as director of Project Hartwell, focused initially on antisubmarine warfare and completed at MIT in 1950 with funding from the Office of Naval Research (ONR).[58] Several others present at Woods Hole were also veterans of wartime research projects.

These involvements provided a model and many of the personnel for what would become large-scale consultancies involving scientists, social scientists, the U.S. military, intelligence, and propaganda agencies. The model was later applied to social studies education as an arm of the propaganda effort, that is, improve manpower development on a broad scale, improve social science instruction, and win the cold war, assuming, of course, that students gain strong inquiry skills and reach the proper conclusions. In the case of Bruner, participation in Project Troy was "a rather heady experience" and led to a regular monthly dinner meeting "at the St. Botolph's Club in Boston the first Friday evening of each month for the next 15 years," which he later described as "the best club I have ever belonged to."[59]

In ensuing years, other theorists added to the mix, creating building blocks for the new reform and fleshing out the rationale. In a practical sense, the involvement of social studies could be marked with several publications, signaling that the social studies field, or at least some persons in positions of leadership, was largely in agreement with the many critiques of the 1950s, especially intellectual critics such as Bestor who called for a return to academic study.

The era of the new social studies was introduced most clearly when an article by Charles R. Keller, director of the John Hay Fellows Program and a former college history teacher, was published in *Saturday Review*. Keller's article was titled "Needed: Revolution in Social Studies," and appeared in 1961. His thesis was that social studies was "in the educational doldrums," while exciting revisions were being devised in mathematics, science, English, and the foreign languages. The problem, as Keller saw it, was partly traceable to the fact that "social studies" was a "federation of subjects: history, geography, political science, economics, sociology, anthropology, and psychology, often merged in inexact and confusing ways."[60] Keller went on to write that social studies teachers too frequently "depend" on textbooks, leading to "unimaginative, unenthusiastic, pedantic teaching . . . a cover-all rather than a selective approach." The remedy, according to Keller, was "a possible revolution in social studies." "We should begin," he wrote, "by eliminating the term 'social studies,' which is vague, murky, and too all-inclusive and substitute for it the term 'history and the social sciences,' which is exact and hence meaningful." Courses should stress "the conceptual rather than the fact-by-fact approach . . . and the unique structure of subjects . . . Students will learn how historians and social scientists go about their work . . . The emphasis should be on learning and discovery rather than teaching, and on analysis, critical thinking, and interpretation."[61] Many of Keller's recommendations proved a prophetic blueprint for the new social studies reform movement, and a clarion call for reform along the lines already begun in other subject areas.

Prior to the appearance of Keller's article, reformers were already engaged in pioneering work in a few isolated places. Lawrence Senesh, a scholar in economics at Purdue University, was busily creating an economics program for elementary age students, drawing on the disciplines in creating a progressive oriented program and textbook series, *Our Working World*. Edwin Fenton, a historian at Carnegie Institute of Technology in Pittsburgh who had been given responsibility for preservice teacher education in history, was bothered by the pat assertions found in high school history textbooks and by the boredom and loathing of his own students for many history and social science courses. In an attempt to bring history to life and rekindle student curiosity he introduced primary source documents as a means of stimulating students, asking them to experience the work of historians, and to make sense of raw data. Fenton's experiences using primary source documents led to publication of a book titled *32 Problems in World History* and an eventual leadership role in the new social studies movement.[62]

As early workers in the new reform, Senesh and Fenton provided a few clear directions and precedents: both were professors in the academic disciplines who became deeply involved in school reform; both gained credibility by implementing ideas in classrooms as "demonstration teachers;" both started small, in their own backyard; both focused on the obvious vehicle for reform, the course textbook and materials; both brought intellect, enthusiasm, and charisma which enhanced diffusion; and both drew on the structure of knowledge and inquiry in the disciplines.[63] Though Senesh and Fenton were working in relative isolation, their projects were path-breaking efforts that would help give shape and form to the emerging focus on the social sciences.

THE RISE OF PROJECT SOCIAL STUDIES

In his inaugural address, President John Fitzgerald Kennedy offered a stirring call to meet the challenges of the times, to "bear any burden" in the cold war struggle against communism, and he asked all of the nation's citizens to, "Ask not what your country can do for you, ask what you can do for your country." As it turns out, the Kennedy administration played a key role in the emerging school reform movement, and in the emergence of the new social studies, a role that mirrored Kennedy's call to the citizenry in a number of ways. The administration's role in curriculum reform involved several government agencies whose roles had already been established during the Eisenhower administration, along with a new group, created under the auspices of the President's Science Advisory Committee (PSAC). What would come to be called Project

Social Studies emerged from cooperation among three main groups, the NSF, the USOE, and the PSAC. Cooperation and communication among these administrative agencies was facilitated by the Panel on Educational Research and Development appointed by the PSAC in early 1962.[64] In hindsight, it appears that the Panel was the key group behind development of a wider reform and Project Social Studies. The reform also involved several nongovernmental agencies that played a supportive role, contributing to the reform by sponsoring meetings, contributing funding, and supplying some of the key players. Perhaps the most influential among these groups were the American Council of Learned Societies (ACLS) and ESI, which together sponsored a key meeting at Endicott House in 1962.

Among the key players in the broadening of the science education reform to include social studies and the humanities, Jerrold Zacharias was most indispensable, and most central. Other key players included Jerome Wiesner, president of MIT and president's newly appointed science adviser; Alan T. Waterman, head of the NSF; Sterling McMurrin, Commissioner of Education, who was succeeded by Francis Keppel in late 1962; Jerome Bruner, the face of the reform; and Martin Mayer, a scholar at the ACLS and among the most outspoken participants.

It was, to be sure, a sort of "official" curriculum reform, given the fact that it had the sanction and support of government officials, combined with some private funding, a condition that would remain true throughout the reform period. For those involved, these were heady times. A generation earlier, it would have been hard to imagine being given such power to influence the direction of the nation's school reform movement. The justification for broadening the reform was an extension of the cold war rationale behind the science and math reforms that preceded it. It was thought that educating more scientists and mathematicians was necessary, but not sufficient to maintain the U.S. position as leader of the free world. The PSAC played a key role, facilitating emergence of Project Social Studies by managing collaboration among the groups and persons involved. The reform of social studies was modeled on, first, the PSSC and other science reforms, and second, Project English, which preceded it only by a relatively short time. Like the earlier reforms in science and math, Project Social Studies largely sidestepped the education establishment, or its leaders coopted it by inviting the participation of only specific educators whom they thought would be supportive of the tenor and general orientation of the reform. And, like the science education reform that preceded it, Project Social Studies benefited greatly, as we shall see, from the political impact of another cold war incident, in this case, the Cuban missile crisis.

The USOE had been involved in the schools, and in educational research for some time. What it had not been involved in prior to the early 1960s was large-scale programmatic curriculum reform. The Cooperative Research Program of the USOE was created in 1954, authorized by Public Law 531, passed by the 83rd Congress, July 26, 1954. The law authorized the USOE to enter into cooperative research contracts with colleges, universities, and state educational agencies. The program had supported hundreds of research projects by the early 1960s, many dealing with curriculum experimentation or reform. Also, Title III of the NDEA of 1958 had contributed to program improvement in science, mathematics, and modern foreign languages, and those curriculum improvement programs had been steadily influenced by NSF activities in support of science and mathematics reform through the PSSC, Illinois Math, and projects in chemistry and biology. By the early 1960s, the USOE and NSF had developed a "very satisfactory working relationship," with the goal to help raise the quality of American education.[65]

In all of its emerging efforts at curriculum reform, the USOE and NSF had to be mindful of the sensitivity involved in developing government-led reform projects, while at the same time "safeguarding state and local prerogatives." Congressional approval for federal involvement in curriculum reform activities had been slow to materialize, and it had been difficult to win congressional support due to concerns over a federal takeover and the long tradition of local control in education.[66] Discussion of the course improvement activities of NSF and USOE reflected a high level of sensitivity on this topic, and included four general guidelines, which had been applied successfully by Dr. Harry Kelly and his associates at the NSF:

1. Federal funds may be used for research and development, for production, experimentation, and dissemination of information, but not to propagandize for any particular curriculum.
2. Federal funds may not be used in any way that can be construed as pushing a particular curriculum on the schools.
3. Participation by any institutions or teacher in any project supported by the program must be entirely voluntary.
4. Any materials produced with Federal support must make their own way on their own merit. Final decisions on what use will be made of such materials must be left to the local educational authorities.[67]

These 1961 guidelines illustrate several difficulties posed by a federal role in curriculum reform, and expose the vulnerability of such programs to controversy and critique. Moreover, in a bit of foreshadowing, they highlight some of the issues that would plague the reform movement in the years to come, especially as it was broadened to include social studies.

In his presentation to the National Conference on Curriculum Experimentation in Minneapolis on September 27, 1961, J. Boyer Jarvis, Special Assistant to the Commissioner of Education, cited a letter to Senator Hubert H. Humphrey of Minnesota from Professor Paul C. Rosenbloom. In the letter, Rosenbloom suggested that the course content improvement programs in science and math, supported by NSF grants, should become "the model for corresponding programs in the social sciences and the humanities," with grants from the USOE. Noting that many of those present had long before "entertained the same idea," Jarvis stated that Commissioner McMurrin hoped that the USOE could "do for other basic subjects what the National Science Foundation has done . . . for science and mathematics."

As we have seen, the move toward a broadened curriculum reform had been brewing for some time. During the 1960–1961 fiscal year, the USOE was engaged in planning "Project English," limited in its beginnings, to research and demonstration projects financed through the Cooperative Research Program and the establishment of two or three curriculum development centers. Though a great deal of preliminary planning took place within the USOE, formal establishment of "Project English" was delayed pending final action of Congress on the 1962 budget appropriation to HEW. Following budget approval, "Project English" was officially launched, breaking new ground in the curriculum reform movement by broadening it to another curriculum area beyond science and mathematics, and established a pattern for later efforts in social studies and other subjects.

After the launch of "Project English," USOE administrators hoped that efforts could be made during the next session of Congress to give the USOE both the authority and the funds to support curriculum improvement projects "in all basic subjects other than science and mathematics." Among the basic subjects to be part of the reform, Commissioner McMurrin included "the study of politics, history, and philosophy," which he viewed as "'essential to the quality and character of our culture,'" along with the "cultivated appreciation" of great literature, art, and music, which he viewed as "a basic element of genuine national strength."[68]

The rationale for broadening the curriculum improvement program was presented quite succinctly by McMurrin at a meeting of the House Committee on Appropriations in May of 1961. Commissioner

McMurrin stated that the task facing leaders of American education was to provide schooling that would serve the "best interests of every individual" and at the same time "contribute to the fundamental quality of our culture and add genuine strength to our national character." This included "maximum cultivation" of each individual's "intellectual, moral, artistic, and spiritual capacities" to produce "a genuinely free person" and yield "the protection and perpetuation of those institutions that are essential to a free society." Thus, he went on, the school's "primary task" is the "dissemination of knowledge and cultivation of the intellect." Only when this central purpose is clearly established will a school produce the results "in personal and civic character that we rightly expect of it." For McMurrin and others at the USOE, the rationale for a broadened reform was succinctly summarized as follows:

> Let us never forget that the ultimate aim of American education—including all of our experimenting with the curriculum—is the development of individuals whose personal competence and commitment are dedicated to the general welfare of free men in a free society, and to the strength of this Nation as the responsible leader of the free world.[69]

As these statements indicate, the reform was aimed primarily at development of the intellect, with the hope that this would lead to both the development of civic character, and the "perpetuation" of the institutions essential to a free society, a conserving goal. All of this, including the aim of reform and improvement of the curriculum broadly, would, it was hoped, contribute to strengthening the nation as "the responsible leader of the free world," a central theme of President Kennedy's inaugural message. Though it was never said, it was strongly implied when these comments are considered in their historical context, that all of this was necessary because of the ongoing cold war confrontation with the Soviet Union.

From the perspective of USOE staffers, Project Social Studies was one of a number of new programs, each of which represented a new direction for curriculum reform, and a higher level of involvement for USOE and the federal government. According to one internal document described as a "progress report," nine major educational concerns had served as "themes for the form and direction" of the new programs. Among these concerns were "The Quality of Teaching," "The Quality of the Curriculum," "Education for Freedom and World Understanding," the arts, educational opportunity, urban education, and technical education. In its section on "Curriculum Improvement," the report described programs in several areas including science, mathematics, English, and social studies. In the section labeled "Social Studies," the report stated, "During 1961 the Office planned Project Social Studies—a substantial effort which will be launched in Fiscal year 1963 to improve the curricula and teaching in all levels of the social sciences; elementary, secondary, and higher."[70]

As we have seen, the growing reform effort was firmly rooted in a philosophical and contextual base. It was, in part, a response to critiques of education during the postwar period, from academics and leaders outside the field, as well as from a host of individual axe-grinders. Just as the effort for Project Social Studies was building steam, McMurrin invited Arthur Bestor to address the professional staff in the Office of Education, in the summer of 1962. Perhaps this invitation, which Bestor accepted, was in some ways an indication of the direction that the reform was taking. Bestor's critique of schooling was especially caustic when it came to social studies. As you will recall, he argued that the entire social studies program should be jettisoned in favor of disciplines-based courses in history and the social sciences. In his letter acknowledging Bestor's acceptance, McMurrin seemed to steer something of a middle course, offering what appears to be a qualified acceptance of Bestor's position. He wrote:

> I am looking forward to hearing you speak. I am sure that the professional staff will agree with your estimation of the preservative power of historical understanding. On the other hand, I am not entirely sure that the majority also will draw the conclusion that the subject should be completely divorced from what are termed the social studies.[71]

Bestor's emphasis on intellectual values and his call for a focus on the disciplines were consistent with the general direction of the reform movement in social studies up to 1962. However, as the conferees at Endicott House would later agree, courses focused on the individual disciplines were sometimes not very practical, especially at the lower levels, given the sheer number of disciplines competing for space and time in the overall curricular sequence.

THE PRESIDENT'S PANEL

Another group playing a key role in the emerging reform was the Panel on Educational Research and Development appointed by the President's Science Advisory Committee (henceforth, the Panel). The curriculum reform entered a new phase when President Kennedy appointed Jerome Wiesner as special assistant for Science and Technology. As the president's science adviser, Wiesner would have special responsibilities, "giving particular attention to trends and developments as they affect national security and welfare," and the "relative progress of Soviet and U.S. science and technology." He would advise "top-level policy deliberations and would attend meetings of the National Security Council, the Cabinet, and the National Aeronautics and Space Council. In addition, he was given full security access to "all [government] plans, programs, and activities" involving science and technology.[72] This passage illustrates the importance placed on educational reform by the administration, and the "insider" status of one of the prime arbiters of the curriculum reform movement. Wiesner, Killian, and Zacharias had all served on the PSAC during key periods of the 1950s. And, early in the Kennedy years, Zacharias and Bruner were both appointed to serve on the PSAC, as well as its Panel on Education.

On November 27–28, 1961, Wiesner hosted a Special Meeting on Education at Room 210 of the Executive Office Building in Washington. The meeting was called to discuss ways of improving course content and learning materials in a wide variety of subject matter fields, at all levels. The meeting was chaired by Jerrold Zacharias. After opening remarks from the three principal administrative leaders of the government agencies involved, Wiesner from the PSAC, Waterman of the NSF, and McMurrin of the USOE, the discussion centered on "the status of teaching and learning of some twelve disciplines at various age levels": their deficiencies, on-going remedial actions, needs, and mechanisms. The deficiencies would lead to discussion of "the possible role of the Federal government in improving American education." A chart circulated at the meeting asked those in attendance to grade the status of each of the twelve disciplines at each of seven different age levels as "good, indifferent, poor, or non-existent." A second chart asked for comment on and description of various curriculum improvement projects in a dozen specific categories, and in various stages of development. The 40 participants included something of a who's who in the curriculum reform and included members of the PSAC, representatives of the NSF and USOE, and a number of other interested persons representing learned societies, and universities. Among those in attendance were Bruner, Francis Friedman, Francis Keppel, dean of the Harvard Graduate School of Education, and Martin Mayer of ACLS.[73]

Following what must have been a wide-ranging, comprehensive discourse on the status of the subjects at the "Special Meeting" in late November, Wiesner invited a subset of the group to what were called, "invitational meetings," and to serve as White House consultants on the new "Panel on Educational Research and Development."[74] An

"Organizational Meeting" for the new subpanel was held on February 21–22, 1962, at Room 208 of the Executive Office Building. At the start of the meeting, McMurrin, from USOE, stated that the Office had "long recognized the enormous value" of the NSF science and mathematics reform efforts, and, hence, had developed "a special interest in the non-science fields—languages, social studies and the humanities—as well as a general interest," and would look to the Panel for wisdom and advice on the improvement of education through "the improvement of course content materials." He stated that the Office needed specific help on "things to be done; how the Office should go about them; and in what priority." Waterman responded that the Foundation would provide "aids to navigation and logistic support to the Panel, but hoped that the Panel would "take a broad view in defining its own role." Panel members during its first year of existence included Zacharias, Bruner, Frederick Burkhardt, Francis Friedman, Francis Keppel, Martin Mayer, and Ralph Tyler.[75]

Later in the meeting, there was considerable discussion on the role of the federal government in supporting projects in the social sciences. The question was raised, "Can Government, as a sponsoring organization, be separated from the content of the materials that are developed?" The Panel decided that one approach to that question was to "ensure that good materials are produced, but not to prescribe their use." Moreover, it decided that in the social sciences it would "be desirable to support several groups in each area of the curriculum so as to give the schools more than one choice." This was an important decision that would have implications for the diversity of projects that would eventually receive support.

Dr. Flynt of USOE discussed another problem facing the Office's programs. Because of a lack of flexibility in its charter when compared to the NSF, it had to get a legislative mandate for new activities. For that reason, the Office had moved ahead cautiously and "very selectively" in developing school curriculum improvement projects. He also discussed plans for "Project English" in some detail, which served as a fairly immediate model for "Project Social Studies." In "Project English," the Office supplied "venture capital" for scholars to undertake curriculum improvement projects, and expected several "curriculum study centers" to be established in collaboration with university-level English departments. On agenda items for future meetings, it was decided that the Panel would discuss "the political and economic realities of public support of various projects," which was a critical component.[76]

In a meeting held on April 22, 1962, the Panel adopted a rather forceful statement, forwarded to the triumvirate of Wiesner, McMurrin, and Waterman, arguing that several steps "should be taken at once." These included "vigorous Presidential support" of the Educational Quality Act of 1962 (H. R. 10145) and that "centers of research and development be established," linked to schools and colleges. These recommendations established operational goals for the Panel rooted in what were described as the three most serious "operating problems facing elementary and secondary schools today": "inadequate quality and quantity of teachers"; the problems of schools located "in the slums of cities"; and "the lack of a program and method of suitable scale to create and test new curricula." The hope was that establishment of R&D centers would help "to attract first-rate personnel" to the program of curriculum improvement and "give entry to the solution of these serious problems." The Panel's memorandum outlined its plans for R&D centers at which "scholars able to analyze their fields be joined by psychologists and educators to create and test both new curricula and new methods of instruction," envisioning them as centers of "basic as well as applied research into learning," with links to schools and colleges "so that trials of new materials may be continuous and the entry into the existing educational structure may be put under study and experiment."[77] These were ambitious goals, and the panel made a rather forceful statement asking for what it believed was needed to transform the initial curriculum reform projects into an effective movement to change schools.

At its next meeting, on May 23, 1962, the Panel turned its attention to projections of the funding needed to fully implement its educational reform agenda. Bowen Dees reported preliminary projections and the Panel itself developed estimates of "gross annual needs" for improvement of science teaching. Its total projections came to $550 million per year, with $260 million for College, $170 million for High School plus grades seventh, eighth, and ninth, and $120 million for the Elementary grades. These projections assumed "re-training 10% of present teachers per year and high quality initial training" of beginning teachers during each annual increment of the program. Though the projections amounted to something of a wish list, it gave substance to the scope and size of the Panel's reform, and reiterated previous projections by Zacharias, consistent with his hopes for a full-blown and generously funded curriculum reform movement.

The Panel also heard a presentation from Dr. Flynt and Mr. Hughes on the USOE's projected programs for 1964 through 1967. Their presentation included considerable discussion of the Cooperative Research Program. Flynt noted that the "Improvement of Educational Quality Act" would provide the Office with "more flexibility and authority to undertake programmed research" than did the Cooperative Research Act, which was designed to sponsor basic studies. It was difficult, he noted, for the Office to sponsor new projects such as "Project English" and "Project Social Studies" under the 1954 Act, a difficulty that would be alleviated with passage of the new legislation. Flynt also mentioned that "if it is not passed this year," the Office would "resubmit the 'Quality bill'" to Congress with "a request for considerably more funds."[78] In a final note of some importance to the development of Project Social Studies, it was announced that the next meeting of the Panel would be held on Saturday and Sunday, June 23 and 24, at Endicott House, Dedham, Massachusetts, with the purpose of hearing the results of the Endicott House Conference on "course content improvement in the social studies and the humanities."[79]

CONCLUSION

By the late spring of 1962, the general outline of the project that would eventually become the new social studies had taken shape. Backed by the military-industrial-academic complex with strong support from government and professional groups, the theoretical moorings and modus operandi for the reform were clearly established. It was a reform shaped by the cold war context, employing a wartime research model, and framed by systems development theory. It was a movement for improvement that turned a blind eye to both the educational establishment and the social and historical context of schooling. It was a reform that favored the elite and sought to develop the "best and the brightest" students to serve the nation's needs. School curricula was thought of as something like a weapons system that could further the nation's strategic interests by developing scientists, engineers, and regular citizens who could think scientifically and who had the right commitments. Institutions such as the NAS, NSF, and the USOE and key individuals, notably Jerrold Zacharias; Jerome Bruner; and the triumvirate of Wiesner, McMurrin, and Waterman were instrumental in transforming what started in science and mathematics into a broader reform that would eventually encompass social studies. But, as we shall see in the next chapter, the final shape and definition for the reform was far from settled, and would emerge in a somewhat more developed form after the meeting at Endicott House in June of 1962.

Figure 1   Arthur E. Bestor

Source: (Photo courtesy of the University of Illinois at Urbana-Champaign Archives, Record Series number 39/2/26 box 6)

Figure 2   Jerrold R. Zacharias

Source: (AIP Emilio Segre Visual Archives, Physics Today Collection)

Figure 3   Alan T. Waterman, director, National Science Foundation, 1950–1963

Source: (National Science Foundation Collection)

Figure 4   James R. Killian, President's Science Advisor, 1957–1959

Source: (Library of Congress, Prints and Photographs Division [reproduction number: LC-USZ62-49170])

Figure 5   President Dwight D. Eisenhower

Source: (Library of Congress, Prints and Photographs Division [reproduction number: LC-USZ62-117123 DLC])

Figure 6   Aerial view of clouds raised by test explosion of an atomic bomb, Bikini Atoll, 1946

Source: (Library of Congress, Farm Security Administration-Office of War Information Collection)

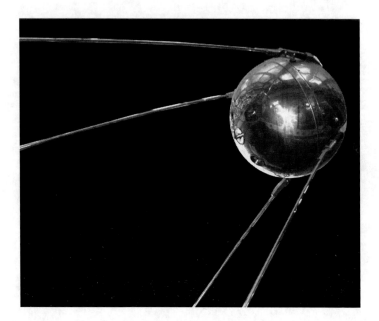

Figure 7   Sputnik 1
Source: (National Aeronautics and Space Administration Collection)

Figure 8   Vice Admiral Hyman G. Rickover
Source: (United States Navy Photo)

Figure 9   Whitney Estate, Woods Hole, Massachusetts
Source: (Woods Hole Historical Collection)

Figure 10   Jerome S. Bruner
Source: (The Schlesinger Library, Radcliffe Institute, Harvard University)

Figure 11   President John F. Kennedy

Source: (Library of Congress, Prints and Photographs Division [reproduction number: LC-USZ62-117124 DLC])

Figure 12   Jerome B. Wiesner, President's science advisor, 1961–1964

Source: (Photograph by Robert Knudsen, White House, in the John F. Kennedy Presidential Library and Museum Collection)

Figure 13   MIT Endicott House, Dedham, Massachusetts
Source: (Photograph by Maureen T. O'Brien)

Figure 14   Edwin P. Fenton
Source: (Photograph courtesy of Ted Fenton)

Figure 15   Donald W. Oliver

Source: (Photograph by Joe Wrinn, Harvard University)

CHAPTER 4

SHOWDOWN AT ENDICOTT HOUSE

DURING THE PERIOD BEFORE AND AFTER the Woods Hole Conference, a series of meetings took place, with the general intent of broadening the curriculum reform projects to include other areas, such as English and social studies. The single most interesting and relevant of these gatherings occurred at Endicott House in June of 1962, planned to run from Friday evening, June 8 through Sunday morning, June 24. The Endicott House meeting was the first comprehensive conference during the reform movement to examine the need for improvement in social studies in some depth. During the Kennedy administration, Jerrold Zacharias, who served as chair of the President's Science Advisory Committee (PSAC), sponsored a number of meetings aimed at further developing and broadening the educational reform movement.

The Endicott House meeting was an immediate outgrowth of a January 1962 meeting at which Zacharias recommended development of an Educational Services Incorporated (ESI) social studies program. That meeting's inception is traceable to a Summer Study on African Education held in 1961 at Endicott House, sponsored by ESI, and attended by 15 African and 30 Western scholars and educators. Major educational initiatives in the sciences, mathematics, and language were launched in Africa as a result, despite what was later described as meetings that were "tumultuous and emotional—with all the emotions that are generated when anticolonialism and cryptocolonialism clash."[1] However, the Africa study found that it could not make any useful recommendations in social studies and the humanities in part because no major new programs in teaching those disciplines had yet been developed. Moreover, Zacharias, who would later organize the Endicott House meeting on social studies, noticed a lack of clarity among American academics about what made for an effective program in social studies, and was "appalled" at the "fuzzy-headed thinking" among American social studies educators. Zach's disappointment with social studies led to a series of discussions among a small group of ESI insiders with Frederick Burkhardt and Gordon Turner of the American Council of Learned Societies (ACLS). The discussions led to a meeting at Massachusetts Institute of Technology (MIT) in January 1962, attended by some 20 scholars and educators. The meeting generated sufficient enthusiasm to warrant appointment of a steering committee charged with "creating and directing a major program."[2] The steering committee, at its first meeting on February 14, led by Burkhardt and supported by a small Ford Foundation grant, decided that it would attempt to stage a two-week conference in June, at which, so it hoped, some agreements could be reached on a program of social studies reform for the schools. In addition, should some agreement be fashioned at the June meeting, a smaller work group would continue for the rest of the summer.[3]

A preconference overview of plans from conference sponsors ESI and ACLS stated that the immediate objective was "to explore the feasibility of an interdisciplinary attack upon problems of curriculum reform in the social studies and humanities." The overview acknowledged the "vast" scope of the subject, and the greater "difficulties inherent" in an attempt to create a reform program in social studies and humanities, and suggested that "a multiplicity of approaches will be necessary." It also acknowledged that a "unified approach" appeared to be "particularly necessary" in the subject, because of the improbability of separate courses in each discipline.[4]

THE ENDICOTT HOUSE CONFERENCE

The Endicott House Conference was held in June 1962, at a secluded estate ten miles from Harvard Square with 47 scholars and teachers representing a broad spectrum of disciplines in the social sciences and humanities, and a wide range of views. The conference was sponsored under the joint auspices of the ACLS and ESI and funded by an Officer Grant from the Ford Foundation. It was held at the MIT-owned Endicott House in Dedham, Massachusetts, the former estate of a wealthy shoe manufacturer. Jerome Bruner describes it as "a charming if incongruous place . . . You may find yourself talking to an African intellectual about Nigerian education as you both stand in the "gun room" under the stuffed heads of African beasts shot by Mr. Endicott, who had . . . modeled himself on his vigorous contemporary Theodore Roosevelt."[5]

According to a written statement circulated with conference invitations, the purpose of the meeting was as follows:

> The June Conference is intended to identify problems of curriculum reform in the Social Studies and the Humanities, at the primary, elementary or secondary school levels, in terms of the substance of the various subject matters; to determine and adopt programs of curriculum reform; to establish lines of action that will lead directly to the preparation of materials (textual and otherwise) and their experimental use in schools.[6]

Unlike the conference at Woods Hole, it was not the primary purpose of the conference to "issue reports or recommendations." Instead, it was intended to be the "first phase of an active curriculum reform program." It was, in form and substance, another of Jerrold Zacharias' summer studies, once again applying the wartime research model by gathering the "best minds in the field" for an intense period of examination and reflection. Moreover, the work of the conference was to continue in an ESI planning group and become the centerpiece of the ESI social studies program.

The meeting was attended by several leading scholars in the humanities and social sciences. Some months prior to the meeting, a number of papers were circulated among those scheduled to attend. These were papers commissioned by ACLS that dealt with a wide variety of secondary school subjects. Some were on specific subjects, such as history or English; others proposed new courses in Russian history or Chinese and Far Eastern culture. Along with these was added a copy of what came to be called the "gospel according to St. Jerome"—Bruner's *The Process of Education*. Before the conference ended, the list of readings grew exponentially, with an "avalanche of papers, monographs, and reports," all centered on the topic at hand.[7]

Participants at the meeting included several well-known scholars including psychologists Jerome Bruner of Harvard, and Richard Jones of Brandeis; historians Edwin Fenton of Carnegie-Mellon, Charles Keller of the John Hays Fellows Program, Eltig Morison of MIT, Leften Stavrianos, Northwestern, and Herbert Heaton, University of Minnesota; anthropologists Robert Ascher and Alan Holmberg, Cornell; sociologist Robert Feldmesser, Brandeis; geographers William Bunge, University of Iowa, William Pattison, University of California, Los Angeles, and William Warntz, American Geographical Society; political scientist Norton Long, Northwestern; classicists Gerald Else, University of Michigan and Harry Levy, Hunter College; writer Mark Harris; lawyer Saul Menlovitz; and art historian Joshua Taylor of the University of Chicago; educators Dorothy

Fraser, City University of New York, Sister Mary Jacqueline, Webster College, Robert Havighurst, University of Chicago, Merrill Hartshorn, executive director, National Council for Social Studies, and school principals Frank Brown (Florida) and Alexander Moore (Indiana). The group also included Jerrold Zacharias, ACLS scholar Martin Mayer who was writing a book on the social studies field at the time, Francis Keppel, then president of the Harvard Graduate School of Education, and Frederick Burkhardt, president of the ACLS.[8]

The steering committee planned to begin the meeting with two full days of scheduled reports, prepared in advance, to be given by selected representatives of the various disciplines, each of which would provide fodder for discussion by the full group. However, as it turned out, most of the first week was devoted to prepared reports followed by open discussion, with the discussion more rancorous and time-consuming than the planners ever imagined. In a preliminary session, the conference "cocked a jaundiced eye" at a scheme describing the history and social studies courses in the present secondary school curriculum, then decided to move directly to a consideration of the various broad areas covered by the label "Humanities and Social Studies." The conference spent no time trying to devise a program that could fit into the current scope and sequence, instead throwing the door open, right from the start, to deciding what ought to be taught through the whole 12 years of schooling. Content and method were the touchstones, and scope and sequence would have to follow.[9]

On Saturday, June 9, the first full day of the conference, controversy emerged almost immediately after Robert Feldmesser, a sociologist, presented the very first paper of the conference titled "Sociology in the Schools." Rather than offering a plea for sociology in the school curriculum as most expected, Feldmesser instead presented a case for all the behavioral sciences. He argued that with the exception of "a course here and there," the social sciences had virtually no presence in American high schools. He then suggested that social studies was made up, almost entirely, of "indoctrination" courses, filled with judgments defending or extolling the values of our society, and that this was not science. Though his audience found little to argue with on these points, he went on to suggest that one of the reasons that scientific attitudes toward social phenomena did not take root in schools was the fact that "history bulks so overwhelming large" in the curriculum. This comment was met with "that echoing kind of silence" often found inside a cold storage locker. So that there would be no misunderstanding, he summarized his position with these words:

Nevertheless, I shall say it again in the strongest possible terms: we shall make no progress in transforming the social studies into social science until we slaughter the sacred cow of history.[10]

Feldmesser argued that history was so dominant that there was no room for a scientific approach to the study of human behavior. He proposed, instead, the inclusion of the social sciences at all levels, even though it meant a reduction in the amount of time devoted to history. Feldmesser added restrictions and qualifications to frame his argument somewhat less aggressively. He made it clear, as described in the conference report, that he was "not attacking history as such; his animus was directed toward the attitude that blandly assumed that because history was being taught, social studies students were learning science." And, as he and several other social scientists argued again and again in the following days, the historical approach, occupied with "peculiarities and unique events" was not what they meant by "the science of human behavior." More to the point, what was being taught in schools had, in their view, "nothing to do with the behavioural sciences."[11] Feldmesser argued that children, from the earliest years, should be exposed to the methodology and conceptual structure of the social sciences and be encouraged to develop a critical, questioning attitude toward the social world. History, he argued, was not serving that function.

Most of the historians who were present at the conference were offended by Feldmesser's charges, and the conference soon erupted into "a shouting match between the disciplines," with history on one side and the social sciences on the other.[12]

One of the few historians to concur with Feldmesser was Edwin Fenton, who agreed that there was entirely too much history in the school curriculum.[13] Zacharias found this contentiousness upsetting. His work with scientists had centered on finding ways of engaging students in the excitement of science, and he was unprepared for the turf battle that was emerging between historians and social scientists over what to teach. Elting Morison later remembered Zacharias' frustration:

That conference . . . was an experience for Zack . . . Here there was this bunch of highly verbal types, most of them from universities, most of them without a clue of what was happening in the schools . . . and most of them loathing each other's fields . . . and everybody fell into defensive postures and forlorn postures, and sad postures, and Zack and never seen anything like this—the humanities at bay.[14]

Despite the acrimony on both sides, the discussion that followed gave the conference its first shot of adrenalin, and offered an initial direction. Discussion centered on the definition of "scientific generality" and the meaning of the statement that "history is the study of unique events in time." Out of the give-and-take emerged a realization that "what was being sought in each discipline was a technique for presenting it that would develop in (and reproduce for) the student, as nearly as possible, the experience of a professional worker in the field. The way a problem is attacked, the tools and techniques employed, the awareness of relevance in the chaos of detail." All of these things to be experienced would be the substance of the teaching-learning process, rather than passive acquisition of inert knowledge. Along with this came the feeling that if the conference could not work up the "ways and means of achieving such a goal, it might just as well pack up and go home."[15]

During its first week, while the dispute between historians and social scientists was still being debated in meetings, and discussed informally during coffee breaks, the conference heard presentations from several scholars on developments in their respective fields. It heard approaches outlined in English, the classics, and art, in which some similarities emerged, "a common spirit, or shared angle of vision . . . not unlike the idea underlying Long's 'disciplined capacity to see.'" In English, Sister Jacqueline and Mark Harris emphasized doing—the act of creating or actively responding to a piece of literature. Bragdon's point that a good history course should also serve as a "studio for practice in expository writing" was one of the first comments supporting interdisciplinary work. The classicists—Else, Levy, McKendrick, and Bock—emphasized new methods of teaching Latin by which students would read examples of poetry and prose for their literary quality rather than to study rules of grammar. In art, Taylor and Hayes proposed the aim of "the experience of the work of art in and for itself."[16]

By the time the humanities had finished their presentations, a new orientation began to emerge at the conference among the behavioral scientists, and the term "interdisciplinary" began to be heard rather frequently. A rapprochement was brewing among sociology, anthropology, archaeology, political science, and psychology. By Saturday, June 16, at the end of the first full week, the feeling was that there was little to be gained by emphasizing differences among the various disciplines, but that units of material could be developed so that "each of these sciences could have its special approaches and techniques explored while at the same time reinforcing the others."[17] Geography and economics, for a time, remained outside this alliance. As for geography, it seemed that a general vagueness about the discipline meant that few of the attendees could visualize just how it might fit into an interdisciplinary scheme. And in economics, its advocates firmly believed, with support from the report by the Task Force on Economic Education, that economic understanding could not be gained without a deeper study of the subject by teachers and students. The conference heard reports from geographers Pattison and Warntz, and examples that made the behavioral relevance of geography readily apparent: the representation of distance as a function of time or cost; the mapping of population densities as a way of revealing for children the implications of their own daily experiences.[18]

In economics, the conference heard an overview of macroeconomic concepts from the Economics Task Force booklet as the "minimal and necessary" ideas that all citizens should understand. Their presentation was then subjected to a sharp critique by Mayer, who said that macroeconomic concepts were "relatively meaningless to young people," and argued instead for a case study or "micro" approach, focused on specific examples of economic phenomena as a means to understanding concepts. By examining the postwar rise of the ballpoint pen, television, the expansion of soy bean production, and the hula hoop craze, students could come to a better understanding of how prices, and profits, affect supply and demand. Wagner responded that he "doubted the value of such extreme dependence on case-study or microphenomena" because it led inevitably to a "bits-and-pieces knowledge of the subject," and he questioned the value of any method that might ignore vital policy matters such as "income distribution, wage rates, and the comparison of differently based economic systems." This sharply argued exchange, and the discussion that followed, was "one of the highlights of the conference." Ascher summed up the pedagogical lesson the dispute emphasized: "If we can learn from such a debate, why can't high school students?" It seemed that the conference was moving toward an affirmative answer to that question.[19]

While there would be several points on which the members of the conference generally agreed, it seemed that the ambitious effort to work out a total curriculum for a 12-year sequence was beyond possibility. This was, in the words of the conference report, "one of those expendable constructs that was almost bound to be erected and demolished in a conference like this one."[20] Ironically, this task, which would seem a logical subject for the systems analysis approach being employed, at least nominally, was never really completed by the scholars of the new social studies, and would later serve as a subject of critique.

On the teaching of history, the conferees agreed, there was room for the use of "hardware," the unstructured primary materials with which historians typically worked. The conference report offered a brief and simple illustration:

> Suppose, for example, that ten pictures are displayed in a random pile. Five of these can be arranged in a chronological order; the rest are unrelated to this order and, probably, to each other. The problem: to find the order. The use, wherever possible, of similar unstructured collections of data was warmly endorsed. This teaching device will certainly be adopted in the behavioral science and history sequences that will grow out of the conference's work.[21]

The conference was also gaining some clarity on what it did not want in schools. History and social science teaching that stressed coverage of long lists of unrelated facts that provided superficial treatment of a long laundry list of topics and left students as passive recipients of predigested conclusions. That was clearly what the nonhistorians in the group did not want. Unwittingly, historian Leften Stavrianos provided critics with a broad target. During the early part of the meeting, he distributed copies of his recently published high school text, a survey of world history titled *A Global History of Man*. The book received a largely negative reaction from the conference. As Zacharias later recalled the reaction: "What a clamor! We just raised hell with that poor thing because it was a collection of bits—everything—all of history, all of mankind. You know, Atilla the Hun, dates, did this, and this—and [gesturing] that much print! You turn that loose in a school and you've got nothing."[22]

By Saturday, June 16, after continued wrestling with the split between the social scientists and historians, and after making no progress on a total-curriculum scheme, the conference seemed to be losing its sense of direction. Fatigue was taking its toll, with the inherent difficulty in coping with such a daunting task, and conferees embracing what seemed to be intrinsically conflicting foundational disciplines. As the conference report put it, "The mind reeled trying to decide just what was being applied where in conjunction with what else." And so, on Saturday, June 16, the conference found itself wondering about the "readiness" question: what ideas might be taught in what order and at what age level. Havighurst was asked to address the topic, and did so at some length, effectively illustrating the complexity of the question and adding to the difficulty of resolving the several dilemmas that were percolating.[23] Hoping to calm the conflict between the behavioral sciences and history, the group decided to suspend formal meetings until the morning of Monday, June 18.

As it turned out, that decision was a wise one. During the ensuing period, Zacharias asked Elting Morison, an MIT historian and a veteran of Woods Hole and other summer studies, whose work had brought him in contact with scholars from diverse disciplines, to address the meeting on Monday in an effort to try to bring about some sort of consensus. After discussing the situation with Bruner, Morison addressed the conference on the morning of Monday, June 18, making the case for a move toward common ground. After stating that "the intellectual processes in every discipline are very much the same," he suggested that the conference focus on those similarities. Both historians and social scientists examine data and derive ideas from them. Thus, a new approach to social studies could bring about a "marriage of the disciplines." As Morison later recalled, " I remember saying that I thought you could write most of the history of the United States by a careful investigation of how the battleship Kentucky was built in 1900."[24] Morison accepted the behavioral scholars' distinction between their disciplines and history as a search for generalization vs. a concern for the particular, and argued that the school curricula should devote more attention to the social sciences. If that meant a reduction in the hours devoted to history, it was unlikely to result in any loss to the student because insight and skill developed much more out of intensive and in-depth study rather than broad "coverage" of a field. More history and social science could be taught through Henry Bragdon's notion of "postholing"—concentration on a few carefully selected topics. Morison ended his speech by suggesting that the conference break up into working groups, "to consider those ideas which it will be necessary in the next half-century for citizens to be possessed of."[25]

In the discussion that followed, there was an effort to define more closely the educational value that was being sought. Norton Long proposed that it be stated as "a disciplined capacity to see." Morison then added his own encapsulation of inquiry, "the organization of material out of a mess," a phrasing that Zacharias no doubt approved. Clearly, a reasonable consensus of those present was emerging. The goal was a new, active, and thoughtful approach to pedagogy, and the enemy was the predigested material contained in textbooks and other traditional school materials. Against this common foe, the historian and behavioral scientist could overcome their disagreements and work together.[26]

Following Morison's address, and the sparkling discussion it inspired, it seemed the conference was heading into its second week with some unity on important matters. The next morning, Tuesday, June 19, Jerome Bruner addressed the conference. Bruner's book, *The Process of Education*, seemed to have its strongest influence when the conference stopped to consider pedagogical problems. His remarks that morning were in a similar vein. Bruner devoted much of his talk to illuminating the learning process. In general, the process was one of increasing simplification. A pattern is sensed when sorting through a mass of irrelevancies, and the child proceeds through stages of development: from motor activity, through recognition of images and development of language skills, to manipulation of abstractions. Transfer of learning occurs after dealing with several similar instances. One of the most significant ideas Bruner emphasized was the notion that "[t]here is, at any stage of development, a readiness for learning appropriate to that level." This raised the question, whether readiness can be "put ahead in time?"[27]

In the discussion that followed, the standard pedagogical pattern of the "expanding world" or expanding horizons was raised. In this pattern of curricular organization, the child's awareness is presumed to broaden outward with increasing maturity, from the home to the neighborhood, and so on, to the larger world. Bruner was quite dubious about this assumption. How true is it, he asked, that the child "lives" psychologically in the home? He suggested that the child's mind is just as apt to be occupied with imaginative and fantasy worlds, just as real for him, if not more so, than his immediate surroundings. Fish are the last creatures to see the water in which they are swimming. And, Bruner went on, there is no reason to assume that the young child's interest cannot be held by a topic made imaginatively meaningful. Moreover, Bruner thought, it is "very doubtful that only what is physically real in the child's environment can constitute the base from which his learning begins." Most of these ideas had been raised at Woods Hole, but they were reconsidered at Endicott House, with a focus on the social studies curriculum.[28]

By this time in the proceedings, the conference had reached a point of general agreement on a number of key principles: on the general benefits of interdisciplinarity, especially for the lower and middle grades; on the value of introducing the "habits of mind" peculiar to each discipline; and, most importantly, on the value of depth through "postholing," in which the raw materials of knowledge would be put into children's hands for guided inquiry via an inductive method.

Additional evidence that the conference took on a life of its own is provided by an item in the appendix of the conference report, "Toward a Dictionary of Endicottese," which began with the suggestion that every society develops its own language, a "set of signals used for purposes of aggression, obfuscation, release of inhibitions, enhancement of status, and (sometimes) communication of meaning." The conference at Endicott House, and the language that was used, had all these qualities.

The terms listed in the dictionary suggest the conferees had both a sense of humor about their disagreements and an ironic awareness of the difficulty of the task before them. FRAME OF REFERENCE was "a nasty term; not used in polite society." HARDWARE, the label the conferees gave to original source material, was "a ripple tank for the social sciences."[29] MACROPEDAGOGY was "what everybody agrees upon about education before getting down to disagreement," or "the struggle as to which discipline gets its hoods into the whole child when and where." MICROPEDAGOGY was "the science of how to get a child cooking." A POSTHOLE was "a means whereby historians try to bury social scientists with kindness. Example: 'A posthole in fifth century Greece will of necessity bring in anthropology, economics, etc.'" SAINT JEROME was described as "a misrepresented disembodied prophet occasionally represented in the flesh." A ZACK was "a monetary unit variously estimated as amounting to $200,000 to $250,000" suggesting the attendees were very aware of the grant money that would be available for continuation of the project. INTERDISCIPLINARY was "a state devoid of discipline in which it is permissible to interrupt whoever is speaking." And, T, or "training teachers, something so manifestly impossible that its discussion is forbidden for fear of damage to the morale of the community." The materialization of jokes about their work suggests that someone, probably the conference leaders, used humor as a means to help overcome the divides that erupted. Though differences remained, humor undoubtedly played some role in what eventually transpired.[30]

On Tuesday, June 19, following Bruner's remarks and ensuing discussion, the conference broke into four working groups, each comprised of a "fairly representative cross-section" of the various disciplines. The work groups, or "panels," were given only the most general charge: each group was to report back to the conference "as many specific proposals for curriculum revision as it could agree upon." This was with the understanding that only a rudimentary outline could be expected, and future groups would carry on, "filling in the outlines with the concrete teaching material." Zacharias assured the group that this approach had worked successfully during the early stages of the Physical Sciences Study Committee (PSSC) project.

Most groups apparently focused on summarizing the main ideas on which they could agree. Proposals ranged from new approaches to teaching the classics, to a new approach to American studies in eighth grade, to a plan for an interdisciplinary behavioral science course for the high school. However, one work group, Group A, developed an interesting and, it appeared, workable six-unit sequence for the elementary school titled "The Human Past." The group's makeup may have contributed to its creativity, as it included a broad cross-section of scholars, a writer, Mark Harris, and a curriculum developer, Evans Clinchy, the ESI staff member who coordinated the conference and presented his group's report.

Final reports were presented on Saturday, June 23. The report of Group A began with Clinchy's description of its six-unit curriculum proposal, focused almost entirely on postholes. The proposal began with the introduction of the concepts of space and time in kindergarten or first grade by use of aerial photographs of the school and neighborhood, the hourglass and clock, a homemade hourglass, and discussion of questions about space and time in the child's own world. In second grade, the posthole focused on "The Stones and Bones Unit," which began with a box of stones and bones based on the excavation of the caves of Choukoutien, in China, where the bones and implements of the Peking man were discovered. From the conference report:

> Hard evidence. The first thing the children see of this unit is a box filled with artfully contrived replicas of human-looking bones and chipped and broken rocks. All jumbled together. Job is to put the bones together in a meaningful pattern . . . Slowly it is discovered that one set [the oldest human skeleton] was dug out of the ground along with those stones. This creature lived a long time ago (no matter just when). What was he like? What did he do?

The unit involved lessons on primate life; a film on the excavations at Choukoutien; more extrapolation from hard evidence; a game in which children simulate a hunt without language (communicating by gesture and grunt only), thus inventing a language; and closed by showing an adapted version of the film "*The Hunters*," asking children to draw parallels.

In third grade, the students would study a "double posthole" based on excavations of ancient Jericho and a living culture such as the Hopi. Through hard evidence, films, special books, and games, students would continue the strands begun in the previous unit, analyze evidence (another box of materials—bones, pieces of houses, scraps of pottery, etc.) of culture and social organization "to show how rich and different a nonliterate culture can be . . . in an attempt to make the children really see and feel the Hopi view of life and the world.

The unit for fourth grade would focus on "The First Cities," on what happens when cities begin to develop. Students would compare the Sumerian city of Ur with the later civilization of the Akkadians, again using excavated material, films, special readings, and gaming to explore the development of "urban technology, organized war and conquest." They would explore "distinct social classes, human personalities and highly specialized divisions of labor, a great written literature, and probably advanced forms of neurosis," along with lessons in cultural diffusion. Again, students would stick closely to the excavated evidence, but they would also be encouraged to wonder at the "awe" and "mystery" of the past.

Fifth graders would explore "The Crete and Greece Unit," based on two postholes, one at Knossos and Mycenae, the other at fifth century Athens, with a focus on Athenian society in its cultural and historical setting. It would make extensive use of films, literature, gaming, and "excavated hardware." The purpose would be to introduce children to "the feel, the sights, sounds, smells, taste, thoughts and emotions of the Greek world, to show how this world came about, how it differs from our own yet how much it has affected what we are today."

The sixth grade "Collision of Cultures Unit" would drop the posthole approach and attempt a "panoramic sweep of history," to illustrate what happens when a powerful culture (Europe) "impinges upon and virtually destroys . . . less powerful cultures" (the Western hemisphere). It would trace the emergence of the Maya, Inca, and Aztec, and the clash with Columbus (the beginning of the end for these cultures) using "collateral historical and anthropological readings, films, original documents, excavated materials, etc." and would provide background for American history, social science, and study of the contemporary world. As was true for each unit in the sequence, the final unit would pick up and trace through the strands begun earlier.

The written version of the presentation from Group A also contained several interesting "Additional notes":

1. There would be no textbooks. Instead, written material would be presented in facsimile form or in a series of inexpensive paperbacks, at different levels of difficulty, so that every child would find something readable, and no child would exhaust all the material. The written material would also help connect the postholes, filling in gaps.
2. The approach is "not amenable to objective testing," but might use new kinds of testing requiring the use of comparison, discrimination, and analogy.
3. The units would require extensive use of film, as the best way to "take you someplace new" and as "the best way to bring the working stiffs—the archaeologists, anthropologists, historians, etc.—right into the classroom."
4. The "most difficult part of the entire sequence will come when teachers first try to use it and realize that the teaching job has been radically changed. Suddenly they are not supposed to *tell* the children much of anything," instead encouraging children to find out for

themselves. There is no "body of knowledge" that must be covered and learned, then tested. Instead, teacher will attempt to move the class forward with assistance from films, materials, and readings.

The note ended with the following statement:

> [The task] of keeping a loose and possibly formless mass of children and materials together, these burdens are immensely increased. Just how the teaching patterns are liable to work out is impossible to say at this point, but it is not liable to be an easy job.[31]

While these additional notes offered practical advice and sounded the voice of realism, they also offered a prophetic warning, one that would prove critical to the prospects of real and lasting reform of the American social studies classroom: it was not going to be "an easy job."

Evans Clinchy's presentation of the report from Group A seemed to capture the imagination of the conference. Martin Mayer later described it as "far and away the most interesting moment" at Endicott House: "Not everything in such a sequence would work . . . not everything in the proposal was historically or anthropologically valid, and many other patterns of elementary instruction can be imagined. But the scholars at Endicott House felt their hearts lift as the sequence of these units was described in a brisk, matter-of-fact manner by Evans Clinchy; surely teachers and children should have a chance to share this excitement if they can."[32] Clinchy also recalled the enthusiasm for Group A's presentation:

> They all applauded at the end—and [it] gave them the feeling that maybe the whole two weeks had not been wasted. It was really on the basis of that—the enthusiasm engendered around the elementary [proposal]—that everybody [felt]: Hell, let's go on and keep trying to do something.[33]

The discussions, and the conference, might have ended with a consensus, but for one dissenter, Richard Jones, a Freudian psychologist from Brandeis, who had been part of Group A, but whose separate minority report, which followed Clinchy's, while supportive of the general outline of the proposed curriculum, especially its emphasis on imagination, evidence, and habits of mind, expressed reservations about "student readiness" to deal with what could prove highly emotional and conflict-laden material. Though the sequence was created with "scientific integrity" in mind:

> Now we have young children occupying themselves under our guidance with bones, teeth, weapons, dirt, human refuse, etc. There are no

more honest materials, we feel, with which to introduce children to the disciplined study of the human past. This said, however, we can safely make two predictions: (1) that the children will be called upon to manage highly emotionally charged images in their attempts to master these materials and the inferences to be drawn from them, and (2) that we shall be accused of alarmism for noticing that.[34]

Though he cast the first prediction as *"opportunities to be exploited* and *not obstacles to be avoided,"* he pointedly noted that it would require a teacher skilled "in enlisting vivid and highly individualized images . . . of injury, of death, of burial, of carnage, etc., in the service of the learning process." He concluded his remarks by suggesting that this challenge *"may be critical"* and called for special attention to it in teacher training.[35] As we shall see, these warnings would foreshadow an Achilles heel in the entire project of social studies reform.

Jones' concern with "readiness" and the emotional risks of inquiry was not well received by the conference. The scholars at Endicott House excitedly debated the merits of various plans for teaching the nation's young, but "they were loathe to consider the affective consequences of social science inquiry on the young." Some were even hostile to the suggestion of emotional risk, and at least one participant, probably Zacharias, urged the group to be "man enough" to disregard Jones' "psychophantasms."

Jones appealed to Bruner, who was scheduled to speak again the following day, to support the need to consider children's emotional reactions. Jones believed that Bruner would support his case for trying to reach the "whole child" and for considering what would later come to be called the "affective domain," because he knew Bruner's eloquence in addressing the heart as well as the head, but it was not to be. The next day, at the conference's final session, Bruner gave what Jones later described as a "first rate Piagetian talk" about the enactive, iconic and symbolic modes of knowing, but chose not to reopen the controversy.[36]

The conference closed on Sunday, June 24, failing to meet its loftiest goal of a completely new scope and sequence for social studies, K-12. But it did make significant progress toward the development of a broadened curriculum reform movement, which had been Zacharias' dream all along. Given the complexity and contentiousness of the task at hand, the diversity of perspectives and disciplines represented, and the limited time, it was a productive meeting. The split between the social sciences and historians had been, at least partially, overcome, with the realization, achieved through genuine dialogue, that both were concerned with the same subject, "man, his origins and achievement," but with differences in methods and conceptual frames.[37] This resolution of the conference's main crisis cleared the way for a general consensus around a notion of interdisciplinary integration, applicable especially to the elementary and junior high levels.

A second area of consensus seemed to emerge around the notion that children, even in the earliest grades, should be introduced to the "habits of mind" that were peculiar to each discipline. For example, if the subject was the formation of the colonies on the Eastern seaboard of what is now the United States, the "purely historical materials"—analysis of written documents [the Constitution, diaries, etc.]—would be handled according to historical rules of evidence, whereas sociological and anthropological materials—how people lived—would be handled in a way that gives children a sense of how a sociologist works and what is meant by various concepts such as "role" and "norm," even if those terms were never used. In the high school, most courses would be discipline-based, while there could also be integrated courses such as one that was recommended for the tenth grade including psychology, sociology, and anthropology. Moreover, in most cases, courses that were broadly disciplinary in history, for example, could draw on insights from the behavioral sciences.[38]

A third area of "general agreement" reached at the conference was on the proper method of introducing children to systematic bodies of knowledge. In fact, according to the conference report, it appears that everyone attending was already in agreement on this prior to the conference. This was the belief that a "linear approach to a subject" in which the teacher starts at the beginning and "dashes roughshod to the end while expecting the student to digest great globs of knowledge by rote along the way, was hopelessly inadequate." There was simply too much to cover. Superficial treatment left too many questions unaddressed, and did little to further deep structural understanding, critical thinking, or habits of mind. It would be much more effective, the conferees agreed, to select a specific topic or time period and delve into it with "some depth and completeness," along with a specific attempt to get at the "underlying concepts or principles" of a discipline. "Post-holing" would help students remember and make better use of the material studied.

Perhaps equally important, the "post-holes" themselves would not be presented in a conventional way, but would, as much as possible, "put the real raw materials [or hardware] of knowledge into the children's hands." With the raw materials, "and without formal lecturing" the students would begin to "*do* things—to sort out the bones and put them together in some meaningful fashion, to use the stone tools." Only after they had begun to sort materials on their own and made some tentative order, sequence, and connection would there be a more formal process. Some of the raw material and much of the process of formalization could be presented through films, which would add "vividness" and an "intel-lectual tone." Thus, by this inductive method:

> The children would be seeing and doing things for themselves, but would also be absorbing, many of the approaches and habits of mind of the scholarly disciplines—the nature of rules of historical evidence, how an archaeologist assesses his materials and makes controlled extrapolations, how an anthropologist studies a culture different from our own.[39]

Slowly and perhaps only "rarely" is the student "burdened with techni-cal jargon and complex nomenclature," and then only when the student already has a firm grasp of the principles to which the nomenclature refers. This was summed up for the conference when, at one point, Bruner put a sequence of three words on the blackboard: "Action—Imagery—Notation." That is, the children "do something, form images and ideas from their actions, *and only later do they notate it with an accepted technological language.*" In this way, concepts and principles that have typically been reserved for the college level can be introduced much earlier.[40]

Despite the initial acrimony and differences, the conference had come together around some notions of pedagogical style, favoring an inquiry approach to teaching in a vein similar to that begun in science and math, and continuous with work already begun in social studies. Like the con-ferees at Woods Hole a few years earlier, the scholars gathered at Endicott House were a select group of leading scholars most of whom were in sympathy with the general orientation of the reform, and supportive of broadening its scope to include the humanities and the social sciences so that schools could improve what they were doing. Though the cold war manpower development rationale seemed a "distant concern," it was still present in the form of proceedings and whenever discussion turned to funding.[41] There were a few professors of education among those invited to Endicott House, though the list of who was included snubbed most of the education establishment. Donald Oliver, whose work at Harvard ran in a conspicuously different direction than the largely discipline-based reform, was invited, but did not attend. The discussion might have evolved in a different direction, had Oliver, or Larry Metcalf, or Shirley Engle been present for the meeting.

Though the conferees at Endicott were in general agreement on the direction the reform should take, the conference received mixed reactions from some who had been involved in schools. One attendee, Franklin Patterson, remembered it as a "quasi riot." Another, Charles Keller, a historian who served as director of the John Hay Fellows Program that provided scholarships for advanced work to promising history teachers, felt offended by the attack on history and was upset that so few of those present had a full awareness of the innovative work already underway to improve its teaching. Keller had spent several years scouring the country for good history teachers, and he was the most knowledgeable person in attendance on the current status of work in the field. As Fenton recalled later, Keller "was so angry at Bob Feldmesser that he heard nothing else that happened through the entire convention."[42] Keller viewed the discussions at Endicott House as an intrusion by scholars into a domain that they did not know or understand. As at Woods Hole, they had little knowledge or appreciation of the history or social context of schools and of previous attempts at reform.

Wayne Altree, on the other hand, who was one of the most experienced classroom teachers at the conference, was "warmly enthusiastic" about the discussions that had occurred. A veteran of previous reform efforts, he later recalled the experience:

> [The conference] communicated to me a vision of what a curriculum could be as a continuous enterprise from the first grade until you got out of graduate school. It was a fresh idea . . . that maybe the process . . . of inquiry was more important than the current data that we were trying to get across. [That] there were systematic ways of constructing experience. Also, there was a tremendous sense of things going on in the social sciences that the schools were unaware of. This whole business of the interdisciplinary thing was new, that there was an organic way to marry the disciplines other than the crude way in the schools.[43]

Much later, Jerome Bruner recalled the conference at Endicott House, and its relation to the growing reform movement:

> Conferences—from Versailles to the little gathering at Endicott House—generate a dynamism of their own. The compromise "plan" for a social science curriculum to run from kindergarten through high school was its instrument. It boasted a starting six year sequence on "The Human Past," not a chronology but a series of "postholes" dug deep into revealing eras in the past . . . It was a noble vision. It was to unite the social studies and social science. Like the beautiful truths of physics, the beautiful materials of these epic eras would catch the imagination of students.
>
> In those heady days of 1962, anything seemed possible. Seminars were organized to "get the ideas right." An astonishingly gifted collection of people gave their time.
>
> What happens so easily in planning groups is that they get taken over by the centrifugal forces they generate. Only a powerful central idea can

prevent it from happening, and there was none. "Stones and bones" become "stones and bones" for their own sake, with mind for little else. The master plan of Endicott House became an exquisite collection of unconnected scholars' pieces: here a distinguished documentary on the emergence of maize culture in Mexico, there some stunning bits on scroll notation and dwelling patterns in Sumeria, later . . . film footage of baboon . . . and of the Netsilik Eskimo in Pelly Bay . . . What it did not make was a curriculum.[44]

At Endicott House an elite group of social scientists and historians, with little knowledge of schooling, its history, social context, and inner workings, and perhaps even less knowledge of schoolchildren, met at the former estate of a captain of industry, and gave direction to a reform that had the official backing of both government and private foundations as the trend of choice for school change. The conference, and the attendees, had a special elite status, of which they were very aware. The funds which were forthcoming to support the growing reform would mushroom quickly, as would its scope and reach. In the end, the meeting produced a few insightful suggestions about where the reform of social studies might head, but did not create an overall blueprint, much as Bruner's comments suggest.

GURUS ON GARDEN STREET

During and following the Endicott House Conference, the founda-tions for the new reform and an intellectual infrastructure continued to emerge. In the summer of 1962, as planned, Zacharias' new ESI social studies group continued meeting regularly to develop a refined, concrete proposal to submit to the Ford Foundation, eventually evolving into the Man: A Course of Study (MACOS) curriculum and other projects. Following Endicott House, the newly formed ESI social studies group began meeting at 12 Garden Street, on the edge of the Cambridge Common, to continue their discussions. Several of the participants at Endicott became regular visitors including Jerome Bruner, Evans Clinchy, Elting Morison, Franklin Patterson, and Zacharias. These "Gurus of Garden Street" worked to clarify, expand upon, and refine the ideas developed at Endicott House and prepared a proposal for submis-sion to the Ford Foundation.

One hopeful sign for the reformers came with a "First Experiment" conducted with a summer, 1962, kindergarten session. The purpose was to explore the reactions of a classroom full of young children to filmed ethnographic material, without the accompanying soundtrack, a narration that was "much too highflown and irrelevant." According to a report of the experiment written by Evans Clinchy, the children watched the film with what "seemed" to be "intense interest." In the evaluation, he wrote, "it seemed that the lack of sound was a positive benefit—there was nothing getting between the children and the people on the screen," and the children's level of interest and understanding went "far beyond" conventional films.[45] Meanwhile, curriculum development and related meetings continued apace at various locations around the country, and spread across the curriculum. In 1962, the California State Department of Education published a new social studies framework based on eight social science disciplines and recommending generalizations that students should derive from social studies courses.[46]

THE PANEL

While the Gurus of Garden Street continued their work on development of the Educational Services Incorporated (ESI) elementary social studies program, the Panel on Educational Research and Development of the PSAC, which had launched its work the previous spring, reconvened to determine its next steps. At its meeting held on September 9, 10, and 11, the Panel made a recommendation to include, in a group of projected winter meetings, a conference on the possibility of developing new curriculum materials in the social sciences. General approval of the plan had been given the previous July by the Panel's three principals, Wiesner, Waterman, and McMurrin. Apparently the dissent and controversy that occurred at Endicott House did not dissuade them from continuing efforts to pursue curriculum reform in social studies. The thinking of the Panel was that the winter conference on the social sciences might begin by "attempting to define a hard core of findings in the social sciences—sociology, anthropology, economics, and psychology—that is generally accepted by people competent in the field." It might then "consider whether this material is worth teaching in the schools, or even teachable in the schools." It could "leave open" the matter of whether the material should aim to become part of existing courses, or new courses in the social sciences. And, finally, it could consider use of materials "besides textbooks, such as films, laboratory apparatus" and other formats.

The plan was for the winter conferences to prepare reports for the Panel, which would transmit them to "the three principals: namely, the President's Science Adviser, the Director of NSF, and the Commissioner of Education," with the hope that the reports would offer guidelines for developing new approaches in each area. It was also hoped that the reports would estimate the size of the job to be done, and suggest "mechanisms—physical arrangements and sources of support—for actually carrying out new research and development that follows these guidelines." Finally, and somewhat informally, the conferences would serve to identify some of the people "who have the most to contribute" to solving educational problems and improving the curriculum in the schools.[47]

A memo from Wiesner to President Kennedy dated September 19, 1962, reiterated the plan, which was given the president's verbal approval the same day. As Wiesner stated it, "The idea behind the conferences is to get outstanding people who are not presently involved in elementary and secondary education, but who are in fields relevant to education, to put their knowledge and imagination to work on the problems of education." He cited a few of the country's outstanding scientists, Seaborg, Purcell, and H. J. Muller, who had been drawn into science education activities and suggested that, in a similar fashion, "many scientists and scholars who could make contributions to education" if they could be brought in, "should not work in isolation, but with outstanding professionals in the field."[48]

A note written by Wiesner a week or so later, expressing concerns about the level of "scientific literacy" among teachers in "nonscientific subjects" added:

> What I believe is this: It probably makes sense to extend this approach to such other subjects as history and social studies, although, obviously this must be tried before we can be sure. And, if the team approach makes sense, does it also make sense to include scientists from appropriate disciplines on the teams, with the purpose of including scientific materials, when relevant, directly in the course materials, and so insure their accuracy and even their mention? What I would like to see is a conference or two organized to consider these questions, with the conferences designed to include school teachers, historians, natural and social scientists, people presently involved in developing new curriculum materials, and others in relevant pursuits.[49]

Thus, Wiesner's support for a broadened curriculum reform included a broad "scientific literacy" component.

What had started with the PSSC and its initial foray into curriculum development was now growing into a much wider, more expansive reform. Still, it retained the same modus operandi: begin with a summer study or other conferences; identify the best and the brightest in the disciplines; turn them loose to develop curriculum materials for the schools, largely circumventing the educational establishment. The phrase "outstanding professionals in the field" was almost always defined as those in the relevant academic disciplines, and seldom included scholars in education. And, an important new development, the broader plan was given the administration's full approval.

Plans for the winter conferences also included brief descriptions and a list of invitees. The description of the conference on the social sciences read, in part:

> The past quarter of a century has seen considerable growth in the volume of research in the social sciences. By the social sciences is meant sociology, anthropology, economics, and psychology . . . Fair sized programs are now underway to bring the new developments in the natural sciences into school, but comparable programs . . . in the social sciences have yet to be started. The conference will explore the possibility of developing appropriate curriculum materials in the social sciences for school.[50]

Political science and geography were later added. The conference would attempt to list some topics in the social sciences that are "typical of the best work now being done," of the kind that "can be presented satisfactorily in some form in the schools." It would then ask some of its members, or groups of members, "to sketch very roughly some blocks of curriculum materials for use in teaching these topics." The conference would meet again in a month or so to appraise the resulting sketches. And, if the work "looks promising" longer working conferences could be set up with the aim of turning the sketches into something more substantial, some "blocks of materials ready for a first round of testing in the schools."[51]

The description of the proposed conference on history stated that the conference would examine the current teaching of history in the schools including "objectives, coverage, techniques of instruction, sequential development," and "explore whether some of the general features of the current efforts to improve instruction in science and mathematics are applicable to improve instruction in history." Some of those general features included

- Forming teams of gifted teachers, outstanding scholars in the field, and other people in relevant areas;
- Including not only textbooks, but other aids such as films, new kinds of laboratory apparatus, new sets of examinations, and teacher's guides;
- Attempting through the materials to get the student to approach the subject in the same manner, if on a reduced scale, as the creative, professional worker in the field;

- Attempting to provide understanding, not merely so many facts and manipulative tricks; and
- Setting up special institutes at colleges and universities to retrain teachers.[52]

What was taking shape was a comprehensive plan to apply the PSSC model to social studies, in combination with the general approach taken by the ESI social studies program, in an effort to revolutionize the field. But, that revolution was to be aimed in a certain direction, led by scholars in the academic disciplines. Though the plan appeared sound, it also raised many questions. It was, to be sure, a hierarchical and top-down approach to reforming schools, diffused somewhat by the mantra of "voluntary participation." There was also, unmistakably, an elitist quality to the reform, whether it was selection of the "best and brightest" in each field, or its germination at a few elite universities. The direction in which the curriculum improvement effort was headed had become very clear. The remaining questions, and the immediate fate of the reform, had to do with securing congressional support and the necessary funding. Finally, there was the question of whether, how well, and to what effect all this would work in the Nation's schools.

THE MISSILES AND MINDS OF OCTOBER

As this series of meetings was developing, the cold war manpower development concerns that had surfaced in the previous decade continued to be aired. At about the same time, a new crisis in the cold war was nearing the boiling point. The Soviet Union had placed missiles in Cuba that were capable of hitting U.S. targets. The Kennedy administration learned of the missiles and demanded that they be removed. The October 1962 confrontation that followed was an episode of brinksmanship that brought the world to the precipice of a Third World War. Though the Soviets eventually removed the missiles, the incident and its aftermath stimulated a new and intense wave of cold war fear and concern. Moreover, the missiles themselves were another representation of growing Soviet success in science and engineering technology, much as the Sputniks had been.

A new report issued in December 1962 by the PSAC titled "Meeting Manpower Needs in Science and Technology" confirmed continued growth in Soviet scientific and technological manpower. With "unprecedented requirements" to serve the nation's needs in "economic progress, military security, space exploration, medical advancement, assistance to developing nations, and education," the report conveyed a sense of "utmost urgency" and stated: "The accelerating rate of demand for engineers, mathematicians, and physical scientists with superior talent and advanced training is rapidly outstripping our ability to produce them."[53] It cited recent reports indicating continued Soviet "accelerated training of large numbers of science-oriented professional and semi-professional personnel." It noted that the implications of "their production of large numbers of B. S. engineers had been carefully studied in the context of both 'cold' war and 'hot' war."

Cited by President Kennedy in a January 1962 news conference, the report singled out the need in the three fields of engineering, mathematics, and physical science, but also noted the need for "more and better instruction in science (and other subjects too)," and stressed that its arguments for "strengthening American science applies equally to other fields of learning . . . [and that] . . . it is essential to give full value and support to the other great branches of man's artistic, literary, and scholarly activity."[54] Behind this most recent "Manpower" report was another secret CIA survey showing dramatic gains in Soviet manpower development in science and engineering in the period from 1939 to 1959. According to CIA figures, the total number of Soviet engineers had grown over the 20 years by 237 percent, with overall growth in engineering, technical, and scientific fields of more than 150 percent.[55] This information, combined with heightened cold war tensions, led to increased national concerns over improving education and contributed to a general willingness to provide federal funding and leadership.

LEGISLATION

Attempts to gain greater congressional support for the curriculum development program had failed in previous years. The "Improvement of Educational Quality Act of 1962" never made it through Congress. However, following the brinksmanship of the Cuban missile crisis, and the sense of foreboding that accompanied it, the school reform movement was to benefit once again from a fresh sense of urgency directly linked to the cold war.

At least two additional changes probably made passage of an education bill with significant increases in funding for curriculum improvement a strong possibility. The first of these was a change in strategy within the United States Office of Education (USOE). Former proposals typically emphasized general aid for the schools. As a key December 5 staff memorandum reported, "This approach has failed in the past; it failed last year. It will probably fail again." Instead, the memo suggested, "We believe a new *selective approach* targeted at particular educational problems . . . would achieve better results." And, the memo continued, "It would minimize some of the old battles and add more strength to the justification by stressing the national manpower, economic, and social contributions of education to the society. We think it could be enacted if the problems are sharply pictured . . . solutions are specific, and the Administration puts full force behind the achievement of specific objectives." The memo suggested "maximum *use* of *existing legislative* authority" with "add-ons," an "*omnibus bill*" with "a *continuum* of measures" which would broaden the base of support. It also advocated utilizing a "*project approach*" of directing federal funds to colleges or school districts for initiatives aimed at specific needs, especially emphasizing economic growth, manpower, and social welfare objectives. Among the specific problems targeted were research and curriculum development.[56]

The second change was the appointment of Francis Keppel, dean of the Harvard Graduate School of Education, to the position of commissioner of the USOE, on November 24, 1962. Keppel had been involved with the PSAC Panel on Education and promised to bring new vigor to the Office of Education partly because of his stature among both educators and scholars. Despite the hopefulness that accompanied his appointment, in his first news conference after taking office Keppel cautioned the nation not to expect "any radical, dramatic reforms." "Education," he was quoted as saying, "is a long slow process—reforms just do not take place immediately . . . We can only move forward to the extent that we have the quality to do so." He was also quoted as saying, "The fundamental problems in American education are connected inevitably with money, but the greatest influence on whether a child wants to learn is in the home." Finally, he noted, "I feel most strongly that the new Congress should pass an aid to education bill. This is very, very, very important."[57]

Reactions to Keppel's appointment were somewhat mixed, highlighting some of the issues faced in any attempt to increase federal involvement in education. One editorial, in the *Washington Post*, applauded his appointment and urged the administration to make federal aid to education a basic legislative aim of the 88th Congress, despite the "religious controversy" over aid to parochial schools. Others were less celebratory. *The National Observer* asked, "Will it be education or indoctrination?" and questioned the administration's plan to upgrade the Office of Education and the status of its Commissioner. The editor cautioned that any discussion of national level education policy "presupposes the existence in Government of an all-wise authority who knows exactly how and what Johnny should be taught. The danger is that Johnny won't be educated, he will be indoctrinated."[58] Another editorial warned, "Brace yourself for a renewed, high-powered, high pressure drive for Federal aid to education—and the inevitable control of the local school buses and the local teachers by Washington and the well heeled, untiring 'teachers union'" [the NEA] of which Keppel was a member. The writer went on to state that freedom of education could only be maintained by "freedom of local boards and local teachers from theories, compulsions and ambitions of the Washington spenders."[59]

THE PRESIDENT'S MESSAGE

President Kennedy's message on education, delivered on Tuesday, January 29, announced his submission to Congress of a comprehensive education bill—the National Education Improvement Act of 1963—implementing the legislative strategy that the USOE "Staff Memorandum" from the previous month had called for. The omnibus bill proposed the first significant expansion of the federal role in education since the National Defense Education Act, and included provisions similar to those contained in previous attempts to get congressional approval. However, this time the president's call for a larger federal role was framed with a broader argument that included both national security and domestic concerns, again, hewing closely to the strategy suggested in the December 5 staff memorandum.

Circulated for comment among the three principals of the growing education reform, the president's message began with the statement, "Education is the keystone in the arch of freedom and progress. Nothing has contributed more to the enlargement of this nation's strength and opportunities." In his introduction, the president argued, "For the nation, increasing the quality and availability of education is vital to both our national security and our domestic well-being," then cited both the benefits of "excellence" in education and the costs of ignorance and illiteracy. Predictably, he worked in a reference to "one of our most serious manpower shortages . . . the lack of Ph.D.s in engineering, science and mathematics." He called for greater investment in education as an "investment in economic growth." And, in a key passage, he broadened the manpower rationale with the following statement:

> In the new age of science and space, improved education is essential to give new meaning to our national purpose and power . . . the twisting course of the cold war requires a citizenry that understands our principles and problems. It requires skilled manpower and brainpower to match the power of totalitarian discipline. It requires a scientific effort which demonstrates the superiority of freedom. And it requires an electorate in every

state with sufficiently broad horizons and sufficient maturity of judgment to guide this nation safely through whatever lies ahead.

In short, from every point of view, education is of paramount concern to the national interest as well as to each individual. Today, we need a new standard of excellence in education, matched by the fullest possible access to educational opportunities enabling each citizen to develop his talents to the maximum possible extent.[60]

And so, Kennedy offered a broad and compelling justification for an expanded federal role. The phrase "a citizenry that understands our principles and problems" and the words "broad horizons" and "maturity of judgment" were broad, fairly direct references to the need for improvement in the social studies.[61]

The president's message introduced a large and comprehensive bill whose goals touched on improving both the "quality" and "quantity" of education, and "increasing the educational opportunities of potentially every American citizen." It included planks on expanding opportunities in higher education, improving educational quality, strengthening public elementary and secondary education, improving vocational and special education, and enhancing continuing education. Section III on "Improvement of Educational Quality" offered a clarion call for expanding the nation's educational research efforts, as follows:

Highest priority must be given to strengthening our educational research efforts, including a substantial expansion of the course content improvement programs which the Government has supported, particularly through the National Science Foundation. Two interrelated actions are necessary:

1. I have recommended appropriations in the 1964 budget for substantially expanding the National Science Foundation science and mathematics course materials program and the Office of Education educational research program.
2. I recommend legislation to broaden the Cooperative Research Act to authorize support of centers for multipurpose educational research, and for development and demonstration programs; and to broaden the types of educational agencies eligible to conduct research.[62]

In short, the bill included everything the Panel had asked for, including an expanded NSF budget for course improvement projects, expanded authority for the USOE to sponsor curriculum improvement projects in nonscience areas, expansion of NSF teacher training institutes "in the natural sciences, mathematics, engineering and social sciences," and broadened authority for the USOE to develop and sponsor teacher institutes.

In the conclusion of his speech, Kennedy revisited the question of rationale, arguing that while education "is and must always be a local responsibility," these efforts must be reinforced by "national support" to maximize "individual and national well-being" in an era of "economic expansion, population growth and technological advance." After stating that the "necessity" of the program did not "rest on the course of the cold war," he went on to note that a recent report from the NSF had found that the Soviet Union was "graduating 3 times as many engineers" as the United States, with "an annual flow of scientific and professional manpower more than twice as large as our own," thus reiterating the cold war manpower rationale behind the curriculum improvement program. The president closed his address by suggesting that the program was "reasonable and yet far-reaching," that it offered "Federal assistance without Federal control," that it provided for "economic growth, manpower development, and progress toward our educational and humanitarian objectives," and that it would "keep America strong and safe and free."[63]

Though the education bill had been formally introduced, the battle for its passage had only begun. While the bill was being considered by the Subcommittee on Appropriations of the House Appropriations Committee, chaired by Congressman John E. Fogarty, Jerrold Zacharias offered to testify at a hearing before the Committee. In a cover letter accompanying his written statement, Zacharias described the PSSC and noted that he had become "engaged in similar activities directed toward overhaul of the social studies and humanities curricula, where problems are even greater than those to be found in the natural sciences . . . the needs are urgent, and the costs will be great." He then offered his wholehearted endorsement of the Cooperative Research Program's appropriation, and attached a five-page, single-spaced written statement. In that statement, Zacharias argued:

> We need to give at least as much attention to social studies, to the humanities, to language, as we are now giving to science. I say "at least as much," but I myself believe we must give far more attention to these fields, for they are far more difficult than science, to teach and to learn. And let me be sure to make it clear that I believe them to be as important as science and technology, and in all but the most material respects even more important.[64]

He closed his statement by describing the ESI program in social studies and the humanities, making the case for federal support for that program, which had received funding only from private sources.

Though the administration's omnibus education bill died in the House of Representatives and was not passed into law, the president's message provided a strong rationale for the influx of funding and support that would eventually broaden and extend the growing social studies reform movement.[65] Funding for National Defense Education Act (NDEA) projects sponsored by the NSF and USOE was extended and expanded in late 1963, a few weeks after Kennedy's assassination, and again in 1964, and would continue into the 1970s.[66] This was a critical juncture in a fledgling social studies reform that had begun with isolated projects at a few universities, led by pioneers such as Senseh and Fenton. The president's message contributed to the build-up of massive federal funding and support for the reform, and ensured that it would be a major influence on the field for some time to come.

PROJECT SOCIAL STUDIES

"Project Social Studies" was officially announced in October 1962, prior to the genesis of the new education bill, the same month as the Cuban missile crisis. At that time, the USOE Cooperative Research Program invited colleges, universities, and state departments of education to submit proposals for *two* curriculum centers and for a limited number of projects in basic and applied research. Little more than six months later, the USOE announced that awards had been approved for seven curriculum centers, eleven research projects, and two developmental activities, with contracts running from three to five years, beginning in 1963. The seven curriculum centers were established with the aim of fulfilling one or more of the following purposes:

(1) To redefine the aims of social studies curriculums at one or more grade levels;
(2) To develop sequences of presenting subject matter that are based on what is known about human development and the teaching learning process;
(3) To work out methods and prepare materials to meet specific needs;
(4) To try out new methods and materials and evaluate them; and
(5) To disseminate information about the most promising methods and materials.

The seven curriculum centers included a center focused on curriculum development for "able students of history and the social sciences" in grades ninth-twelfth at Carnegie Institute of Technology under the direction of Edwin Fenton; a center at the University of Minnesota under the leadership of Edith West established with the aim of identifying the structure of each social science discipline, and developing materials; a project to develop a social science curriculum with 30 teaching units based on the analysis of public issues and led by Donald Oliver at Harvard; a project at Syracuse University under the direction of Roy A. Price with the aim to identify basic concepts which should be communicated to students in the social studies program, and to develop "illustrative materials for three grade levels"; a center to concentrate on economics at the ninth grade level at Ohio State University under the direction of Edward J. Furst, which will "analyze the structure of economics as a discipline" and develop materials; a center at Northwestern University under the direction of Jonathan McLendon to improve instruction about U.S. society in grades fifth, eighth, and eleventh, aiming to eliminate the duplication that occurs in the teaching of American history; and a center at the University of Illinois under the direction of Ella C. Leppert aimed at developing a five-year sequence for the secondary school designed "to help students understand the basic structure of the social order, the dynamic nature of societies, and the effects of social change."[67]

The Office of Education also sponsored a series of conferences involving leading scholars and focused on various aspects of the emerging reform. A conference at Stanford aimed to develop a statement on the "functions of the social studies" curriculum, to explore "reasons for public reluctance to permit the social studies curriculum to be realistic," to consider the need for "more and different instructional materials," to throw light on the problem of "preparing teachers," and to outline "the research that is needed."[68] Conference planners at Syracuse University acknowledged many "well conceived" efforts but were concerned that "much is being done without a sufficient base in research findings."[69] Many conference participants were project directors, consultants, or scholars in the social sciences, and focused on themes such as teaching inquiry and the scientific mindset, and learning theory focused on cognition and conceptual learning. Meanwhile, several scholars devoted attention to the ideas presented by Bruner and discussed at Woods Hole. Joseph J. Schwab delved into the "structure of a discipline" in the sciences, and Earl S. Johnson explored the concept of "structures" in the social sciences, calling them "elements in the discourse of reason."[70] Another important conference at San Jose State College considered the structure of knowledge in four major areas of the curriculum and included two important theoretical papers, one by Joseph J. Schwab of the University of Chicago on the structure of the disciplines, and another by Michael Scriven of Indiana University on the structure of the social studies.[71] These papers and conferences contributed to the general ferment out of which the new social studies emerged.

CONCLUSION

What had begun as a cold war era science education reform aimed largely at manpower development concerns was growing into a much broader reform movement with a strong theoretical base and modus operandi that would touch virtually all the disciplines. In social studies, the reform promised to shake up what was seen as a complacent field, dominated by progressive rhetoric and a curriculum of life-adjustment, and bring renewal if not revolution.

During the late 1950s and early 1960s the curriculum reform movement broadened to include social studies and other areas, embracing Jerrold Zacharias' early blueprint for reform through a series of meetings involving elite members of the governmental and academic establishment held at Easton and Woods Hole, and including participation and financial support from key members of the National Academy of Sciences, the National Science Foundation, the U.S. Office of Education and other authorities. A key but contentious meeting at Endicott House set the direction for social studies reform. Activity at the highest levels of government and on the PSAC led to new legislation and expansion of the reform with the announcement and institutionalization of Project Social Studies. The broadened reform received support from scientists; scholars in a variety of other disciplines; and key players in government, business, and the expansive military-industrial-academic complex who proceeded from the halls of power to implement a wide-ranging top-down reform. Several contextual factors played a role in the widening of the reform at that time. The Cuban missile crisis, ongoing concerns over manpower development, the demands of educational reformers, forward-looking presidential leadership, and a yeasty focus on emerging issues and problems led to an enlarged effort at curricular reform.

And so, a vast, expensive, and promising social studies reform movement was underway, with support from a consensus among government, private foundations, and leading universities. As we shall see in the next chapter, the materials created during the next several years by these and other projects would bring a new excitement to many classrooms, an animation that was rare in the typical social studies classroom of the past. As reform led to reform, the old problems of schooling were replaced by a new set of difficulties, some of which would eventually, and, it seemed, almost inevitably, undermine the reforms and lead in new directions.

PART III

INTO THE SCHOOLS

CHAPTER 5

THE PROJECTS

IN THE OCTOBER 1962 ISSUE OF *SOCIAL EDUCATION*, the same month as the Cuban missile crisis, a small, two-paragraph "Announcement for Project Social Studies" was printed on the lower half of one page. The announcement said, in part, "The United States Office of Education has announced the initiation of Project Social Studies, which is designed to improve research, instruction, teacher education, and the dissemination of information in this field." The announcement stated that the United States Office of Education (USOE) would work with "colleges, universities, State education departments, and, through the latter, the elementary and secondary schools of the Nation." The announcement went on to read, "Current plans call for the early involvement of associations in education and the academic disciplines to advise the Office in laying its plans for Project Social Studies." The announcement also stated that funding was obtainable for research projects, curriculum study centers, conferences, and seminars.[1] The fact that the announcement corresponded with the height of cold war anxiety is not lost in retrospection, though at the time the depoliticization of education made it seem a rather innocuous research and development notice, with exciting opportunities for teachers and scholars.

The earliest social science projects had begun to receive financial support prior to the announcement of Project Social Studies, and obtained funding from the National Science Foundation as well as private foundations such as Ford or Carnegie. As we have seen, following Sputnik there was a significant increase in the number of curriculum development projects funded by the National Science Foundation (NSF) and USOE in science and math, with new projects starting up in 1958 and 1959. Senesh and Fenton had already begun work on their projects in the 1950s, and received at least some private funding in support of their efforts. A similar enterprise, the Amherst history project, had its beginnings in the 1959–1960 school year under the leadership of Van Halsey. Halsey and a group of historians and teachers began a series of meetings that resulted by 1963 in development of ten two-week units for a revised United States history course. The units were organized topically and included suggestions for teachers as well as student readings composed mainly of primary source documents. The units were published by D. C. Heath, beginning in the fall of 1963.[2]

Three additional projects were initiated in 1961, all emanating from professional associations. All three were eventually awarded funding from the NSF. The first, the High School Geography Project (HSGP), involving the Association of American Geographers and the National Council on Geographic Education, was begun under direction of Nicholas Helburn of Montana State University in Bozeman. The second, Sociological Resources for the Secondary Schools (later changed to "Social Studies"), began operation at Dartmouth College in New Hampshire, with Robert Feldmesser as director. The third was the Anthropology Curriculum Study Project (ACSP), begun at the University of Chicago under the direction of Malcolm Collier.

Following up on the announcement of Project Social Studies, in July 1963, Gerald R. Smith of the USOE reported that seven curriculum centers, eleven research projects, and two developmental activities had been approved for funding. The curriculum study centers, their directors, and their charge, included:

- Edwin Fenton, Carnegie Institute of Technology: "prepare materials and make suggestions on reading materials for able students of history and social studies in grades 9–12."
- Edith West, University of Minnesota: "use an interdisciplinary team of experts to identify the structure of each of the social science disciplines" and prepare and evaluate materials, grades K–14.
- Donald W. Oliver, Harvard University: "plan a social science curriculum based on an analysis of public issues" and develop "a curriculum including approximately 30 teaching units organized around 5 persistent social problems" for grades eighth, ninth, and tenth.
- Roy A. Price, Syracuse University: "identify the basic concepts which should be communicated to students in the social studies program and prepare illustrative materials for three grade levels."
- Edward J. Furst, Ohio State University: "analyze the structure of economics as a discipline, prepare materials and disseminate information" for grade ninth.
- Jonathon McLendon, Northwestern University: "work at improving instruction about U.S. society in grades 5, 8, and 11 . . . Attempt to

eliminate the unnecessary duplication that occurs in the teaching of American history at these grades."

- Ella C. Leppert, University of Illinois: "work out three sequential courses for a social studies program for the secondary school . . . designed to help students understand the basic structure of the social order, the dynamic nature of societies, and the effects of social change."[3]

Four additional new projects were funded in 1964. These included a project at San Jose State College to develop a twelfth grade, one-semester course in economics; the Amherst history project; a Massachusetts Institute of Technology (MIT) project to develop a two-semester course on social phenomena and the social environment; and a project at the University of California at Berkeley to develop materials for teaching about Asian nations and cultures. By 1965 some two-dozen projects made up the new social studies movement, funded by the NSF, the USOE, or private foundations. Most notable among the new additions was the Harvard Education Development Center's Man: A Course of Study (MACOS), for which Jerome Bruner served as intellectual architect. The vast majority of the projects conformed to the general theme of the "structures of the disciplines," but there was some variety in orientation. Perhaps the least compatible with the discipline-based focus was the Harvard Project with its concentration on public issues as the central emphasis of citizenship education.

OVERVIEW

Clearly, a transformation of some sort was brewing, but what was its nature? During the years of the new social studies projects, journals periodically published reports from individuals involved in the projects and assessments of the work of the projects as a whole. In 1964, for example, *Social Education* published a brief summary of the Harvard Project written by Oliver and Shaver. Then, in April 1965, *Social Education* dedicated virtually the entire issue to a "Report on Project Social Studies," with a lead article and overview provided by Edwin P. "Ted" Fenton and John M. Good. Their report opened with a bold and self-assured statement: "The curriculum revolution which began in mathematics, the natural sciences, and modern foreign languages about a decade ago has at last reached the social studies. More than 40 curriculum development projects of national significance promise to revolutionize teaching about man and society." Calling the sum of the projects "the new social studies," in what appears to be the first use of the term, Fenton and Good provide a succinct synopsis of some of the general themes of the activities supported by Project Social Studies and other funding sources:

- "*The emphasis on structure.* With the single exception of Donald Oliver's project at Harvard, each of the HEW curriculum projects in the social studies seeks to identify the structure of social science disciplines or to build a curriculum around social science concepts. The directors have taken their cues from Jerome Bruner's influential volume *The Process of Education.* Thus far, however, no consensus about structure has emerged." Some identify the term with generalizations drawn from the social sciences, others use the terms, concepts, and structures interchangeably, and others imply that "structure is synonymous with the social scientists' mode of inquiry."
- "*Inductive teaching.* Most teaching in traditional social studies courses continues to be expository . . . The new social studies has abandoned this system of instruction. In its place has come a set of teaching strategies diversely called the discovery method, hypothetical teaching, or an inductive approach."
- "*Emphasis upon the disciplines.* With the exception of Harvard, all of the projects intend to teach generalizations and concepts drawn from the disciplines of history and the social sciences. In the courses which are being designed, students will organize knowledge as historians, geographers, political scientists, economists, anthropologists, sociologists, and psychologists . . . All of them (the projects) have scholars on their staffs . . . most of them intend to integrate materials and techniques from various disciplines within each course.

  Several of the projects emphasize another aspect of the disciplines, the mode of inquiry of history and the social sciences . . . The emphasis is shifting away from the accumulation of facts for their own sake to learning facts as part of the thinking process of scholars."
- "*Emphasis upon sequential learning.* Many traditional social studies curricula pay minimal attention to sequential and cumulative learning experiences . . . Each project has tried to develop a hierarchy of learnings to be taught in sequence beginning with the simple and moving toward the more sophisticated."
- "*New types of materials.* Project staffs are writing a host of new materials of a bewildering variety." Some supplement a traditional text, others replace it. Materials consist of "readings, games, films, tapes, transparencies . . . The majority of projects have embraced a multimedia approach."
- "*New subject emphases.* Increased emphasis upon knowledge and methods from the social sciences. In the past, history, geography,

and civics have formed the heart of the social studies curriculum. Now anthropology, sociology, economics, political science, and other disciplines clamor for a place."

- *"Giving maximum aid to teachers.* Each project recognizes its responsibility to help teachers learn to manage the new materials" . . . and materials are field-tested and revised.
- *"Evaluation."* Each of the 12 Project centers has a psychometrician on its staff to evaluate its work. Most groups try out their material on experimental classes and test their results against control groups.

The main points raised by the article gave a thorough yet concise overview of the new reform. As in earlier works, the authors made little mention of the contextual origins of the movement. The final paragraphs of the article pointed to several "fresh problems" generated by the projects, foreshadowing much of what would eventually result. These problems included:

- How can teachers and school administrators choose intelligently among the flood of new approaches coming from publishers' presses?
- How can we incorporate the work of the best of the projects into an integrated and sequential curriculum when the directors of the projects may have begun from quite different premises?
- How can we reeducate current teachers and change preservice education to prepare the next generation of teachers for the challenges of the new social studies? Summer institutes and generous grants . . . may help to solve some of the problems . . . but they cannot hope to solve them all. Only the practicing classroom teacher can translate the plans and raw materials now being developed in the curriculum projects into the day-by-day reality of the classroom. This challenge may well occupy the entire profession for the decade that lies ahead.[4]

One additional problem, discussed earlier in their report, was the lack of clarity about what was meant by "structure." These quandaries mentioned in the description by Fenton and Good, especially the last one, posed dilemmas that would haunt the new social studies movement as long as it lasted.

After 1965 another cluster of projects was christened. By 1967 more than 50 national projects were in progress, though curricular materials were slow to appear and were not issued in significant numbers until 1967. Haas writes that the projects developed after 1967 all claimed fidelity to the principles of the new social studies, but in actuality, moved off in all imaginable directions.[5] My own review suggests that although there were many variations and permutations of the general themes of the new social studies, the general parameter of discipline-based inquiry appears to have held fairly constant as a working guideline for the vast majority of projects.

Most of the projects included field tests, summer institutes, and some forms of teacher in-service education to familiarize teachers and assist in dissemination of materials. Most project directors and others had for years expressed the need for new in-service and preservice education. Hilda Taba observed a "serious gap between what teachers are now doing . . . and what is expected of them." Ted Fenton combined in-service educa-tion with curriculum materials development. During the peak years, thousands of social studies teachers across the nation attended in-ser-vice conferences, summer institutes, or teacher fellowship programs. Moreover, many of the earliest published products of the new social stud-ies era were designed as methods textbooks intended for use with preser-vice teachers. Among these were books by Fenton, Oliver, and Shaver, and Massialas and Cox focused on secondary teachers, and a volume by Clements and others on inquiry in elementary social studies.[6]

From 1964 to 1967 a few of the materials of the new social studies projects began to appear in print. Among the earliest were economics materials by Senesh for grades first to third, and the Amherst history series. By 1967, sets of curriculum materials and theoretical works came into print from a variety of projects in anthropology and history, and 12 paperback unit booklets were published by the Harvard Project. By the end of 1967, a rather extensive literature existed on the new social stud-ies projects and growing numbers of curriculum materials were in print. By that time the United States Office of Education (USOE) had funded a total of 58 projects and the NSF was financing 6 curriculum develop-ment projects. Also, additional federal funds were made available for in-service education programs consistent with the philosophical pattern of the reform movement.[7]

From a distance it appears that the new social studies movement reached its zenith in 1967. In this year, the total number of funded projects appears to have peaked. New social studies topics and concerns dominated both *Social Education* and the National Council for the Social Studies (NCSS) annual conference. Moreover, for many of the initial projects, grant periods were at or near their end. The years following 1967 would largely be spent dealing with publication, dissemination, and diffusion of materials. After 1967, one of the largest projects, the HSGP, elevated dissemination and in-service education to top priorities.

The HSGP made use of at least two styles of working with teachers. They held conferences to familiarize teachers, methods professors, and curriculum supervisors with their materials, and they developed leadership teams in specific school districts that would study and work with materials and devise a team plan for implementation. The HSGP also developed a number of means to disseminate information about the project and materials including a newsletter, press releases, a 16 mm film, videotape demonstrations, a sampler kit, position papers, brochures, advertisements, and journal articles. Although it often occurred belatedly, most new social studies projects engaged in some form of diffusion and teacher education.[8]

A second wave of projects obtained initial funding from 1968 to 1972, including a Social Science Program based in Berkeley, funded by NSF; "People and Technology," and "Exploring Human Nature," at the Harvard Education Development Center, funded by the renamed Education Development Center, Inc. (EDC) and USOE; the "Human Sciences Program, BSCS" in Boulder, CO, funded by NSF; and, "Comparing Political Experiences," at Indiana University, funded by NSF and directed by Judith A. Gillespie, Howard Mehlinger, and John Patrick. During the same period, several other curriculum development projects in fields with links to social studies also received funding.[9]

Several of the newly subsidized projects added selected use of modern social problems as topics for study and as criteria for selection of social science content. Adding to the general excitement, nonproject social studies curriculum workers, teachers, and teacher educators labored in the field, often providing conferences and workshops with support of grants from the USOE, state departments of education, and local school districts.[10]

If 1967 was the zenith of enthusiasm for the new movement, the years following, through the mid-1970s, represented a continuing presence with activity at a lower level of intensity. As we shall see, events in the society, many of which directly impinged on schools, may have weakened teacher enthusiasm for the new social studies and its general focus on inquiry rooted in the structure of the disciplines, a step removed from the conflicts and dilemmas of the social world.

OUTCOMES

Outcomes of the projects are more difficult to describe with certainty. There were two evaluations of the new social studies projects published in *Social Education* in the early 1970s. Sanders and Tanck grouped the projects into four categories: "comprehensive, discipline-oriented, area-oriented, and special purpose." By far the largest group of the projects they surveyed was in the discipline-oriented category. Their summary of the general features of the projects included the following main points:

- The projects place "greater emphasis on ideas on methodology" from the social sciences. "History and geography have not been abandoned but have become relatively less dominant as the subject matter of the social studies."
- "Many of the projects take an interdisciplinary, integrated approach to curriculum development." Many discipline-oriented projects weave ideas and methodology from other disciplines through their courses and materials.
- "Concern for the structure of knowledge is characteristic of most projects." This may include concepts, generalizations, and modes of inquiry.
- "Practically every project claims to use discovery or inquiry teaching strategies, but they define the terms in several ways and give varied emphases to them." Several stress specific inquiry skills such as classifying data, judging sources, formulating and testing hypotheses, etc.
- "A concern for values is evident in many of the projects." Some tend to promote particular values, others seek clarification and analysis of values, including the student's.
- The projects admit "more social realism and conflict" to the curriculum. The lives of common people and the daily experiences of students are given more attention. "Some formerly closed areas such as violence, profanity, social class and status, sex, and personal-social conflicts are treated more openly."
- "The patterns of thinking required of students are more creative, subjective, and divergent. Students are often asked to make their own value judgements, hypotheses, plans, or analyses. Although most activities still lead to closure, increasing numbers do not."
- Cross-cultural studies and emphasis on the non-Western world are discernable trends.
- "In-depth studies of selected topics" are favored rather than general surveys. "Interpretation of primary sources is favored over secondary description."
- "The traditional spiral of expanding student horizons is often altered or abandoned," with considerable variety in grade placement.
- "The projects have developed a greater variety of materials." Textbooks have been frequently abandoned in favor of a pamphlet or booklet for each unit. Texts are largely collections of readings and resources rather than narrative. Audiovisuals and games are an important part of some projects.

- "The major projects provide all essential instructional materials rather than relying on school libraries or community resources."
- "Considerable attention is given to teacher preparation and guidance."
- "Materials from almost every project were field tested in classrooms" and revised. "Virtually all the major projects have been successful in finding a publisher willing to market the materials."[11]

In the concluding portion of their article, Sanders and Tanck cite a few problems that had arisen among teachers using project materials. To wit, one staffer wrote, the projects "all invite students to inquire into a body of evidence in much the same way as a scholar working in the discipline does. Yet, with increasing frequency the feedback I get from teachers who are using these materials is that a noticeable portion of students are turning the invitations down cold or are at best reluctant guests at the banquet tables of inquiry and discovery." Another wrote, "We have learned, to our chagrin, that what appeals to an adult may seem either too obvious or too obscure to an eighth grader. We found, too, that we had to stretch our educational imaginations to the utmost to devise ways in which the material would induce student interest, but also not lead the student to an inevitable answer."[12] Opposite the first page of the article was a photograph from a classroom and the question, "Can the Social Studies Projects 'open the doors of the classroom' to innovative ideas?" The answer, at least according to this early appraisal, was "yes, sometimes," given a wise and thoughtful use of materials by skilled, knowledgeable, and committed teachers. The materials, it seemed, were far from "teacher proof."

One lasting contribution from these projects was an expansion and conceptual building of the mandarin, social science approach to social studies along with a massive level of materials development. In fact, given the financial and intellectual resources devoted to their development, it is not surprising that many of the curricular materials produced under the aegis of the projects were outstanding, and remain brilliant examples of inquiry-oriented social studies. Mostly, two generations later they have been disposed of. Some are still collecting dust in libraries, curriculum centers, and storage closets where they maintain a somewhat hidden existence.

DESCRIPTION AND DISCUSSION OF SELECTED PROJECTS

In this section, we will examine three of the most prominent projects, selected on the basis of my perception of their influence on the thinking of social studies educators and lasting influence on the field. For each project,

I shall discuss: (1) origins and development, people, ideas, motives, and sources of funding; (2) theoretical foundation—rationale; (3) project description; (4) classroom materials and publications; (5) and popularity.[13]

TED FENTON AND THE CARNEGIE-MELLON PROJECT

Ted Fenton, the key figure behind the Carnegie-Mellon Project, was perhaps the most well-known social studies figure of the entire period. The origins of Fenton's social studies work can be found in two experiences during the 1950s. During graduate school at Harvard in the early 1950s, he taught at the Brimmer and May School in Boston, a small private girls school, where he first "discovered (or invented, I can't remember which)" use of historical documents. Then, at Carnegie-Mellon, beginning in 1954, he began using a syllabus for teaching the freshman European History course developed under the leadership of Paul Ward, head of the history department. It was a syllabus filled with questions calling for evidence and decision making, and with readings from original sources.[14]

In 1958, Fenton and Ward attended an AHA-sponsored conference on the Advanced Placement (AP) Program. Encouraged by Charles R. Keller during a shared ride to the airport, Fenton launched into organizing and securing funding for an AP history project in Pittsburgh. With initial grants from the Fund for the Advancement of Education and A. W. Mellon, Fenton and a small group of colleagues in three high schools developed courses in American history, European history, and a sophomore course called "Introduction to the Social Sciences." During the next few years via an alliance with teachers and professors at the annual AP conference, and continued collaboration with Pittsburgh schools, which had won a large grant, the project grew dramatically.[15] Fenton's early focus on developing materials for world history led to publication of *32 Problems in World History*, which he later described as "an attempt to bring elements of inquiry into the world of the narrative textbook," drawing on skills he had learned in "my Carnegie Tech days" of working with Paul Ward in teaching the freshman European history course. Reflecting on his first four years of experience in teaching at Carnegie-Mellon, and his work with Paul Ward, Fenton later wrote:

So what did I learn about teaching history? Almost everything I know.

(1) Use narrative texts sparingly. They inhibit inquiry and critical thinking and lead to recitation and lecture courses.

(2) Plan courses carefully in advance and present them to students in a syllabus that includes reading assignments and questions to guide study.

(3) Teach students to inquire into the past. As the philosopher and historian R. G. Collingwood puts it in *The Idea of History* (1956), "History is a kind of research or inquiry . . . we ask questions and try to answer them."

(4) Give directions for study to students in a written syllabus containing questions on which to focus.

(5) Teach students skills such as note taking and essay writing.[16]

In 1963, the Fenton Project was awarded a grant from the USOE as one of the seven initial curriculum development centers funded under Project Social Studies. Under Fenton's leadership, the staff of the Carnegie-Mellon Social Studies Curriculum Center developed a four-year series of high school courses for able students, which was described as "a cumulative and sequential curriculum," much of which was outlined by Fenton himself in an earlier memo. The courses were titled:

Ninth grade: Comparative Political Systems and Comparative Economic Systems;

Tenth grade: The Shaping of Western Society and Studies of the Non-Western World;

Eleventh grade: The American Experience;

Twelfth grade: An Introduction to the Behavioral Sciences and The Humanities in Three Cities: Ancient Athens, Renaissance Florence, and Modern New York.[17]

The rationale "developed slowly during the life of the project" but centered on several key propositions: the project defined "able" students as the top 20 percent; it set the overall goal of "helping each student to develop to the limit of his ability into an independent thinker and an informed, responsible citizen of a democratic society," a broad goal that was divided into "four subdivisions—attitudes, values, inquiry skills, and knowledge." Much of the curriculum that was subsequently developed centered on a "mode of inquiry" by identifying some 19 analytical concepts drawn from the disciplines, and then developing analytical questions with each concept to guide the search for and use of data.[18] As Fenton defined inquiry, and put it into practice in his materials, it focused on thoughtful use of analytic questions for inductive thinking, moving from observed data to a general thesis or principle. Teams of writers and teachers from Carnegie-Mellon and the public schools developed materials, tried them in schools, revised, and tried them again. In 1966, the Fenton-led team of curriculum developers contracted with Holt, Rinehart, and Winston to develop a version of their materials that would have somewhat broader applicability in schools, aimed at "average and above average" learners.

This led to publication of a series of textbooks and materials, which greatly broadened the reach and influence of the project.

The center set out to develop a curriculum that made strong use of primary sources, and student materials reflect that aim. The readings in textbooks include a variety of resources—historical accounts, excerpts from speeches and essays, documents, magazine and journal articles, memoirs, fiction, and poems. Each set of readings is accompanied by a short introduction and several study questions. Study questions may begin with one item asking for information, but the focus throughout is on interpretation and implications. For example:

> What hypothesis have you formed about Renaissance attitudes and values from the previous two readings?
> Do you think the evidence in this reading supports your hypothesis?[19]

Many of the lessons also used handouts, filmstrips, picture cards, and recordings or transparencies from audiovisual kits, which were intended to be an integral part of each course.

Subsequently, Fenton and his associates developed a curriculum and materials for "slow learners." This work led to publication of a junior high school textbook titled *The Americans: A History of the United States*, and *Living in Urban America*, a text in sociology. Fenton would later comment that this was the work of which he was "most proud."[20] Yet, one of Fenton's former students, Anthony Penna, later described the development team as "oblivious" to the "pejorative" nature of the "slow learner" classification, and decried the "perniciousness" of the bureaucratically organized system in which "the culture of the school . . . perpetuated this caste system."[21]

Throughout his social studies materials, Fenton and associates emphasized inductive reasoning, guided inquiry, values analysis, and persistent issues. The sequential and cumulative curriculum they created via the Holt Social Studies program was reminiscent of Harold Rugg's work in the 1920s and 1930s, but with a stronger focus on the disciplines. As the Fenton team was engaged in creating and testing their inquiry materials, Fenton was also engaged in writing for and speaking to professional audiences. He authored an impressive string of articles appearing in *Social Education* and other leading journals; he edited a volume titled *Teaching the New Social Studies in Secondary Schools: An Inductive Approach* (1966) in which he forecast a "pending revolution" in social studies and presented selections from several leading theorists and reformers; he also wrote a slender volume titled *The New Social Studies* (1967), which provided an

overview of the reform, descriptions of the materials and teaching strategies that were being produced, and raised important questions about key
issues ranging from objectives to teacher education.

His leadership of the Carnegie-Mellon curriculum project and professional writing and speaking engagements placed Fenton at the apex of the
new social studies movement. Moreover, Fenton seemed less influenced by
the antieducationist bias shared by many of the founders of the curriculum
reform movement and much more attuned to the realities of teaching.[22]
Despite his own grounding in the discipline of history, his high school curriculum combined materials from several key disciplines for thoughtful instruction, and went beyond the disciplines to explicitly address value dilemmas
and choices. This was, largely, a discipline-centered and Deweyan approach.

MAN: A COURSE OF STUDY (MACOS)

One of the most highly regarded new social studies projects, MACOS
had its origins in the discussions of the social studies curriculum at
Endicott House in Dedham, Massachusetts, in June of 1962, and in the
curriculum development work that occurred just afterwards, sponsored
by Educational Services Incorporated (ESI), at the Garden Street house
in Cambridge. Douglas Oliver, an anthropologist at Harvard, was named
to lead the elementary school team that developed a framework for six
courses of study under the general theme *Evolution of Man and Society*.
As originally designed, the first grade course focused on study of the
Netsilik Eskimos of Pelly Bay, Canada. Asen Balikci was commissioned
to make a set of films that would depict the Netsilik's traditional lifestyle
and culture. The second grade course was based on study of Australian
aborigines and African Bushmen. A third grade course, titled "Becoming
Human" explored baboon communities via film; fourth fifth, and sixth
grades included study of early agriculture and animal husbandry, the
beginnings of city life via archaeological studies, and ancient Greece,
respectively. In 1964, Jerome Bruner took leadership of the elementary social studies project when Oliver left following the death of his
wife. In 1965, Peter B. Dow, a young teacher and head of the History
Department at Germantown Friends School in Philadelphia, joined the
project after hearing Bruner speak at the Annual Meeting of Friends in
Philadelphia in 1964. Dow, whom Bruner would later describe as "the
answer to my prayers," would soon become project director.[23]

Under Bruner's leadership, the aim of constructing a comprehensive
social studies curriculum for the elementary grades was set aside to focus

on creating one course for fifth grade to be called, *Man: A Course of Study* or MACOS. The course examined three questions:

1. What is human about human beings?
2. How did they get that way?
3. How can they be made more so?[24]

As Dow later framed it, "At the heart of *Man: A Course of Study* was this notion that you could get kids to turn around on what it means to be a human being . . . Maybe understand something about the origins of humanness, and as Bruner hoped, maybe have them think about how you create a more humane way of life." The course and student materials dealt primarily with the first of these questions, and was centered on ethnographic films and materials gathered in field research. Using anthropological sources, teachers and students explored the roots of human social behavior through intensive study and comparison of animal groups and primitive human societies. Again, according to Peter Dow, "This idea of taking kids to the frontier of research required that we have very different kinds of materials . . . to try to provide an experience in the classroom that came as close as possible to the ethnographer in the field. So film became the central teaching method of the course."[25]

The course materials introduced fundamental questions about the nature of humans in contrast with animals. The course began with a unit on the life cycle of the salmon and asked students, via contrast, to examine questions about the nature of human development. The second unit focused on the behavioral patterns of herring gulls, extending discussion of parenthood by looking at a species whose family structure is similar to humans. Free-ranging baboons were the subject of the third unit, raising questions about the functions of dominance, aggression, sharing, reciprocity, territoriality, and other behaviors and offering many provocative contrasts for examining human social practices. The culminating unit investigated the concept of culture through an in-depth study of the Netsilik Eskimos. Drawing on materials from the Danish explorer Knud Rasmussen who studied the Netsilik in the 1920s and film-based ethnographic studies conducted by Asen Balikci from 1963 to 1965, commissioned by ESI, children further explored what it means to be human by examining similarities and differences in the lives and social practices of a group very different from themselves. The films, which would later be at the heart of the MACOS course, were outstanding.

The developers of MACOS sought to actively engage students in a process of inquiry. By exploring materials and questions students were involved in hypothesizing, observing, collecting and interpreting data, categorizing, and developing tentative generalizations while wrestling with powerful organizing concepts from the discipline of anthropology. The aims of the course were summarized as follows:

- To give pupils confidence in the powers of their own minds;
- To give them respect for the powers of thought concerning the human condition, man's plight and man's potential;
- To provide them with a set of workable models for analyzing the nature of the social world in which they live, the condition in which man finds himself;
- To impart an understanding of the capacities of man as a species in contrast to other animals;
- To instill concern for the human condition in all its forms, whatever race or culture.[26]

The developmental outline, concepts, and materials contained in MACOS were strongly influenced by the ideas of Jerome Bruner. According to Bruner, "The curriculum of a subject should be determined by the most fundamental understanding that can be achieved of the underlying principles that give structure to that subject." Moreover, he theorized, "The best way to create interest in the subject is to render it worth knowing, which means to make the knowledge gained usable in one's thinking beyond the situation in which the learning has occurred." Bruner reflected on the purposes of the course many years later, and stated, "As somebody said, what are you trying to do, make these kids into contemporary philosophers? And the answer was, why not?" While Brunerian principles guided the creators at every stage of their work, as they developed materials, framed questions, and prepared lessons, in much of the day-to-day development work, others took the lead.[27] One of the overarching aims of the course was summarized some years later by Asen Balikci: "We were firmly convinced that with these new tools (and) with the Eskimo (films) we would be able to effectively oppose racism and ethnocentrism in America. We really believed it."[28]

Course materials fell into three main categories: film and other visuals, written materials, and games and other active devices. Film was the primary source of data. They were in color, with natural sound and minimal commentary. In anthropological terms, the films were used primarily as a simulated field experience. As Dow put it, "One of the things was to get rid of the textbook. Get rid of these compendiums of codified knowledge that we were transmitting to kids and engage kids more directly in the process of knowledge generation."[29] Instead of a text, there were 23 booklets, written in a variety of styles and including many illustrations. Some of the booklets supplied evidence for various questions, others focused on concepts. Still other materials included field notes, journals, songs, poems, and stories. Learning activities included games and construction exercises that allowed children to work individually and in small groups with minimal teacher direction. Seven teacher manuals provided background in subject matter and instructional suggestions. Throughout the course, the materials and activities placed a great deal of the intellectual responsibility on students. By design, all of the materials stressed Bruner's three modes for expressing and obtaining knowledge—the enactive, iconic, and symbolic. In Bruners' own recollection, the project design team coalesced around the challenge of creating an engaging curriculum, as Bruner later wrote:

> My precautions against films as a "passive" medium spread to all the other things we were doing—posters, pamphlets, books, "field notes," class plans. Were they sleep-producing? We were all seized by the battle against passivity—from the cutting rooms through the design studio to the lesson planning for our tryout summer session. It became a pedagogical style rather than a theory.[30]

The project received funding from several sources; at first from the Ford Foundation then later and most prominently from an NSF grant beginning in 1963, which assisted in the course development and dissemination, and in funding workshops and regional centers so that teachers could use the materials most effectively. Though the materials were originally created for fifth grade, they were also used effectively at various levels through high school.

A survey of teachers and other social studies professionals placed MACOS among the highest rated new social studies materials in surveys conducted in 1973 and 1974.[31] One reviewer, writing in *Social Education* in 1972, wrote:

> It is the analyst's opinion that MACOS is one of the best curriculum projects developed to date; the course has the potential of completely changing the learning climate of the school. As a result of working with the materials, students will be more interested in school; teachers will be more apt to involve students in the learning process and less apt to dominate the class; school districts will be less likely to think of social studies curricula in the terms of a single textbook, and will be more willing to support the social science laboratory concept in future curriculum selections.[32]

This was high praise indeed. If it was true, and evaluation data reported by EDC suggests that it was, then MACOS was a huge success. It meant that a revolution in social studies was indeed possible, given the right materials and the necessary funds for workshops to prepare teachers for an inquiry mode of teaching. At its peak in 1972, the MACOS curriculum reached an estimated 400,000 school children, a strong indication of its success.[33] In retrospect, it stands as a shining example of the kind of engaging and provocative work that is possible.

DONALD OLIVER AND THE HARVARD PROJECT

The Harvard Social Studies Project had its origins in a seminal article by Donald Oliver that appeared in the *Harvard Education Review* in 1957, titled "The Selection of Content in the Social Sciences." Oliver critiqued the approach to content selection by the American Historical Association (AHA) Commission and an NCSS Committee. He suggested both "failed to consider adequately the school's right to mold personal values of the student," and had confused the term "knowledge" and the relationship between "knowledge and values." He argued that both groups failed to take into account the "ferment and conflict over competing ideas and values" that is allowed under a creed of mutual tolerance, and to "consider the difficulty of adequately describing American society." Instead, Oliver wrote:

> We propose that the relationship between personal values, the general canons of tolerance of our society, and the determination of public policy for the regulation of human affairs be made the center of the social studies curriculum in the public school. The basic core of content would consist of the study of existing and predicted conflicts caused by differing definitions and interpretations of the meaning of liberty, security, and public welfare.[34]

This would be accomplished by teaching students to recognize and define areas of human conflict, to define alternative means of regulating human affairs on specific political and social issues, and to make thoughtful predictions about the consequences of various alternatives. The central objective of the approach was "to introduce young people to the fire and controversy that rages within a free society over ways of regulating human affairs." The hope was to provide students with a way of approaching conflicts and controversies that is more "'rational' than blind adherence to some ideology . . . learned during early socialization."

As with the Rugg program, disciplinary boundaries would, of necessity, be broken down. The approach combined valuing and social science with an emphasis on ethical considerations. It was, Oliver asserted, a "tough-minded scientific approach."[35]

The general orientation of the Harvard Project ran counter to most of the other new social studies projects developed during the era, calling for analysis of public controversy as the central focus of citizenship education. The project developed under the leadership of Oliver and several of his graduate students including James Shaver, Fred Newmann, and Harold Berlak. Initially funded by a private grant, funding was later augmented by support from Harvard and by the Cooperative Research Branch of the U.S. Office of Education.

Oliver and his associates developed an elaborate and definitive rationale for their alternative approach to social studies that included both an unambiguous concept of citizenship education and an explicit link to relevant social theory. "The model citizen," they posited, "is one who, in the manner of an intelligent journalist, engages in dialogue with others in an attempt to reach positions on controversial public issues." The function of the dialogue is "to provide clarification," to facilitate the "justification of one's position," and to understand the positions and justifications of others. A successful dialogue requires use of "various forms of inquiry, analytic and argumentative skills"; "a fund of information to support claims and definitions"; and a "repertoire of analogies" to support or refute arguments.[36]

The Oliver-Shaver rationale, as explicated in *Teaching Public Issues in the High School* (1966), portrayed public controversies as "latent dilemmas ingrained in a cluster of values" that are sometimes referred to as the "American Creed." Citing the work of Myrdal and others, they argued that there is broad agreement on general values such as human dignity, freedom of speech, the sanctity of private property, majority rule, and the rights of the minority. However, the consensus is threatened when two or more values come into conflict in dialogue on a contested public issue, or when one value is given precedence over another. The history of American society, they suggested, is that of a pluralistic community held together by a shared commitment to a liberal, constitutional political tradition in which value conflicts are negotiated and, in some cases, resolved.[37] Thus, the curriculum they developed focused on "analysis of public issues which have at their core legal-ethical dilemmas."[38]

The teaching strategies used by the Harvard Project centered on rational discourse and envisioned a "model" classroom discussion setting that might best be described as a "seminar or coffeehouse round table." In response to the pessimism often expressed regarding the value of discussion, they argued that "opinion" issues can be "resolved through rational discourse." In support of their approach, they argued, "There are objective standards for judging the rationality and validity of positions." They went on:

> Briefly, a position or opinion that is supported by reliable evidence, that is consistent, that takes into account analogous situations, and that offers useful definitions of vague terms is more valid than a position that is unsupported by evidence, inconsistent, insensitive to analogies, and uses ambiguous language.[39]

In implementing the jurisprudential model, the "teacher becomes a facilitator" and cannot appear as a "truth-giver" who has "all the answers." Instead, the teacher's role is to assist in clarification of issues, to ask for substantiation for a particular point of view, and to help students understand the complexities of issues. The teacher's opinions must be somewhat tentative as well, open to revision via the process of exploring the issues with students. The approach emphasizes conflicting values and "clarification of two or more legitimate points of view as they bear on a public policy question," with teacher and materials acting as catalyst. "Our focus, then," Oliver and Shaver wrote, "is on the dialogue, either between teacher and students or among students."[40]

With Socratic discussion at its heart, the approach made extensive use of "case study materials." Case study materials were defined as: "investigations of single institutions, decisions, situations, or individuals." The object was "to gather somewhat detailed information about a relatively small class of phenomena" and to examine it intensively. It was an application of the postholing approach that historians in other projects were using, only with the focus on enduring public issues. In the Harvard Project, case materials included stories and vignettes, journalistic historical narratives, research data, documents, text, and interpretive essays.[41] The project endorsed use of a wide variety of teaching strategies, and cautioned, "Despite our emphasis on discussion, it is certainly inadvisable to have student discussions every day." Other types of lessons used included traditional lecture, reading cases aloud, writing analogy cases, "hard-probing Socratic dialogues," games and role-playing, films, writing briefs and position papers, and various small group discussion formats. All of these strategies would be used in an "open-ended inductive" or "discovery" approach that would "allow students to search for and reach conclusions on their own" instead of having conclusions given to students by the teacher. The project staff contrasted their "open-ended" approach with a "closed inductive approach" in which the teacher leads the student to the "right" conclusions, however subtly.[42]

The materials produced by the Harvard Project centered on a series of booklets titled the *Public Issues Series*, published by Xerox Corporation. The booklets were heavily concentrated on historical topics, and, according to a *Guide to Teaching*, were intended to be used as "supplementary experiments for U.S. History" or even as a replacement text for certain topics." Notably, this was a step back from the position taken by Oliver and Shaver that the jurisprudential model should serve as a substitute for history courses, but probably helped market the materials to a broader spectrum of teachers.[43]

Each unit booklet, printed on newsprint paper and written in a highly readable style, contained a variety of relevant case material from history, the social sciences, and analogous and contemporary situations. For example, *The New Deal* contained four historical journalistic narratives (on causes of the depression, the NRA, AAA, and WPA), one fictional story (a town facing job losses), one authentic story (of WPA bureaucratic bungling), and one contemporary journalistic narrative (on contemporary poverty programs). Each booklet also contained questions for reviewing the facts of each case.[44]

At the end of each section, the booklets contained thoughtful discussion activities and questions titled "Persisting Questions of History" that raised key issues of the unit and posed analogous situations. At the end of each booklet a section titled "Review, Reflection, Research" suggested additional questions and activities. Throughout the materials their creators posed thoughtful questions of fact, definition, and value. Often, a central value-laden policy question of an enduring nature was at the heart of the unit. For example, in *The New Deal*, one of the central questions was, "How responsible should the government be for the economic well-being of its citizens?" A related activity asked students to consider several different approaches to the problem of poverty, and asked, "Which policy do you think should be adopted by the government?" The initial set of pamphlets, published in 1967, focused mainly on topics in U.S. history including *The American Revolution, The Railroad Era, Religious Freedom, The Rise of Organized Labor, The Immigrant's Experience, Negro Views of America*, and *Municipal Politics*. In the ensuing years, pamphlet coverage broadened to include a range of topics that might be used in other history and social science courses. By 1972, the series had published 30 pamphlets on a range of topics addressed in history and social science courses.

The Public Issues Series was one of the most popular sets of materials created during the era of the new social studies. In surveys, the materials ranked in the middle and upper one-third of all new social studies materials, and in a final survey conducted in 1975, it ranked near the top of the list.[45] Sales of the booklets were high (they were relatively inexpensive) and reportedly reached a total of over 8 million pamphlets.[46] The pamphlets also received a great deal of use in classrooms. One survey reported that 20.2 percent of teacher respondents had used the materials with students, a higher percentage than with any other project.[47]

INFLUENCE

Judging by my own exposure to the materials, and an ongoing and unscientific examination of social studies curriculum labs and materials closets, from 1975 when I began my teaching career, to the present, it would appear that MACOS, the Senesh books, and Taba social studies were the most influential at the elementary level. On public issues and instruction in government, the Public Issues Series, from the Harvard Project, and the textbook *American Political Behavior* by Mehlinger and Patrick appear to have been most influential and most widely distributed. I am told that the *Public Issues Series* was the best seller among all of the new social studies materials. For U.S. history and culture, the Fenton textbooks were widely distributed, as were materials from the Amherst Project. In the social sciences, materials from SRSS and the HSGP were widely used, and were popularized by a compilation of lessons aimed at preservice and in-service teachers titled *Experiences in Inquiry*.[48]

SHORT-TERM INFLUENCE AND USAGE

The materials were evaluated by teachers and other social studies professionals under the auspices of Irving Morrissett and the Curriculum Information Network (CIN) and jointly sponsored by *Social Education* and the Social Science Education Consortium during the first half of the 1970s. In surveys, respondents were asked three questions (1) How well did these materials work with your students? (2) How do these materials compare with other social studies materials you have used? and (3) Would you recommend these materials for use by others? Over the course of three surveys conducted from 1973 to 1975, most of the project materials received positive responses, but some were more positively received than others. Rankings based on the three surveys showed consistently high rankings for the HSGP, the Public Issues Series, and the MACOS materials. American Political Behavior and Sociological Resources for the Social Studies (SRSS) ranked toward the middle, and the Fenton materials received a lower than average ranking. Other materials that received relatively high rankings included the *Holt Databank*

System created by William R. Fielder, *The Promise of America* textbook series authored by Larry Cuban and published by Scott-Foresman, and the *American Adventures Program* authored by Thomas Ladenburg and published by Scholastic. That these smaller ventures were ranked among the most useful in classrooms suggested that individual teachers and publishers, given a creative hand and wide distribution from a commercial publisher, might be just as influential on classroom practice as the most highly funded federal projects.[49]

Use of materials was also assessed in a study conducted by Thomas Switzer and others that examined the extent to which social studies teachers in five Midwestern states were cognizant of and using curricular materials developed by ten of the most prominent social studies projects. Projects in the study included the Amherst Units in American History, the ACSP, Berkeley's Asian Studies Inquiry Program, Carnegie-Mellon's Social Studies Curriculum Project, Harvard's Public Issues Series, the HSGP, Indiana's American Political Behavior, Law in American Society Foundation's Justice in Urban America Series, San Jose State's Econ 12, and SRSS. Among the study's respondents, only the Carnegie-Mellon materials had been "heard of" by more than half, while more than 40 percent had "heard of" the Harvard and Amherst materials. The study also found: respondents who taught a subject dealt with by a particular project were more likely to have heard of and examined the project's materials; projects producing interdisciplinary materials had a higher percentage of respondents having heard of the materials; and that even for the Harvard Project, the most widely used, only 20.2 percent of the respondents reported using the materials. Carnegie-Mellon materials were reportedly used by 18.7 percent, Law in American Society by 17.6 percent, and Indiana materials by 10.4 percent. All of the other materials surveyed were reportedly used by less than 10 percent of respondents. These were sobering results, indicating that remarkably few teachers were using project materials. Use as reported by subject taught provided a slightly more encouraging picture, with 36.4 percent of sociology teachers using SRSS materials; 33.3 percent of geography teachers using HSGP materials; and 64.3 percent of anthropology teachers using ACSP materials.[50]

Despite their eventual disappearance from the classroom, the theorists, projects, and classroom materials of the era had a profound long-term influence on the field of social studies education. Several individuals of note played a leading role. Jerome Bruner had perhaps the widest and most extensive influence, serving as a sort of point man for the reform, playing a key role in meetings and curricular work, authoring seminal books such as *The Process of Education* and *Toward a Theory of Instruction*, and mentoring Peter Dow. Ted Fenton was the single most recognizable figure among the social studies reformers, and served to bridge the gap between discipline-based and issues-centered theorists. His materials including both the Holt textbook series and *The Americans* were widely adopted in schools and his professional writing resulted in several key articles and books, including *Teaching the New Social Studies,* and *The New Social Studies.* If there was a "Mr. Social Studies" during the period, he was it. Donald Oliver had a singular creative influence on the reform through the Harvard Project and the seminal book *Teaching Public Issues in the High School* written with James Shaver.

With a multitude of creative projects, curriculum developers, and scholars, the era of the new social studies had a profound influence on thinking in the social studies field. This is perhaps its most enduring influence. As of this writing, the period serves as an exciting and unusual chapter in the history and development of the field, and as a case study in reform, its success and failures. Federal involvement increased exponentially during the period, establishing a precedent and leaving perhaps the single greatest lasting influence. Research and development centers established during the period took on new meaning and prominence. Finally, the period and the materials produced, despite some variety in theoretical orientations, have come to stand as the single best representation of the structure-of-the-disciplines approach to the field.

CONCLUSION

As a concluding section for this chapter, we will examine the influences of the theories and materials from the period of the new social studies, assessing both their potent strengths and their most glaring flaws. A comprehensive overview of the projects and the reform should include a variety of concerns ranging from conceptualization to the pedagogical innovations embodied in the texts and materials produced. As we shall see, many of the strengths and dilemmas of the projects and materials were ultimately traceable to the origins of the reform.

CONCEPTUALIZATION

From a theoretical perspective, the projects and materials of the era of the new social studies tended to rely strongly on Brunerian theory and the ideas set forth at the Woods Hole and Endicott House conferences. The central ideas included strong notions of inquiry or discovery learning, an emphasis on interactive forms of pedagogy, and a rationalist, structuralist approach to the disciplines, emphasizing the "structure" of the various social science disciplines as the heart of the reform movement, though what "structure" meant varied considerably. Other key principles included the assumption that children of any age could explore conceptually complex disciplinary knowledge in an appropriate manner, and that depth-of-study through postholing was preferable to broad and superficial treatment. While interdisciplinarity was generally prized, what it meant and the degree to which it was embraced also varied widely.

Rationales for the projects were, in many cases, only partially developed. As we have seen, the general intent of most project designers was to replace the ill-conceived social studies taught in schools with scientific or academically grounded discipline-based courses. It was, in essence, the antidote for progressive social studies, with its emphasis on "problem-solving," which had been severely criticized during the 1950s. Projects tended to focus on one discipline, a particular course, or units that could be used in a variety of courses. An in-depth rationale for citizenship education was developed by the few projects that had strong involvement from social studies educators (i.e., Oliver and the Harvard Project; Engle and the Indiana Project).

Along with the frequent lack of a strong, in-depth rationale linked to citizenship education, the projects and the movement as a whole gave little attention to issues of scope and sequence. Of course there were exceptions such as the EDC curriculum and the Fenton (Holt) series, but these were the exception rather than the rule. Most projects did not attempt to create a new scope and sequence, and what emerged was a modified version of what had become the standard sequence, with many schools and districts going their own way, replacing individual courses with new offerings, but, and frequently, leaving the overall scope and sequence something of a hodge-podge.

FUNDING

Of course, none of this intense work would have been possible without massive financial support. By 1968, the federal government had spent more than $3 billion on a multitude of educational improvement projects, and funding continued well into the 1970s.[51] Firm estimates of the total funding devoted to school curriculum improvement projects during the era of the new social studies are difficult, but the sum over the course of the broader reform movement was likely in the hundreds of millions of dollars. Moreover, both the amount of funding and the level of federal involvement in the curriculum were without precedent, and represented part of a major shift in both the control and direction of schooling in the nation.[52] Unquestionably, the money that funded the new social studies was a continuation of the funds unleashed by Sputnik, and the support was delivered with the same essential, though now broadened and largely forgotten, purpose in mind, to win the cold war by upgrading the quality of the educational system, drawing on the best minds available from each discipline. The new social studies was the citizen education wing of the national security–inspired reform movement, employing a wartime research and development model and engaging many of the same persons in positions of leadership.

STAFFING

Most of the directors of the reform were, by design, leading scholars from the social science disciplines. This choice was something of a double-edged sword. It gave the reform its strong connection to the disciplines and led to versions of inquiry method and materials exploring disciplinary concepts and topics, but also meant that key scholars and theorists from schools of education, who might have helped fashion more successful projects, were discounted, left out, or given minor roles. Though there were exceptions, the conscious decision to bypass the educational establishment was rooted in a disdain for schools of education and "educationists," reflecting the critiques of education that inspired the reform.

PEDAGOGY

All of the projects focused on development of innovative pedagogy, and used approaches to teaching focused on inquiry, discovery, critical thinking, or inductive reasoning. Most projects embraced a healthy focus on open-ended questions, concepts, and interactive lessons designed to inspire student thought. Many made strong use of multimedia sources. Beyond this general focus, there were some significant differences. A few devoted significant portions of their work to "guided inquiry," in which students were led to conclusions similar to those reached by scholars. Others concentrated on open forms of inquiry conducted by scholars that were replicated by students. Many project directors and committees believed that students lacked sufficient background knowledge and conceptual understanding in the disciplines to conduct full-blown inquiry, and therefore created variations on inquiry on a small scale. A few projects made the use of film as a key pedagogical tool, as in the case of the MACOS Project, partially replicating the model provided by Jerrold Zacharias and the PSSC.

DISCIPLINE-BASED

The vast majority of projects, especially those for secondary schools, were discipline-based. This meant that there was a focus on how a specific discipline could best be taught, drawing on concepts, topics, and modes of inquiry from that specific discipline. For example, building on its anthropological base, MACOS used film as a substitute for the field observation necessary in ethnography. The Amherst Project used primary source documents, much as historians would in constructing a historical narrative and interpretation. Many included some interdisciplinary work, reflecting the consensus that emerged at Endicott House.

REVOLUTIONARY INTENT

The intent of the reformers as a whole was "revolutionary." That is, they intended to replace what was seen as a failed approach to social studies in the schools with what they viewed as a superior approach, drawn and crafted from the academic disciplines. This not only raised expectations beyond a reasonable level, it sometimes precluded retention of and building upon anything of value that was already present in the classroom. That the reform was primarily disciplines-oriented tells us something about what it was, and reminds us of the linkages of projects and materials to the origins of the reform, but also tells us something about what it was not. It was clearly not revolutionary in the sense of a strong social reconstructionist orientation, save for perhaps a few projects. However, and quite ironically given the origins of the reform, many of the discipline-based projects ended up leading students to the same kinds of value dilemmas and social justice issues that social reconstructionists such as Harold Rugg, George Counts, John Dewey, and other progressive educators had raised a generation earlier, only they did so through a different lens.

ROLE OF THE TEACHER

In almost all of the materials, to varying degrees, the teacher was thrust into a new and different role, as the lead inquirer and facilitator, rather than the arbiter of truth. In the traditional classroom, the teacher, textbook, films, and supplementary sources dispensed truth via a banking approach, making deposits in the minds of students, informing, but simultaneously dehumanizing.[53] In the new social studies classroom, the teacher was still the director of learning but teacher talk and textual materials were no longer the fountain of all knowledge. Instead, students were more frequently asked to do much of their own inquiring, to make up their own minds, and to draw their own conclusions.

Ironically, given this stance that treated students as intellectuals, many of the projects foisted their materials and teaching approach onto teachers as "the" one best practice, contrasting it with traditional approaches to teaching. Teachers were frequently managed as consumers and implementers of curriculum materials created by "experts" in the discipline, rather than as true intellectuals. They were frequently thought of as curricular instructional gatekeepers, rather than as independent thinkers constructing their own considered approaches to teaching.[54] Though projects varied somewhat in how they treated teachers, the general thrust and intent of most of the projects was to substitute an expert approach for the teacher's own. In the long run, this represented a trend toward the deprofessionalization of teaching, a trend that has only grown stronger in recent years.[55] Moreover, the role of teachers in the development of project materials varied greatly. In some cases, teachers were integrally involved and treated with greatest respect. In other cases, they served as window dressing, providing Project Directors and potential consumers with the illusion of collaboration with practitioners.

EVALUATION

There were at least two forms of evaluation embedded in the new social studies projects. The first of these involved evaluation and revision of project materials via field trials, which sometimes included extensive research and comparison of the experimental curriculum with control groups. This form of project evaluation provided invaluable feedback from teachers in the field-testing phase of each project, and sometimes led to important published research, and in a few cases, significant contributions to the knowledge base.[56] A second meaning of evaluation came in the form of teacher assessment of student learning as a component of the project. A few projects included extensive materials for evaluating student learning. However, this was frequently perceived as a weakness in reviews of project materials. In most schools, teachers were expected to assess student learning and assign grades. Traditionally, assessment focused on recall of factual information, with some attention to other higher-order goals via alternative forms of assessment such as writing or projects. Given the inquiry orientation to pedagogy employed by the new social studies materials, alternative assessments were necessary, but were seldom sufficiently developed to satisfy teachers, who were forced to rely more on student writing, projects, and participation to assess learning and determine grades. Though it seems rather obvious, it is important to point out that reading and grading projects and papers can take a good deal more time and effort than totaling scores on multiple-choice tests.

SYSTEMIC ISSUES AND DILEMMAS

The reformers knew and talked about the fact that the reform of social studies in a massive and largely decentralized school system was a daunting project, but they acted as if the rhetoric of revolutionary change was a reflection of their true situation. In reality, project directors faced a central dissemination problem: How to distribute the materials they had created in an effective manner that would influence classroom practice? Though they enjoyed varying degrees of success on this task, on the whole, the projects had only limited influence on classrooms, and far less influence than their developers had imagined. Perhaps their expectations were too high. Perhaps they failed to adequately understand the culture of the school. Ultimately, it was ironic that a reform whose origins were tied to "systems analysis" would fail partly because of its lack of an effective analysis of the educational system and how it might best be influenced.

TEXTBOOKS AND MATERIALS

The materials were generally of very high quality, but were something of a grab bag, reflecting their conceptualization and the diversity of ideas represented in the general reform. The reading level for most was high, appropriate for advanced or college preparatory classes, and unsuitable for students who were poor readers. There were a few materials created with those students in mind, notably the *Promise of America* textbook series by Larry Cuban, and Fenton's *The Americans*. Materials were highly interactive and engaging, often using multimedia approaches, and frequently focused on questions. As one reviewer described it, materials came in an "almost bewildering variety." To be sure, they represented a much more complex set of resources but most could be readily adapted by a thoughtful teacher.

A NEW LANGUAGE

With their many theoretical and practical contributions, the reformers created a new language that became part of the lexicon of social studies. Among the terms created or popularized during the period were inquiry, discovery, induction, inductive reasoning, critical thinking, postholing, structure-of-the-disciplines, values, jurisprudential, systems analysis, decision making, public issues, and a host of others. Moreover, the new cognitive psychology popularized by Bruner and others brought new ways of thinking about teaching and learning that outlived the materials created during the reform. It was an attempt at a "multidimensional change" that affected curricular traditions, pedagogical practices, staff relationships, and more broadly, the school's role in the society.[57]

On the whole, these general characteristics of the reform and the materials, both strengths and flaws, were, in many cases, traceable to the antiprogressive, "antieducationist," cold war origins of the reform. The revolutionary intent was, in part, based upon a conviction, drawn from Bestor and other critics of schooling from the previous decade, that a new and more rigorous approach was needed with a focus on excellence to be led by discipline-based scholars from the university. If the problem was the educational establishment, then the heart of the problem was the school of education and the third-rate scholars that taught its classes. Reformers had an antieducationist bias that led most of them to sidestep the educational establishment and appeal directly to teachers.

Despite its many flaws and limitations and the general failure to realize their highest hopes, reformers and the materials they created influenced a great many teachers. They created a new level of curriculum development and an excitement about social studies that is rare in the history of the field. Moreover, the project directors and their collaborators have a continuing presence in the literature of the field. Though most of the materials created during the period are no longer in print, and have virtually no presence in today's classrooms, the approaches they championed have had a broad impact on thinking in the field and on classroom textbooks and materials, which often include inquiry questions, topics for decision making, primary source materials, etc.

In retrospect, the materials produced in the era of the new social studies were among the most innovative and influential commodities ever produced for use in social studies classrooms. Despite the historical context out of which they were born, and perhaps partly because of it, projects funded by millions of grant dollars from the NSF, the USOE, and other sources contributed to creation of a rich and multifaceted explosion of curriculum development the likes of which may never be seen again. The projects and materials set a tone for an era of innovation and inquiry that spread to other curriculum materials, textbooks, and curriculum guides.[58] Yet, as in each of the previous attempts to reform social studies, this one too had its critics and problems, as we shall see in the next chapter.

PART IV

CONSIDERING
ALTERNATIVES

CHAPTER 6

CRITIQUES AND DILEMMAS

DESPITE THE EXCITEMENT GENERATED and the national attention focused upon the field, the social studies profession was not unified in support of the reform movement. There were many contemporary critiques of the new social studies, from multiple perspectives. Perhaps the earliest published critique of the new social studies was by Donald Robinson in an article published in 1963, shortly after the launch of Project Social Studies. Sounding a note of caution about the "ferment" in social studies, Robinson observed, "Everyone has a different notion of what the social studies should attempt," and predicted that "curriculum reform will continue to result from diverse, and often contradictory trends." He concluded that social studies classroom practices would persist in being shaped by "a combination of national tradition, suggestive state programs, locally prescribed curricula, the considerable influence of textbooks, universities, and professional organizations."[1] Robinson's comments indicated some of the variables that might blunt attempts at reform, regardless of its direction.

Another early warning came from James Becker who noticed, in 1965, that there was a new consensus emerging on the need for reform in social studies. Yet, ironically, he remarked, "Never before in our history has there been less general agreement about precisely what needs changing and how the changes should be made." He described a "nearly total confusion" and discord over purposes afflicting efforts to define the field. The social sciences, he wrote, were "too young and too yeasty a field to be able to provide us in the schools with a neatly packaged set of goals and objectives." Becker cautioned that prospects were remote for any kind of dramatic change in social studies, or in education more broadly, citing "[w]idely dispersed power, lack of strong central authority, [and] responsiveness to variations in ideological, social, and political outlook" as factors limiting the possibilities for reform. Major departures from typical practice were especially unlikely, in part, because "the society itself is diffuse and decentralized" as were the schools. Becker acknowledged that educational change takes place, but suggested "it seldom moves far ahead of public attitudes and that teacher competence and availability of materials are further inhibiting factors."[2]

DEFINITIONAL DILEMMAS

Some of the critiques may be traceable to the continuing definitional dilemmas that had been part of social studies since its inception. Throughout the 1960s and beyond there was continuing interest and concern focused on curriculum and methods. In fact, many concerns from previous decades continued virtually uninterrupted. Theorists continued to focus on the problems approach though the name often changed from problem solving to inquiry or critical thinking. There was also some attention to interdisciplinary approaches such as core, though various forms of integrated curricula garnered less attention after 1960, with the movement to reaccentuate the academic disciplines.

There was, at the same time, a reinvigorated interest in methods of teaching. This concern focused on topics ranging from methods of grouping students and discussion techniques to use of teaching machines, programmed instruction, and textbook skill development. Among the more innovative additions to the lexicon of instructional methods were the introduction of case method, use of popular music, and a focus on various forms of role-playing and educational games. Simulation games received a good deal of attention by the late 1960s and throughout the 1970s.[3] In the 1970s, aspects of the open schools movement found their way into social studies literature and fostered growing attention to learning centers and open education. On the whole though, the emphasis was on inquiry, interaction, and exploration, and it was influenced and aided by the new social studies movement.

There were also many other developments in social studies, concurrent with the headlines made by the national reform effort. Other trends took place in the shadow of the new social studies, though in several cases they were a mirror of conceptual and practical limitations of the disciplines-oriented movement. As we have seen, not everyone agreed with the Brunerian structure-of-the-disciplines approach. As a consequence, definitional debate on the status and future of the field continued throughout the period.

In a notable special issue of *Social Education* published in April 1963, a number of leaders offered their thoughts in a collection of articles titled

"Revising the Social Studies." The new social studies movement was headed mostly in the direction of lionizing the individual disciplines and largely abandoning the possibility of an integrated social studies. Though the essays included in the special section took Bruner's call for "structure" as a starting point, the kind of structure they described was much different than the discipline-based structures embraced by the majority of the new social studies projects. Instead, they discussed potential configurations for a discipline of social studies, as a unified field of study. The introductory editorial by Lewis Paul Todd warned of "intellectual arrogance" and the dangers of "limited vision," and urged the profession to avoid the disconnectedness that might result from the structure-of-the-disciplines approach.[4]

Shirley Engle's composition outlining his thoughts on the conceptual foundations for an integrated social studies supplied the opening statement and principal focus for the symposium. Engle had previously authored a number of highly regarded articles advocating a Deweyan, reflective, and issues-centered approach to teaching, including the seminal article "Decision Making: The Heart of Social Studies Instruction" in 1960.[5] In his 1963 symposium entry, Engle argued:

> The cornerstone of the structure of the social studies curriculum should be our knowledge: first, that every human society, though it may differ from others in detail, possesses certain basic characteristics in common with other societies; and, second, that the social problems to which serious and responsible social scientists, philosophers, politicians, and citizens devote attention are merely variations of basic social problems which persist from time to time and society to society. Building on this cornerstone, the structure of the curriculum is afforded by a listing of the basic ideas or concepts in terms of which human experience is explained, together with a listing of the persistent social problems of the society . . . Concepts and the problems to which they relate afford the avenue by means of which facts, so called, become relevant and useful. Facts learned out of a context in which they can be put to use in clarifying general ideas and understanding of our problems become merely academic; their learning quickly becomes a bore. The structure of the social studies curriculum should therefore emphasize general ideas or concepts and social problems.[6]

Engle then emphasized one of his two main points: *"The course of study should provide for regularly recurring emphasis on the basic ideas or concepts in terms of which all human experience is explained."* He went on to list nine basic concepts and eight central questions, each of which relate to "the principal areas in which all societies have persistent social problems."

Later in the article, he emphasized his second major point, insisting on the direct study of social problems: *"The course of study should provide that every child will have the opportunity to study and understand thoroughly the important problems which confront the American people."*[7]

The second article in the symposium, written by Engle's protégé, Byron G. Massialas, added to Engle's general notion of a concepts-and-problem-oriented curriculum through the enhancing idea of "models of search, verifiability, and invention which the learner employs in his quest to find dependable knowledge." Massialas urged "the study of value conflicts in our society and alternative approaches to understanding or resolving them," as well as greater attention to "intuitive thinking," as Bruner had argued. Massialas concluded his article by arguing that all students "should directly participate in inquiry, invention, and the act of philosophizing. The study of value conflicts in our society and alternative approaches to understanding or resolving them should also have a definite place in the curriculum." He went on to suggest that such a program would tend to "face realistically the challenge of our twentieth-century civilization. A school system operating within such an orientation would provide educational leadership and act as a major reconstructing agent in society."[8]

An entry in the symposium by Lawrence E. Metcalf delineated current deficits in social studies programs, including "the ritualistic quality of instructional purposes" offered by curriculum planners, a "poor and wrong" approach to student motivation, an "inadequate . . . conception of problem-solving," the continued "domination of history" and lack of attention to the newer social sciences, and the "aimlessness of instruction." Metcalf then described the approach to social studies he developed with Maurice P. Hunt: "The foremost aim of instruction in high school social studies is to help students examine reflectively issues in closed areas of American culture." Metcalf argued that students should be encouraged to reason carefully about the conflicting beliefs involved in such areas as "sex, economics, religion, race, and social class." He suggested that the substance of social studies "would acquire meaning if its relevance to current problems and issues were perceived by students," and advised selection and use of content from history and the social sciences in a manner that "tests propositions and clarifies conflicts."[9]

The symposium also included an article by Paul Hanna in which he lamented the fact that few of the social studies projects began with an "overall design" for the curriculum in mind, and that "one looks in vain for proposals on scope and sequence that have institutional or organizational support." Hanna also discussed his own "wholistic and coordinated" approach for elementary social studies built upon "the expanding communities of men." In essence, he proposed an overlay of "a grid of human activities" on the omnipresent expanding horizons curricular model, with geography and history woven into the overall design. For the secondary school, beginning with grade eight, he proposed a curriculum sequence made up of world geography, world history, and one-semester each in economics and political institutions and processes. Eleventh grade would focus on the nearly universal United States history requirement, and twelfth would be devoted to an issues-oriented course on problems of society, requiring "contributions from all the social sciences and history" and "focused on problems that cut across disciplines."[10]

All contributors to the symposium supported "inquiry" in a general sense, and argued for inclusion of the social sciences and history, though not as the core of the field. On the whole, they gave little support for civics or Problems of Democracy courses, which had by that time earned a passé, old fogey image. Moreover, most of them referred to Bruner and the developments of the new social studies projects briefly, and suggested alternatives to the structure-of-the-disciplines approach as backers of the assorted disciplines were describing it.

There were other important works related to the matter of definition. One, written by Samuel P. McCutchen, a Progressive Education Association (PEA) veteran and National Council for the Social Studies (NCSS) President, proposed a discipline of social studies. He argued that instead of continuing an endless battle of the disciplines for space in the curriculum, social studies should become a discipline in its own right. Social studies, he went on, must "induct young people into today's society, help them to understand it, to find meaningful places in it, and make it livable; that is, move it closer to its ideals." McCutchen identified four "elements" of the new discipline: "the societal goals of America, the heritage and values of Western civilization, the dimensions and interrelationships of today's world, and a process of rational inquiry and the tenets of good scholarship." The final component implied that critical thinking or a problems approach be "taught in a wide variety of content," and at least once, "be made the basis for an organized course."[11]

Each of the articles discussed above could be loosely connected to the meliorist camp. An exchange of letters between William H. Cartwright and McCutchen, and a memo from Erling M. Hunt, all members of the NCSS Curriculum Committee working on developing a curriculum document in 1962, illustrates the lack of consensus within the organization, and differing orientations regarding the place of the disciplines and the general purposes of the field. In a letter from Cartwright to McCutchen on June 17, 1962, responding to McCutchen's proposed curriculum, Cartwright wrote:

> I have been consistent in opposing fused social studies grades 4–11, and have not changed my position. History, geography and government, as school subjects, should be broadly conceived, and should draw on other social sciences as well as areas outside them. But I think we will get a better and tighter organization by using the subjects.[12]

In July of 1962 McCutchen wrote:

> The closer I get to "the methodology of the several social sciences," the less I am sure that I know what is really meant and that each of the disciplines has a methodology distinct from every other . . . I am not sure that any one of these disciplines really differs from the methodology of good scholarship plus that of critical thinking.[13]

Hunt, in a document titled "Criteria for an Adequate Social Studies Curriculum" included as the first item, "Identify and emphasize the values and ideals that have guided the American people and nation, with a view to ensuring a reasoned and disciplined patriotism."[14]

From each of these leaders of social studies we see concerns raised from alternative directions. From Cartwright, a general sense of support for the role of the disciplines; from McCutchen, a questioning attitude toward the disciplines having distinct modes of inquiry; and from Hunt, an emphasis on social efficiency, on socializing students for patriotic citizenship. It was apparent from these diverse perspectives that the definitional dilemma was far from resolved.

EARLY CRITICS

Among the earliest pointed critiques of the new social studies reform movement were those articulated in a group of letters published as rejoinders to the 1965 overview of Project Social Studies by Fenton and Good. Fred M. Newmann wrote that "we must be cautious to avoid seduction by the fashionable emphasis on 'inductive thinking' or 'discovery method'" when the major objectives of most of the projects centered on "communication of the structure of one discipline." Newmann worried that the projects "provide no guarantee that a spirit of intellectual autonomy will be developed," and cautioned that they too frequently aimed at guiding students to predetermined generalizations.

Byron Massialas charged that the projects "concentrate on the empirical and cognitive dimensions of learning" neglecting the normative and affective components. He went on to argue that, with the exception of the Harvard Project, they have done little to consider "the work of philosophers and psychologists," and that "nothing is said about the points of contact between empirical generalizations from the social sciences and value judgments expressed by individuals about society." A second weakness, he charged, lay in the projects' "disproportionate amount of emphasis on the 'structure of the disciplines'" and their neglect of "careful consideration of other sources of curriculum development—the individual and society." Finally, he argued, regarding instruction, most of the projects seemed to assume that "what is good for the social scientist acting as a researcher is good for the child or the adolescent as well."

Richard E. Gross suggested that the projects suffered from a failure to clearly delineate purposes, hazy and somewhat unsophisticated research designs, a tendency to concentrate on average and above average students, and development of "teacher-proof" materials that could reduce the teacher's role to that of technician. William H. Cartwright worried that the projects seemed to assume that practically all of the old in social studies was bad. Carl O. Olson, Jr. envisioned an "articulation nightmare," called for reform on a "K-12 basis," and urged more involvement of practicing teachers, warning that the projects represented a threat to the "integrity of the individual teacher" by emphasizing curricula prepared in advance. Daniel Roselle, who would later become editor of *Social Education*, worried that the projects were "moving in such a variety of directions" and expressed his concern that "national confusion may result." He called for greater "coordination of projects," and for "research into the common vital issues facing man today." Gerald Marker voiced a similar observation, that the projects "go off in all directions" but did not view that diversity of approaches as undesirable, given the "present state of social studies research."[15] These early critiques embodied many of the most significant dilemmas of the new reform, and may have influenced its later direction to some extent.

KRUG'S CRITIQUE

One of the most widely cited critiques of the new social studies movement came from a different perspective than many of the early critics. In an article titled "Bruner's New Social Studies: A Critique," appearing in *Social Education* in October 1966, Mark M. Krug charged that the new reforms had several conceptual flaws. First, he argued that unlike science and math, there was no logical structure of ideas in the social sciences. In the discipline of history, for example, Krug noted, "the few historians who have tried to find some order, rhythm, or structure in history have done so with limited success."

Krug also suggested that the Brunerian approach assumes that students will share the thrill of "discovery" and want to imitate the research procedures used by scholars. He quoted a question posed by Newmann: "Why should a general lay population be taught to perform intellectual operations of a nature preferred uniquely by the academic profession? That is, why should all children be taught to ask and answer the kinds of questions that interest historians, political scientists, economists, etc.?"[16] Krug argued that students need knowledge of history and the other social sciences, and charged that Bruner slighted this need. Bruner, he argued, wanted the behavioral sciences to play the central role in the social studies curriculum. Krug wrote that this would not help students develop the historical perspective needed to understand the world and its problems. Krug's preferred alternative was to restore traditional history.[17]

A subsequent issue of *Social Education* contained letters responding to Krug's critique. Most of the letter writers found Krug's comments interesting and were pleased to see a critical review of new social studies ideas rather than the general "acquiescence" that seemed so common at the time. One wrote that Krug's ideas were "refreshing" and that he had grown tired of the insistent demand of the reform's advocates "that nearly everything that is presently being done be scrapped." Another applauded Krug for his critique, and challenged the notion that the new social studies should "replace" current programs. "What evidence is there that the new programs are effective?" he asked. Others suggested that many educators were embracing the rhetoric of the reform "simply because it is new," and that "too many people are jumping on every innovation that comes around." Another warned, "Too many teachers are being misled in that they are expecting a package deal to tell them how to teach." A final and lengthy letter from a teacher using Bruner's "structural approach" took issue with several of Krug's arguments, especially his suggestion that Bruner's approach would lead to a loss of historical perspective, and pointed out that he and his colleagues were using the "New History" to help students develop even greater "historical perspective." Moreover, he reported that "students become excited by discovering and applying generalizations which show the structure of history," and cited student feedback that was typically either "favorable or enthusiastic." He quoted an anonymous student evaluation:

> In the normal history course I tend to become bored, but in the New History I am stimulated. The discussions we have are always revealing because we are always discovering something. The new discoveries we make are more interesting because we have found them ourselves . . . I think the New History is much more meaningful and significant than the way history is usually taught.[18]

INSIDER VS. OUTSIDER

An insider's perspective on the reform was provided the same year from Richard Brown, director of the Amherst Project. In an article that appeared in *Saturday Review*, Brown addressed several of what he termed, "paradoxes aplenty" in the reform. There were questions, and a need for clarification, on the meaning of the term "discovery":

> Is it nondirective under any circumstances? Or is it in fact strongly directed, not toward an answer to be sure, but by the questions asked and by all of the apparatus and logic of scholarly method? Does it not also embrace both inductive and deductive methods of learning?

Brown expressed concern about the various attempts to develop projects directed by "the old siren-song of interdisciplinary work," and called instead for "a coordinated multidisciplinary approach" with due respect for the "subtly but importantly different" methods of each discipline. Most presciently, he worried that few teachers were "equipped to cope" with the inquiry orientation of the new reform. Trained in "dreary expository courses by academicians and professional educators, many have no idea what it is to ask a question or pursue a line of inquiry. They teach as they have been taught." This, he wrote, was "the most serious obstacle of all to the success of the social studies revolution," and he urged academicians to accept, "a full measure of responsibility for education rather than paying it the lip service—mixed with none-too-gentle scorn—which he does at present."[19]

An outsider's view came from Gerald Leinwand, whose critique appeared in the same issue of *Social Education* as Krug's, and who offered a broad series of queries and pointed critiques, many of which went right to the heart of the reform. Warning of the danger of taking Bruner's seminal ideas and making of them "a cult, an orthodoxy," which perhaps even Bruner did not intend, he suggested that the reform movement had led to the "hasty abandonment of the teaching theories and curriculum designs of the recent past . . . to substitute far too quickly the idea of curriculum as 'discovery and inquiry.'" The heart of his critique, however, centered on the reformers' methods. He wrote:

> To have the student perennially assume the role of the social scientist and discover what the historian or economist already knows is artificial. At its best it is play acting and, if what the student discovers is quite contrary to what he should discover, the entire procedure becomes wasteful—if not downright ludicrous. Essentially, before one can discover for himself he needs background, knowledge, information—as well as the process by which that knowledge has been acquired.

Moreover, Leinwand charged that while a reasonable amount of postholing could enhance the curriculum, structuring the entire curriculum around postholes would lead to fragmentation. Many primary sources would be virtually unreadable for average and below average students who often struggled with reading. He warned of the danger of that we would "sacrifice the common heritage" and the "body of accumulated wisdom and knowledge which can and should be understood and appreciated, though admittedly not unquestioned or uncritically accepted." At the close of his essay he argued for a thoughtful approach to the teaching of history with use of "analogies" and "devices for stimulating insight and imagination." While acknowledging that the social sciences can "contribute enormously" to social studies, he argued, "history remains the integrating discipline par excellence."[20]

A special issue of *Social Education* titled "Questioning the Role of the Social Science Disciplines," published in November 1967, contained several articles examining the new reform from a variety of critical perspectives. Jewett and Ribble offered a cold shower to reformers, providing a realistic critique on the "excitement over the social studies" which, they noted, was not a new phenomenon. Citing the history of conflict over social studies, they argued, "the assumption that a resolution of the conflict will emerge out of the present excitement seems unwarranted from past experience." In their view, "many of the conflicts that exist within the social studies area . . . are the result of the pluralism of the American culture." To these authors, the new social studies posed the threat of deprofessionalizing the teacher through creation of "nationally packaged curricular materials" that could make the teacher a mere functionary, manipulating "teacher-proof" materials.[21]

Jack Allen revisited several earlier critiques, arguing that the new social studies was too little concerned "with the total scope and sequence of the social studies curriculum," that it virtually ignored longstanding conflicts over the field, and that too little research was available comparing student performance to justify the inquiry and discovery approaches. Stephanie Edgerton examined "learning by induction" and wondered whether educators had "confused a method of inquiry seemingly appropriate for the validation of knowledge claims with a method appropriate for policy making."[22]

THE HARVARD GROUP

Some of the most cogent and thoroughly grounded critiques came from scholars involved in the Harvard Project. James P. Shaver, in another article that appeared in the November 1967 special issue of *Social*

Education, raised serious questions about the new social studies projects' philosophical rationale in "Social Studies: The Need for Redefinition." Shaver pointed out the striking paradox between social studies goal statements centered around rational, reflective, intelligent citizenship, and the new social studies projects' lack of "concern with analytic concepts appropriate to analyzing public issues." Calling for a clear recognition that "social studies is general education," Shaver lamented the "general failure . . . to examine the basic rationale for social studies instruction." Too often, he charged, an approach to social studies as the "handmaiden of the social sciences" perpetuated a curriculum perceived by students as "irrelevant to the realities of life." Charging that many of the current "social studies" projects were "actually social science projects," and "scholacentric," he offered little optimism to advocates of a curriculum that would focus on the reflective examination of public issues. Shaver was quick to admit the importance of knowledge from the social sciences to the education of citizens. However, he added, "It will not . . . be organized according to the dictates of the social scientist, but according to the demands of general education . . . as relevant to understanding specific issues facing the society." Shaver concluded his article with an incisive, realistic observation that "[e]ducation for rational citizenship seems foredoomed to continue as a stepsister to history and social science instruction." He concluded, "A citizenry effectively schooled . . . in the analysis of public issues might be too disruptive to our society."[23]

Fred M. Newmann, in another article that appeared in the November 1967 special issue, also addressed the definitional problem and questions of rationale to which new social studies reformers were generally giving little attention. Newmann argued that "principles for the selection of structures must be sought in the realm of educational philosophy, not in the impulse to teach social science." He charged that the social scientist involved in the projects was "committed to spreading his gospel" and trying to inject more of his "structures" into the school, giving too little attention to curricular rationales and dilemmas.[24]

In an earlier paper presented at the Cranbrook Curriculum Conference in 1965, Newmann made similar arguments questioning the rationale for the reform. His critique was perhaps the most thorough and deeply disturbing analysis of the reform to that point in time, and deserves in-depth treatment. After examining some of the possible arguments for "structure" as an educational objective (related to human freedom, emotional well-being, material reward, harmony with nature, and the survival of man), he argued that the reformers had appealed to structure as a "self-evident ideal" and that it was "an insufficient ground on which to justify educational policy." Even with a full explication of a "structural" justification (which Newmann developed), he asked, to what extent would this guarantee fulfillment of the five underlying values on which such a justification could be based? Instead, he argued, achievement of such fundamental goals was more dependent upon a variety of variables that affect the educational process.[25]

Newmann then went on to develop three criteria for assessing models of social studies revision:

1. Each model for curriculum revision in social studies should develop an *explicit concept of citizenship education.*
2. In order for social studies curriculum to be properly justified, it must be developed out of an identifiable social theory. *The theory must be explicitly presented or reliably induced from the proposed concept of citizenship education.*
3. Models of social studies reform must provide *analysis of their own implications for the general process of educational change.*

While acknowledging "some effort to outline [the] structure of separate disciplines" Newmann charged, "[T]here has been no published attempt to justify the 'search' as a primary model for social studies reform."[26] On the basis of what had been said by scholars and curriculum planners to justify the new reform in social studies, Newmann characterized their frame-of-reference as follows:

> The ultimate objective of education should be the cultivation of intellectual excellence. To define intellectual excellence we need only observe activities and products of those men, past and present, seriously engaged in the pursuit of knowledge. From the work of scholars we should formulate models of intellectual excellence and translate them into instruction that will maximize the intellectual development of youth.

He then stated that this position seemed to originate in "an implied reverence for the formal activity called 'the pursuit of knowledge,' a commitment to emulate the intellectual operations of men recognized as great thinkers and men involved in the academic profession."

In stating the heart of his critique, he went on:

> If the position is founded only upon a priori faith, it fails to meet our criteria, for it does not explicitly confront the problem of citizenship education, nor does it emerge from an identifiable social theory. It is based only upon (1) a normative dictum that the function of education should be to continue the search for truth, and (2) a stipulation that the best models of training for this search can be found in the work of those formally engaged

in the search. Stated in this way, the position reflects a parochial value judgment that commits all youth to the asking and answering of questions according to norms and styles preferred by scholars.[27]

Newmann went on to suggest that the academician could provide a stronger justification by arguing:

> The free pursuit of knowledge and unlimited critical inquiry is necessary for the attainment of human dignity and the progress of civilization. It is the essence of freedom and requisite for the good life.

With further elaboration on the ultimate ends of such a justification, the reformers, Newmann suggested, could create "a complex theory of the inquiring man in society." However, he noted, "rarely do we find it developed by those who argue for a social science, discipline-centered approach to curriculum reform."

Newmann then made two additional critiques of the "search for structure model" related to the role and "functions" of the teacher and the "nature of classroom interaction." The reformers, he wrote, were attempting to translate the structures "found in the heads of university academicians" into materials and forms of teacher training that would "effectively transmit the structures into the heads of students. In a devastating image cutting to the heart of the reform, he wrote:

> The model presents an image of the teacher as a transmitter, or possibly a hypodermic needle which injects serum taken from cells of the university into the bloodstream of the student. The teacher has no part in composing the message or the serum . . . [except for the] important function in devising clever methods of transmission and injection.

This was, Newmann was careful to point out, "not to accuse the Brunerian school of construing the teacher as an information-giver or drillmaster" given the stress on "discovery." However, Newmann complained, we must be careful not to confuse emphasis on the "discovery" process with "absolute intellectual autonomy":

> What are students supposed to discover as they study the disciplines? My impression is that they would discover that by using intellectual approaches recommended by scholars at the university, they (the students) will reach many of the conclusions that university scholars have reached by using those approaches. Are we to conceive of the discovery process as a treasure hunt in which the teacher provides motivation and excitement for students to engage in the hunt? . . . We may find that a sizeable proportion

of students consider the treasure useless or uninspiring—in which case the teacher's role as motivator or communicator will become more difficult.

Newmann concluded that curriculum conceived as "a canned product" and the teacher as "a handmaid to the university scholar" would impose significant barriers to attracting "better teaching talent" into classrooms. He then went on to examine an alternative approach, which had developed an "elaborate, definitive rationale" that he identified as the Harvard model.[28]

Oliver and Shaver in *Teaching Public Issues in the High School* not only developed a thorough and well-grounded rationale for jurisprudential inquiry, but also addressed the Brunerian reform and offered a similar critique. They charged that proponents of "structure" assumed that the main ends of education were inquiry and a search for knowledge "within the highly specialized frameworks" found among academic scholars, and argued that the approach "has questionable value for general education in the social studies." They went on to state two major reservations with the reform's focus on the social science scholar as "the model" to be followed: first, that this approach ignores other models of reflection and action, which "obviously are relevant" to social studies; and second, that the social scientists seemed to be generalizing from their own experience, assuming that because structures and modes of inquiry "make the social world meaningful and exciting to [them]" the same would be true for "restless children and adolescents." They went on to argue that after examining the attitudinal, temperamental, and intellectual dimensions running through "any social studies program," that a focus on "the academic scholar as the model of intelligent citizenry seems inadequate."[29]

Following their critique, Oliver and Shaver developed an argument for a broader perspective that would transcend any one discipline. It would consider contributions from various disciplines as well as the "legal-constitutional basis of the modern democratic state . . . [and] the logical-rhetorical element in public discourse, usually referred to as the skill of reflective thinking." Moreover, they argued, social problems must be seen as "more than academic historical or social science problems" but as problems "involving ethical-legal dilemmas for individuals." Each of these elements, they suggested, was part of a broader perspective necessary for thoughtful participation in a democratic society. They believed that the discipline-based reform failed to embrace this broader perspective.[30]

OTHER CRITICS

Also in the November 1967 issue of *Social Education*, Marion Brady, a social studies supervisor, found it "unfortunate that a few leaders in social studies continue to insist that no unified, independent social studies can be created. In so doing," he went on, "they seem to be abandoning the field to the vast administrative-intellectual structures which are the separate disciplines, and time is marked while the historians, geographers, anthropologists, sociologists, and political scientists gather their material in preparation for the coming struggle . . . There are those who feel that out of the competition will come, somehow, *the* new social studies, but it is hard to see such a result from present efforts." What was likely, he went on, was improvement of some of the "traditional fragments," but no emergence of a conceptual framework which would integrate the whole of the social studies and make it intellectually manageable for the student." And, Ivor Kraft, an advocate of open education, called for a social studies built around the "grand theme of . . . man's search of meaning in life," and a curriculum that is "chiefly problem centered and only secondarily discipline centered." This implied the need for "direct, real, and non-artificial . . . confrontations with reality," as well as an opening up of the curriculum in which "no areas of inquiry" are considered taboo.[31]

In the same issue of *Social Education*, Albert S. Anthony, in a lengthy critique aimed specifically at the "new history" noted a "general lack of concern with objectives," an a priori commitment to the field of history, and a rationale that was "rudimentary indeed." He charged that leaders of the "new history" had managed to "overlook the need for a philosophically and pedagogically defensible rationale." Moreover, Anthony charged that many historians were motivated to take up curricular reform by fears that the subject would disappear from schools, with "the villain's role . . . given to certain social scientists (probably in league with the educationists)." The job would be performed not by a direct assault upon history, "but by a gradual infiltration and subsequent takeover. The infiltration will take the guise of interdisciplinary activity oriented around the social sciences." Anthony concluded, "The primary goal of the 'new history' projects would seem to be the preservation of history as a distinct discipline." He went on to suggest that "the doctrine of structure" was appealing to historians because "it holds that the way to salvation in education is via the individual disciplines. This is what historians, engaged in a crusade to preserve history as a school subject, want to hear."

Focusing particularly on deficiencies in the "new history," Anthony charged that the historians involved had neglected to develop criteria for content selection, and had given little more than token attention to "the needs and interests of the child and contemporary social problems." He wrote, "In almost every publication studied . . . the starting point for instruction was some topic or issue from the past which had little direct bearing on the life and experiential background of the student." This was not surprising, he went on, given the aim of the "new history" to give students an opportunity to engage in activity "similar" to that of the professional historian. Anthony called this the "junior historian model," and suggested that its proponents, guided by their urgency to "save history" in the schools, had neglected to give serious attention to "construction of defensible rationale and criteria to guide the teaching of history on the secondary school level."[32]

An article written in 1968 by Leonard S. Kenworthy noted that the changes being suggested for social studies were "so diverse" and in many cases "so unrealistic" that the reform carried "as much peril as it does promise." Kenworthy developed a comprehensive list of questions aimed at teachers and curriculum directors to help in sorting out the various proposals, projects, and materials in order to develop "a comprehensive, cumulative, and coherent" social studies program, and he presented a proposed social studies curriculum, K-12, incorporating many of the newer ideas including "postholing" and "studies in depth," along with a focus on "problems and decisions" of past and present.[33]

CRITIQUES CONTINUE IN THE EARLY 1970S

In the early 1970s, critiques of the reform continued, but with increasing focus on its impact. One social studies teacher and curriculum coordinator, William Goetz, asked whether the new social studies was a "Boon or Bust?," and focused on whether the "revolution" had actually reached the classroom. Despite the arrival of "a wide variety of high quality materials," a good deal of teacher education through summer institutes, and much excited discussion of Bruner and Fenton at conventions, he reported, "there are significant signs that the revolution has not lived up to the expectations of its zealous prophets." In appraising the reform, he offered a list of pointed observations:

1. The social studies revolution started at the top, and offered many proposals from the university couched in academic jargon and dressed in the refinery of scholarly articles. It failed to turn many teachers on.
2. The university has found social studies to be a difficult and complicated business. Extended debates on theory, delays in producing materials, and constant revisions indicate that the transition from theory to practice has been more difficult than envisioned.
3. The new programs and materials are too disjointed from one another, resulting in a bewildering mixture of philosophies and materials.

4. Many social studies teachers simply do not feel a need for "reform" and "revolution." Many outstanding teachers have created their own structures and materials and are skeptical of "canned" and "packaged" materials.
5. Many social studies teachers are unaware of the struggle for a "new" social studies."[34]

Despite all these obstacles, he argued that the new social studies had much to offer: it had introduced important problems involved in the psychology of learning and the design of curricula; forced consideration of the role and methodologies of all the social sciences; brought schools and universities closer together; created new types of materials; and, created a rich discussion about the nature of the field. In closing, he suggested that "[i]t might be time to 'cool' some of the grandiose rhetoric," and the unfortunate impression that "a bright, radically different social studies would emerge overnight and sweep aside all textbooks" and traditional teaching. Finally, he noted, thoughtfully, "Perhaps one lesson we have all learned is that social studies education is a difficult business. To upgrade it substantially will require time and patience . . . [and] the commitment and perseverance of each school."[35]

Another observer, Martin LaForse, in an article critiquing "The New Social Studies Mania" offered a few similar observations but also warned, "certain features of the evolving discovery position ought to be carefully reconsidered" lest they become "a new orthodoxy." LaForse suggested that in most classrooms the students "continued to learn the contents of a traditionally conceived textbook" but now "learned some of it by 'doing.'" In a pointed critique echoing some of the earlier critics, he wrote that key examples of the "discovery process" revealed that "students must become sleuths, searching out contextual clues in order to find out what the teacher has on his mind, or reaching generalizations designed to flow from pre-arranged data packages." In other words, the students "play detective, ferreting out clues, making deductions until finally they find out what the teacher and the material intended for them all along." In most cases, he suggested, inquiry was set up to lead students to a "pre-ordained conclusion." The approach "disallows divergency and initiative," reducing teaching to a "con-game" in which students seek to "give teacher what she wants" and lulling students into inquiries in which they have "little intrinsic interest."[36] He referenced anthropologist Jules Henry, who described the culture of education as one that taught "docility."[37] In his critique, LaForse was suggesting that many of the new curricular "packages" defeated the "essential meaning of inquiry" which is "open-ended" and can take students "wherever they are willing and able to go." In closing, he argued that the reform represented "the premature dissemination of new ideas" that needed further examination and revision.[38]

BRUNER AS CRITIC

Somewhat surprisingly, another contemporary critique of the new curriculum movement was written by one of the founders, Jerome Bruner. In an article titled "The Process of Education Revisited," published in 1971, Bruner wrote that the rational structuralism of the *Process of Education*:

> was based on a formula of faith: that learning was what students wanted to do, that they wanted to achieve an expertise in some particular subject matter. Their motivation was taken for granted. It also accepted the tacit assumption that everybody who came to these curricula in the schools already had been the beneficiary of the middle-class hidden curricula that taught them analytic skills and launched them in the traditionally intellectual use of mind . . . Failure to question these assumptions has, of course, caused much grief to all of us.[39]

Bruner's comments reflect the reformers' utter lack of experience in schools, and their failure to understand the ways that contextual issues impinge on the curriculum. Bruner's closing remarks revealed both a sense of regret over the reformer's naiveté, and deep misgivings over the nature of the reform he had helped set in motion:

> Education is not a neutral subject, nor is it an isolated subject. It is a deeply political issue in which we guarantee a future for someone and, frequently . . . deal somebody else out . . . If I had my choice now . . . it would be to find a means whereby we could bring society back to its sense of values and priorities . . . I believe I would be quite satisfied to declare, if not a moratorium, then something of a de-emphasis on matters that have to do with the structure of history . . . and deal with it rather in the context of the problems that face us.[40]

Ironically, it seemed, Bruner had come to a position much closer to that of many educational theorists in social studies, whose ideas had previously been seen as part of the problem that the new reform would replace.

There were many other critiques continuing to emerge as the reform reached its later phases. In a philosophical analysis, Joseph V. Ellis suggested that not much in the "new social studies" was really new, and that "inquiry," the "simple seven-letter word" on which the movement "built its rationale" had distant roots long before the Sputnik era. Ellis compared the themes of the new with comments from social studies educators of previous decades, and stated, "Inquiry and the asking of pertinent and even at times unanswerable questions have been the hallmark of successful teachers for decades and centuries." He went on to argue that "there is much of worth, sincerity, proven performance, and possibility for the future in the 'old,'" and concluded that "the past and present infighting" was "over semantics" instead of substance.[41]

The following year, a young professor named Terry Northrup wrote a response to Ellis that got right to the point. Northrup agreed with Ellis that "many of the 'new' ideas" were not really new, but asked, "If the 'old' social studies was so good, why was there a need for the "new" social studies? Although there was a lot of rhetoric about discovery and inquiry in the 'old' social studies, the practices of teaching social studies changed little in the 20th century," especially in secondary schools. Northrup then offered a cogent analysis of the new reform, noting that it had developed among social scientists who knew little about the literature of social studies education but understood that "the social studies curriculum was ineffective and outmoded." Within the movement, Northrup noted, there were "two schools of thought":

> One group wants students to *discover* a structure of knowledge of a social science or several social sciences, including the techniques of finding and verifying knowledge. The other group wants students to *inquire* into perceived problems relating to public issues or social problems in order to learn how to make decisions about such value-laden issues . . . there are two positions.

Northrup went on to suggest that the two positions could be referred to as "the structure-discovery position" supported by Senesh, Morrissett, and Bruner, and the "reflective inquiry position" supported by Hunt, Metcalf, Oliver, Shaver, Engle, and Newmann. "From this perspective," Northrup wrote, "one sees social studies in a vastly different light.

> There are choices among goals (learning social science structures *or* learning to make decisions relating to public issues), methods (discovery *or* inquiry), curriculum materials, and approaches to value issues (value free *or* value analysis) . . . The major question is not whether the new social studies is better than the old social studies. Rather, the question should be: Given the teacher's goals and abilities and the student's needs and abilities which version of "new" social studies is most appropriate?[42]

As we have seen Northrup's analysis was accurate regarding the orientation of the new social studies projects: there were (at least) two groups, and teachers were being offered what amounted to an increasingly rich array of choices and materials. Northrup's analysis of the reform reflected many of the ideas of his mentors, Robert Barr, James Barth, and Samuel Shermis, who would later describe three competing traditions in the social studies field, on the basis of their own historical analysis: citizenship transmission, social science inquiry, and reflective inquiry.[43]

Others tried to make sense of the terminology of the reform, which seemed wrapped in a swath of confusion. June Chapin and Richard Gross argued that terms like "inquiry," "discovery," "structure," "induction," and "problem-solving" were being "tossed about with great fuzziness" and used "ambiguously." In an effort to clarify some of the confusion, they reviewed many of the main terms and ideas of the reform movement. "Structure" they wrote, had two main parts: (1) the conceptual framework—fundamental concepts, generalizations, and principles; and (2) the methods of inquiry used by the scholars in a field, and it was not always clear which meaning was being referred to. Projects with a heavy emphasis on history such as the Fenton and Amherst projects emphasized the second part of the definition, focusing on the methodology of how a historian goes about his work. Thus, Fenton defined structure as "a method of inquiry made up of two parts: the formation of a hypothesis and the process of proof." For Fenton, "inquiry with questions" was at the heart of structure of history. Moreover, historians and social scientists, they were quick to point out, had been shaken by their own "identity crises." There were conflicting methodological trends, and a new questioning of the scholarly distance, passivity, and neutrality that had been the norm.[44]

The term "inquiry" was also subject to various meanings. In some projects it was equated with students using a scholar's methods for research. In others it referred to student projects in which "complex forms of thinking" were involved. In still other cases it was primarily an inductive approach. Frequently, it was used interchangeably with problem solving, discovery, inductive thinking and similar terms. According to Chapin and Gross, discovery learning and inductive thinking were parts of the more general process of inquiry. But, they noted, in the new social studies materials, inquiry frequently begins "by emphasizing the inductive process," but then tends to move on to hypothesizing or forming generalizations. They also noted the frequent distinction "between pure or non-directed inquiry versus directed or guided inquiry." In the latter, the teacher provides much of the data through which students may develop a generalization or hypothesis similar to that of legitimate scholars. In contrast, the more "laissez faire" or open type of inquiry involves a lower level of teacher guidance and, usually, a more wide-ranging search for data on the part of students.[45]

"Problem solving," on the other hand, is a higher level of thinking in which the learner confronts a new situation and must apply previously learned rules and past experience to achieve a solution. "Problem solving" had already been subjected to a good deal of research, they wrote, though the results were inconclusive. "Apparently, some students thrive on open-ended problem-solving or inquiry while others both dislike it and have little success. Some researchers have found good motivational effect with this type of instruction but no superiority in retention or transfer." Moreover, they wrote that while problem-solving approaches had been advocated in social studies for many years, "their implementation in classrooms has been limited and ineffectual." In their conclusion, Chapin and Gross stated their hope for a new direction in the reform, with "less concentration upon separate academic disciplines," and more emphasis on "broadfield areas of investigation and analysis," which progressive social studies educators had championed for several decades.[46]

A PHILOSOPHICAL ANALYSIS

Another scholar conducted a philosophical analysis of the new social studies focused on use of the "inductive approach" as an epistemological problem. Richard F. Newton argued that the term "induction" was frequently misused, misunderstood, poorly defined, or sloppily applied. Induction, he pointed out, is not defined as "inference from the particular to the general" as many new social studies scholars suggested, nor was it a method of discovery. It was, instead, he argued, "a non-demonstrative type of inference whose conclusion is ampliative." In plain language, this meant that inductive conclusions were probable at some level, but not necessarily true. Moreover, he suggested, there might be several possible conclusions that would result from a process of induction. The new social studies, he wrote, "seem to be little concerned with the problem of induction," and while it was not totally neglected, it received a "low level of priority."[47]

To make his point, and clarify the use of induction in the new social studies, Newton analyzed selected programs. Fenton, he wrote, "uses the term induction to mean the type of argument which goes from the specific to the general and is nondemonstrative." Using a "hypothetico-deductive model of explanation," Fenton goes "from the hypothesis back to the data in search of confirming evidence," then decides whether to modify, accept, or reject the hypothesis. Newton charged that Fenton "does not discuss the notion that a hypothesis is never fully confirmed," nor does he discuss when to "reject a hypothesis." He critiqued Fenton for failing to thoroughly examine his philosophical premises and for his "free and easy" use of the term "induction."[48]

According to Newton, Massialas and Cox's *Inquiry in the Social Studies*, an influential methods book of the period, did a much better job of examining and explaining their philosophical premises and rationale, drawing heavily on the work of John Dewey. They made clear the "probabilistic nature of induction (inquiry)," and express skepticism about "the orderliness of the universe." They emphasized, Newton wrote, that "an answer may never become true, but only highly confirmed," and that answers are "always subject to continuous revision." They offered, according to Newton, "an excellent discussion of the problems of induction . . . without getting overwhelmed by purely technical problems."[49]

Sociological Resources for the Social Studies (SRSS) also emphasized inductive techniques, defining induction as "reasoning from the particular to the general." Newton argued that SRSS materials tended to place emphasis on the techniques of research used by sociologists, with very little attempt to examine the logic or procedure by which the social scientist "validates his conclusion." Moreover, he charged, some episodes (one in particular) tend to direct students in such a manner that "he reaches a conclusion which has already been designed into the material" with data and readings seemingly aimed at "getting the student to accept certain value positions." Such episodes are best used, he argued, not as an example of open inquiry, but as an exercise in the "logic of validation" in an "empirical framework." Moreover, he charged, the episode tends to leave a "feeling of certainty" regarding the conclusions reached. Another episode, designed to introduce students to one method of "scientific inquiry" provided an "excellent example" of how "the problem of induction" could be addressed in secondary schools.[50]

Newton also reviewed the Harvard Project materials, and while he had many positive comments about the materials and their orientation, he suggested that their use of the term "inductive approach" was problematic because they seemed to use the terms "discovery" and "induction" interchangeably. Their "looseness" in the way the term induction was used seemed to only "add confusion." Moreover, he charged that it was "almost as if the term induction was used solely on the basis of its popularity."

In conclusion, Newton suggested that almost all of the new social studies programs could have done a better job explaining and using the term "induction." He suggested that educators sometimes, it seemed, were guilty of "believing in some type of verbal magic," focusing less on what they are actually doing than on whether it "*sounds* good" or is "fashionable." He urged educators to teach the "inductive problem" as one way to "foster a spirit of inquiry," and suggested that they avoid the kinds of "prearranged puzzle games" that appeared in some of the materials.[51] In another venue, he stated many of the same concerns, urged both teachers and students to become fully "immersed in problems of scientific methodology," and concluded, rather harshly, that much of the materials presented by the new social studies were merely "building toleration levels for unnecessarily involved game playing."[52]

CONCLUSION

And so, as we have seen, many observers, including some insiders, believed there were significant flaws in the new social studies reform. Some pointed to the obstacles and limitations that made any reform difficult, and that supported the persistent patterns of teachers teaching in a traditional manner, much as they were taught. Others critiqued the guided inquiry of many reformers as an artificial search for what social scientists and historians already knew. For most projects, the reform ideas and materials offered a "scholacentric" approach with citizenship education as a "handmaiden to the social sciences." In the main, the projects gave too little attention to questions of rationale—to questions of purpose related to the education of citizens in a democracy. Newmann's suggestion that social studies should focus on "the free pursuit of knowledge" and the aim of "unlimited critical inquiry" needed for "attainment of human dignity" and the "progress of civilization" was a more powerful framing.

Other critics, including Jerome Bruner, found fault with many assumptions underlying the reform—that student motivation was taken for granted as was an audience of students relatively free from the scars of poverty, well prepared and attuned to a curriculum that would ask them to use their minds critically. Finally, the terminology at the heart of the reform was often fuzzy or ambiguous, and use of philosophical terms such as "inductive reasoning" was frequently flawed. As we shall see in the next chapter, a new set of critics would soon emerge who questioned not only the viability of the new social studies, but offered penetrating critiques of the traditional purposes of schooling in American society and the workings of schools as an institution.

CHAPTER 7

REFORM IN PERSPECTIVE

IN THE EARLY 1970S, an emerging alternative perspective developed by critical theorists began to take a hard look at the assumptions, context, and practices of schooling. The budding critical perspective was influenced by American "new wave" literature critical of schooling, and by European critical theory as it was applied to education. In step with the questioning attitude and social turmoil of the late 1960s and early 1970s, these authors were strongly influenced by social reform initiatives of the time, including the free speech, civil rights, and antiwar movements. From this new "critical" perspective, schools were a key establishment institution contributing to the perpetuation of myriad social problems. They primarily served to train students in obedience for social efficiency, and to reproduce traditions rooted in hegemonic institutions that were racist, sexist, capitalist, neocolonialist, and imperialistic. In their eyes, the new social studies was merely the latest reform artifact of a problematic system, despite the avowed aim of furthering inquiry and discovery.

THE NEW CRITICAL PERSPECTIVE

Though many scholars offered their assessments of the educational system writ large, at least three, Thomas Popkewitz, Michael Apple, and Jonathan Kozol, authored interesting critical analyses addressing specific new social studies materials. In the mid-1970s, Popkewitz presented a review from a critical perspective specifically directed at materials developed by prominent new social studies projects. In a thoughtful analysis premised on the notion that social theories "are socially constructed and become a part of our symbolic and interpretive world," he suggested that much of American social theory accepted a "systems" view of the social world, in which all structures and social practices are part of the social system, and individuals are "arranged and socialized into existing institutions to maintain an orderly and stable system." Drawing on the work of Michael Apple, Popkewitz argued that much of organized knowledge in curriculum tacitly accepted this "systems" perspective, and that the vision of society embedded in the curriculum tended to create individuals who would maintain the "ongoing system and its institutional arrangements" via the elimination of conflict. Thus, Popkewitz sought to understand the implications for "individual responsibility and authority" relating to the use of knowledge by examining the approach to knowledge and conflict in three discipline-centered curriculums: *American Political Behavior* (Mehlinger and Patrick, 1972), the Holt Secondary Social Studies Curriculum (Fenton, 1967), and *Investigating Man's World* (Hanna, 1970).[1]

He found that the materials contained "latent" value orientations that made social relationships seem fixed and beyond individual control. They had a tendency to focus on knowledge that moves students away from the particular and local and discourages connections with everyday realities. This distancing and detachment, he argued, gives more power and legitimacy to experts who interpret reality via scientific concepts that are secondary abstractions that move people away from face-to-face contacts, value dilemmas, and conflict situations.

Investigating Man's World, he wrote, "gives no attention to conflict," and instead emphasized "the legitimacy and benevolence of leaders and rules," along with the legitimacy of experts. Despite its stated purpose of fostering inquiry, *Comparative Political Systems* (Holt), offered interpretations made by its authors, with "analytical" work set up in a way that made the teachers and text author's answers plausible. For example, in discussing dissent, the analysis focused on decorum, suggesting that "views which are expressed quietly and at an orderly forum" were the more appropriate forms of dissent. Citing the civil rights movement, in which demonstrators often "broke basic rules of society," Popkewitz argued that judging dissent on the basis of "procedural consequences" made suppression of dissent seem more reasonable and logical. Similarly, *American Political Behavior*, in its section on "Elections and the Behavior of Voters," made voting "possibly the sole, if not major" activity of citizens, and implied that other forms of participation may be shifted to elites as "the masses are asked to accept their own passivity." Likewise, treatment in the same text of socioeconomic status and political participation "unintentionally" gave the impression that "social stratification is an integral and necessary part of the political system." Moreover, he suggested that the fragmentation of social problems into discipline subjects, as in this example, might prevent students from dealing with interrelated problems.[2]

In a section subtitled "Detachment from Social Affairs," Popkewitz argued that the discipline-centered curriculum focused on knowledge that moves students away from the particular and local, and replaces their everyday language with a more esoteric "science" knowledge. This has the "latent function," he suggested, to socialize students into forms of knowledge that discourage connections with everyday affairs and to elevate the role of experts. It tends to train students "to accept unquestioningly" the knowledge of experts and to empower those "who present themselves as knowledgeable" to make decisions. Moreover, drawing on Gouldner's critique of social science Popkewitz suggested that "the very methodological stance of detachment insulates and alienates people from the world being studied." The discipline-centered curriculum represented by the three courses of study tended to legitimate the "expert" and, by intent, have students "define social problems in the manner of the social disciplines," ignoring the fact that social problems are not defined in the "neat packages provided by the disciplines," or that the "focus of discipline are historical accidents."[3]

Popkewitz also analyzed the ways in which the materials conveyed a sense of knowledge as certain, despite their aim of developing "independent thinkers" who can "develop hypotheses." By example, he illustrated the ways in which "the actual tasks of instruction" can subvert that purpose. Frequently, the "tacit function of inquiry is to have children learn the generalizations of a social science as an 'accepted truth'" rather than as tentative propositions open to further evidence, review, modification, or even disputation. While social scientists, for their part, "maintain a stance of skepticism," Popkewitz argued that the work children are called upon to do in the new curriculum materials frequently directs students toward specific, preordained answers, and "posits knowledge as fixed, unchanging, and unyielding." An example from "Metropolitan Studies" found in *Investigating Man's World* contained lessons that offer: a generalization to learn, pictures to promote class discussion, a short reading section, and a discussion question that is "carefully structured to the inductive approach." The text then suggested, "[P]upils will automatically interpret the pictures first, then the text, then return to discussion of ideas that will lead to the unit understanding or a related understanding."[4]

Popkewitz related another lesson from this text to what Jules Henry called "education for stupidity." In a revealing exercise, students were asked to assume they are knowledgeable about serious social problems on the basis of very limited reading and study. After examining six photographs of an urban area, and reading three pages, students are asked, "Why do children drop out of schools? Why do slum dwellers need to help as well as outsiders in solving the slum problem?"[5]

Popkewitz concluded with the observation that the curriculum materials projects' air of "certainty" made it difficult for children to understand the limitations of social science knowledge. In a concluding passage he wrote, "The use of the social disciplines in these curricula seems not so much a change from emphasis on content to process but how that content is organized. The authority of the teacher as knower remains." Citing Paulo Freire, he described the approach of the social science discipline materials as "a pseudo-inquiry, bound up in the predefined questions and data posited in textbooks and worked out in advance by educators and social scientists." It serves, Freire suggests, "to minimize or annul the students' creative power and to stimulate their credulity," and ultimately "serves the interests of the oppressors, who care neither to have the world revealed nor to see it transformed."[6]

Popkewitz, drawing on new insights from critical pedagogy, offered powerful observations that cut right to the heart of the new social studies reform movement. Though not true for all of the projects and materials, many of his insights reflected some of the frequent refrains of critics since the inception of the new social studies, though he gave those critiques a new and more powerful conceptual framing.

APPLE

In developing his critique, Popkewitz drew on Michael Apple and the emerging critical perspective on schooling. In "The Hidden Curriculum and the Nature of Conflict," Apple also gave some attention to social studies materials of the period. Apple's central thesis was that treatment of conflict in the school curriculum "can lead to political quiescence" and acceptance of "a perspective on social and intellectual conflict that acts to maintain the existing distribution of power and rationality" in society. He examined social studies and science to scrutinize the ways in which a "consensus-oriented perspective is taught" through a "hidden curriculum," which fails to provide examples "showing the importance of intellectual and normative conflict." In science, he argued, the contested nature of the scientific enterprise, the theories and modes of procedure, or "structure of disciplines," which is central to making progress in scientific disciplines, "is hidden from students," despite the efforts of reformers. In social studies, much of the literature found in teaching materials "points to an acceptance of society as basically a cooperative system," in which "happy cooperation" is the norm. Much of the content of the K-12 social studies curriculum shows:

[h]ow all elements of a society, from the postman and fireman in first grade to the partial institutions in civics courses in high school, are linked to each other in a functional relationship, each contributing to the ongoing *maintenance* of society. Internal dissension and conflict in a society are viewed as inherently antithetical to smooth functioning of the social order. *Consensus* is once more a pronounced feature.[7]

Apple cited three examples of new social studies materials that illustrated his point. The first was found in the Science Research Associates (SRA) economics kit, *Our Working World*, developed for primary grade students and organized around everyday social interaction. Apple suggested that there is "no better example of the emphasis upon consensus, order, and the absence of any conflict in the social studies curricula," and quoted a passage that read:

> When we follow the rules, we are rewarded; but if we break the rules we will be punished . . . That is why we *learn* customs and rules, and why we *follow* them. Because if we do, we are all rewarded by a nicer and more orderly world.[8]

Apple argued that "even most of the inquiry-oriented" materials show a neglect of the importance of conflict. He cited curricula developed by the Center for the Study of Instruction, which puts forward a "hierarchy of generalizations" that are to be internalized by students through role-playing and inquiry. What is "intriguing" he wrote, is the "nearly complete lack of treatment of or even referent to conflict as a social concern or as a category for thought" in the materials reviewed. He also reviewed materials developed under the aegis of Hilda Taba that do give some attention to conflict, but focus on the "serious consequences of sustained conflict rather than on the many positive aspects also associated with conflict itself," and wrote that conflict is viewed as "dysfunctional," though ever present.[9]

Interestingly, Apple suggested that this inadequate and misleading consensus approach to conflict was "being countered" to some extent by content being taught under the rubric of Black Studies. In this new subject area, he found that "struggle and conflict on a communal basis are often explicitly and positively focused upon." He noted that there was an attempt to present "a comparatively realistic outlook on the significant history and uses of conflict" through a focus on the civil rights and Black Power movements. Even within this new curricular focus, he suggested a range of treatment in that within some presentations of Black historical materials, "those Blacks are presented who stayed within what were considered to be the legitimate boundaries (constitutive rules) of protest," noting a common lack of reference to Malcolm X, Marcus Garvey, and others who offered a potent and more radical critique.[10]

On the basis of his analysis, Apple suggested that it is possible to counter the consensus orientation by portraying conflict as a source of change, as "a basic and often beneficial dimension" of society. He concluded with a number of suggestions: that the comparative study of revolutions could help to focus students on the nature and role of conflict; and that "a more realistic appraisal and presentation of the uses of conflict in the civil rights movement . . . would no doubt assist in the formation of a perspective that perceives these and similar activities as legitimate models of action." In closing, he reiterated his thesis that "schools systematically distort the function of social conflict" and noted that the "meaning structures" created by schools are "obligatory." That is, students receive them from "significant others" in their lives (including teachers) who are part of a process of socialization.[11] Apple's critique was part of an emerging critical perspective. Though his findings on the treatment of conflict provide an interesting and valuable perspective, the extent to which it can be applied to other materials is unclear, especially those rooted in history or an issues perspective, in which a somewhat more realistic approach to conflict may be prevalent.

KOZOL

Another writer whose work became prominent during the 1960s and 1970s was Jonathan Kozol. In *The Night is Dark and I Am Far from Home*, published in 1975, Kozol launched what was perhaps his most strongly worded ethical examination and critique of the mainstream educational system. He described a system of schooling aimed at "state indoctrination" of good citizens who would "learn how not to interrupt the evil patterns that they see before them, how not to question and how not to doubt: to learn to vote with reasonable regularity, to kill on orders and to sleep eight hours without grief." The system of education he described was aimed at "developing "ethical incompetents" who would accept war and social stratification as just the way things are.[12]

Like Apple and Popkewitz, Kozol examined a few of the new social studies materials, describing the newer social studies and its focus on issues as a form of "child manipulation" and "managed choice" offering the illusion of "open" education when in reality what was presented to students was a limited selection of alternatives, something like a smorgasbord. He described it as the pretense of free choice and a kind of "organized public bamboozlement." Kozol critiqued a Xerox publication from the Public Issues Series on "Conflict Resolution" and its suggestion that "people with opposing views do not have to adopt a combative posture." Instead, he suggested that sometimes there is a need to "fight it out," that sometimes poor people, for example, were justified in feeling "hostile" and "bitter."

Quoting Herbert Marcuse, Kozol lamented the fact that public education makes "a virtue of dispassion," and argued that "prison bars . . . can be fashioned out of words and hesitations," frequently denying students the right "to make strong, risk-taking choices." He argued that, in essence, public education was "a 12-year exercise of ethical emaciation."[13]

"The most intense and honest course of research," he suggested, "can be well accepted by this social order so long as it is kept within a set of boundaries no one cares about." Ironically, as an example he cited the Man: A Course of Study (MACOS) curriculum that induced children to do "'wide-open' and 'unstructured' research into such dangerous areas as the life-struggle of the Netsilik Eskimo (long-since destroyed) and the life-cycle of the mealworm."[14] As we shall see, the MACOS curriculum would later stir passionate criticism from parent and community groups.

Kozol also pointed out the hypocrisy and contradictions of much of the literature examining the ways in which "we talk about things we don't intend to change," and in which dissent that becomes "a sociology of dissent." Students "rap" about issues and dozens of books "mediate" between real issues and the discussion of issues in schools. He lamented the fact that "we learn to remove ourselves from the immediate . . . and situate ourselves instead upon a safe and sober ledge from which to look down on the action . . . It is the goal and destination. The poet must be dissuaded from his vision . . . The rebel must be transformed . . . In place of concrete action, school instructs our children in a false form of behavior called CONCERN." Thus inert concern replaces action. As an antidote to this common malady, Kozol cited one social studies teacher that he knew with "one rule and one rule only: Any idea a student genuinely believes, and feels to be his own, must be enacted, executed or applied within the realm of the real world."[15]

He also critiqued the "systems" approach that was a main part of the new social studies ideology, suggesting that the "system is, itself, the primary vehicle of state-control." "Discovery" is described as a "new phrase for an old deception," implying that the new social studies was a fanciful mediation between the classroom and the realities of life, the pressing issues of stratification, oppression, and war, largely preventing ameliorating action and furthering that oppression. Citing Ivan Illich and Paulo Freire, he wrote that school "cannot be, at once 'for freedom' and 'for socialization,'" nor could it be "neutral."[16]

As a solution he offered the alternative of education for social justice with a strong social action component. "Kids who come to strong conclusions in regard to slumlords, housing covenants or racist realtors, lawyers, doctors in the neighborhood . . . have launched attacks, begun with words, gone on to visits, tabulations, press-campaigns, a picket line and blueprints for a boycott," thus turning their beliefs into concrete deeds, though he admitted it could result in dismissal.[17]

THE KEY DILEMMA?

Several other scholars of the period pointed to some of the other important dilemmas of reform. Frank L. Ryan, in an article discussing what he called the "hidden curriculum" of social studies, pointed to the problem of instructional implementation and the persistent pattern of recitation as the major obstacle that would have to be overcome by the new social studies, if it was to make much difference in the typical classroom.

By the early 1970s there was a growing awareness of at least a few of the obstacles faced by any attempt to reform the curriculum. Though the content of instruction (the subjects and topics included in courses, textbooks, curriculum guides, and taught in classrooms) was subject to shifting emphasis, the process of education was much more resistant to change. Ryan raised awareness of the central pedagogical dilemma and challenge to the new social studies in an article that appeared in *Social Education* in 1973. By the early 1970s, materials from the "new" social studies were "conspicuously displayed in numerous schools" he wrote, "but frequently there is no one around to 'get them off the ground.'" Ryan argued that the chief obstacle to extensive use of the new materials could be found in what he called the "hidden curriculum." Instead of the rituals of political and cultural socialization that had previously been labeled a hidden curriculum, Ryan was referring to the "mannerisms, procedures, and ways of dealing with students" that teachers employed in their daily classroom interactions with students:

> What kinds of questions are being posed? How are students asked to respond to questions? How does the teachers react to the students' responses? Which students do the responding? What are the non-responding students doing?

In the typical social studies classroom, he wrote:

> Students are in neat rows of desks facing the front of the classroom . . . [they] take out their social studies textbooks, and the main part of the lesson usually consists of having various students . . . take turns

reading aloud to the rest of the class. The day's reading is followed by a short discussion period in which the teacher asks a series of questions which are ordinarily at the recall level. The teacher's role becomes one of soliciting from the students the facts of the day's reading.[18]

What are students learning from this pattern of instruction? That "facts are the most important part of social studies; that the best way to acquire understandings, and praise from the teacher, is to 'pay attention'; that the primary usefulness of facts is recall for the teacher"; and that social studies is "a bland mixture of information" to be "swallowed unquestionably."

"Of course," Ryan wrote, "such learning outcomes are completely incompatible with the intent of the newer social studies programs." Instead, he wrote, establishment of a new set of teacher behaviors would probably lead to the spirit of learning required "for the newer social studies to flourish." The behaviors cited included:

- "there is a utilization of higher-level questions" that ask students "to think about" the topic being studied;
- "there is a solicitation of multiple and varied ideas from the students";
- students have opportunities to "express their own ideas" and "react to the ideas of others";
- the students examine the reasoning behind responses;
- the teacher relinquishes "center-stage";
- students, as inquirers, generate knowledge, make inferences, and check on the adequacy of their understandings.

Finally, Ryan noted perceptively that implementation of these "new" instructional behaviors was "not always easily attainable," especially when it required "an erosion" of the typical behaviors employed in a "textbook-read-recite instructional environment."[19] The new set of teacher behaviors brought higher risk and a strong element of unpredictability to the classroom, partly because student behaviors would be harder to manage in classrooms that focused on inquiry and discussion.

Ryan's analysis was right on target. The daily behaviors of teachers and students are hard to change. Teachers and students were used to a steady diet of traditional instruction focused on the "right answer" and "banking approaches" in which the teacher was the dispenser of knowledge placing "deposits" in the minds of students. Most had developed a certain level of comfort in the use of a regular pattern of classroom procedures and styles, and were not likely to give up that comfort level easily. A survey of research by Hoetker and Ahlbrand, cited by Ryan, indicated that for at least the past 50 years teachers most frequently posed questions at the factual recall and memorization level, and that the trend was persistent.[20] Moreover, even though the "newer" approaches and materials had a certain cachet, the schools as an institution offered little in the way of incentive for teachers to modify their teaching practices, making widespread adoption unlikely.

DISCUSSION OF CRITIQUES AND DILEMMAS

Looking back, there was, in the new social studies, and in the new curriculum movement generally, much to critique and much to reflect back upon. As a movement to change the curriculum, it aimed, largely, to shape the mindset of a generation into rational, structuralist, and scientific ways of seeing, and subtly away from moral questions, social issues, and social problems.

Unfortunately, the new social studies sometimes led to materials that omitted citizens' questions and perennial social issues and problems from discipline-based studies. Discipline-based experts were lionized as the main source of knowledge. This approach often ignored or minimized student knowledge, community resources, and social issues and problems. It also frequently served to undermine the possibility of interdisciplinary study and to reify education and power relationships endemic to the institution of schools. Many of the critiques reflected blind spots in the new social studies movement as well as the ideological orientation of each critic.

What were the main patterns of critique? After reviewing the critiques that had been brewing since the inception of the reform, there were several often interrelated strands of critique that seem to fall into the following categories: expectations vs. reality; rationale and conceptualization; reform strategy; institutional obstacles; and critical perspectives. The following pages summarize and examine each category of critique.

First, a number of critics from within the educational establishment challenged the grandiose expectations of some of the reformers, suggesting that the excitement over the new reforms was "unwarranted," and that the reformers had created "unrealistic" hopes for change, especially given the long-standing conflicts and disagreements over the field, which the reformers ignored, and about which they knew little. James Becker cautioned that there were slim chances for any radical reform of the educational system, partly because of its large, diffuse, and decentralized nature. Moreover, he suggested that lasting changes tended to come incrementally. A fairly large number of the critics commented on the "diverse" and "contradictory" nature of the reform, and the lack of agreement on goals. These comments were a reflection of what might be called the wisdom of long experience with the educational system, and suggested the benefit of knowledge and understanding of the history of a field that had seen multiple and repeated waves of reform, some of which had little lasting effect.

Second, a number of other critics challenged the reform on philosophical grounds, arguing that the reformers had not developed a clear and thoughtful rationale, that they had failed to adequately delineate the purposes of the reform, and failed to offer sufficient justification for their approach to education. Despite this flaw, critics lamented, the Brunerian approach to schooling had become something of "a new orthodoxy," and a "mania." Several argued that "structure" in itself was insufficient grounds for reform, and that the reformers needed an explicit concept of citizenship education. Several critics argued that the new social studies embodied an approach to reform based on reverence for scholars in the disciplines, like "a hypodermic needle" injecting serum from the university; it was a "scholacentric" approach to citizenship education. The reform assumed, these critics pointed out, that inquiry via the "specialized frameworks of academic scholars" was the main end and should be the chief means of formal education. They ignored the needs and interests of children, or, at best, gave them secondary status. Though critics believed that the social sciences and their approaches to inquiry were of value, they questioned making them the centerpiece of social studies education.

Along somewhat similar lines, other critics challenged the reformers' implied rationale for its "neglect" of normative and affective components of schooling. Still others suggested that there was an inadequate research base upon which to justify the reform. No one had thoroughly examined the outcomes of an inquiry approach rooted in the social sciences in comparison to other approaches.

Educators' comments on the weakness of the rationale for reform were well-grounded. In almost every case, the social science projects linked their work to Bruner and the founding principles from Woods Hole and Endicott House and failed to offer a thorough justification supporting their approach to reform, though they did offer justifications for the study of their particular discipline or the usefulness of their project or materials. Why didn't the reformers offer a more thorough rationale? Perhaps it was partly because they were not well prepared to do so, with little background in education. However, it seems reasonable to assert that it was partly because they didn't have to. It simply wasn't necessary to develop a strong and thoroughly developed rationale statement in order to join the reform movement or to receive grant support from either the government or private foundations. The rationale was already provided. It was situated in the national security need for scientific and technological manpower and the concomitant extension of democracy via various forms of "scientific" inquiry including those provided by history and the social sciences. Logic, reason, and common sense, the materials for building a thoughtful rationale, mattered little in the face of a reform backed by a consensus of the nation's power brokers and deemed to be in the country's best interests. The curriculum reform movement, and its extension into the social studies field, had the backing of powerful foundations and governmental agencies. Behind that backing were the money and support of the economic and political establishment ranging from elite business groups to powerful and influential professional groups in academia. The new social studies movement was, as we have seen, an arm of the cold war effort to win the battle against communism, and to rescue schooling from the "wasteland" of mediocrity. It did not begin with needs and interests of children. Instead, it originated in fear, and its rationale was saturated with the language of manpower development.

Critiques of the rationale for the reform came from at least two quarters. First, and most commonly, it came from those who believed that "public issues" or societal "problems" should be the main focus of the social studies curriculum. This critique was given voice most thoughtfully and thoroughly by educators from the Deweyan tradition, and from issues-centered educators of the Harvard group. A second source of critique of the reform came from those who supported more traditional forms of history and social studies, advocates of traditional history or a broad and consensus-oriented approach to social studies who did not want the nation's common heritage to be given less attention because of a shift to the social sciences.

A third and related area of criticism, partly a result of weaknesses on rationale, focused on conceptualization problems. The reform was fragmented, critics argued, via its segmentation by discipline, by too much postholing, by poor articulation and a lack of attention to developing an overall scope and sequence, and by its academic orientation that seemed at odds with the orientation of the average teacher and citizen. In addition, there was conceptual confusion over the central terminology of the reform. Inquiry, discovery, inductive thinking, structure, and a host of additional concepts were used loosely, and often had different meanings depending on who was using them. In part, perhaps, this reflected a lack of knowledge and familiarity with education. To be sure, most of these terms and ideas were far from new, and had long been slippery even for those with a long history of involvement in education. Moreover, it seemed that most of the reformers made too little attempt to clearly define terms, or to engage in the philosophical analysis of precise meanings. In any event, confusion over the new lexicon was predictable and detrimental.

A fourth area of criticism suggested strategic problems in the design of a workable reform model and in the dissemination of materials and procedures. To one degree or another, most of the projects aimed at developing materials that were at least somewhat "teacher-proof," replacing the teacher's mind with the mind of the project directors and developers, mostly university social scientists. The pattern for materials development, as we have seen, was to gather some of the best minds from the discipline together with some excellent teachers, and set them to work developing innovative materials that would bring concepts and modes of inquiry from the discipline into the classroom. The hope was that once the materials were available, they would be so clearly superior, more engaging, and interesting for teachers and students that their acceptance and adoption would snowball, perhaps slowly at first, but then gaining momentum to become the one best curriculum. Once materials were created, it was often assumed, the rest would be relatively easy. As it turned out, this was far from the case. Teacher-proof materials tended to deny the intellectual autonomy of the teacher, as many critics pointed out. Moreover, many were created with a reform model that purposely circumvented teacher educators and the educational establishment. Given the harsh criticism of schools during the 1950s, especially social studies, and the fact that many reformers were situated at the apex of national power, it appears that the reformers failed to give due consideration to involving professional educators in the planning and implementation of reform. Clearly, many of the reformers had an attitude of superiority toward scholars in education, teachers and other educational professionals. Moreover, despite a profound lack of knowledge of the history and social context of schooling, they thought they knew better and could bring lasting reform. Their thinking, in many cases, reflected a vision of omnipotence and ultimately served to limit the success of their endeavors.

Perhaps the single most glaring failure of the reformers was their general neglect of a variety of obstacles that had limited previous reforms, and that would plague this reform as well. First, the high reading level of many of the materials they produced for classroom use made them difficult to use with students who read at or below grade level. Second, the reformer's work tended to make plentiful use of academic jargon. These two factors gave the new social studies a mandarin, overly intellectual tone, and combined to turn away many teachers who might otherwise have been promising adherents of the reform. Third, many of the projects and materials failed to demonstrate adequate respect for the intellectual autonomy of teachers. It was, largely, a top-down reform in which the teacher was often a gatekeeper, seldom treated as an intellectual.

Many of the inquiry materials developed offered a sort of "artificial inquiry," which was perceived by some teachers and students as a "treasure hunt" at best, or deceptive form of "child manipulation" at worst. Only sometimes was the inquiry truly open-ended. Last, the reformers failed to fully understand and satisfactorily address the most commonplace aspects of schooling that would tend to limit the "instructional implementation" of their ideas and materials. Exposed to "dreary expository courses" throughout most of their own education, teachers tended to teach as they were taught, to replicate the general patterns of instruction they had experienced in schools and colleges. In short, the reformers failed to recognize that social studies education, especially in the transition from theory to practice, is a "difficult business." Reformers simply did not sufficiently account for and make adjustments to these and other obstacles.

A final group of critics, consonant with the social turmoil of the late 1960s and early 1970s, and steeped in a new critical perspective, offered a penetrating analysis of the "systems" perspective that had given rise to the reform, the subtle and insidious ways in which it operated, and the deeper epistemological problems that it created. The critical perspective echoed many previous complaints, but took the analysis to another level of complexity, linking the frequent neglect or elimination of conflict in consensus-oriented school materials and teaching practices to the social fabric. The sense of "detachment" promoted in new social studies materials led, they suggested, to "political quiescence" in maintenance of the existing distribution of power. "Neutrality," they announced, "is an illusion." Rather than being interested in true inquiry, they suggested, schools and most of the recent curriculum materials were really a disguised form of "state indoctrination" and led to the imposition of ethical paralysis through a "banking" approach to teaching. These new critical perspectives offered an alternative, but it was an option that could prove a difficult or even dangerous path for many teachers.

Overall, the criticism of the new social studies that emerged pointed largely to the naiveté of the reformers, and to the difficulties inherent in most any attempt to change schools. Many of the critics of the new social studies offered penetrating insights, and were especially perceptive on questions of rationale and conceptualization. Disappointingly few of the critics gave attention to the many obstacles to reform. Though a few did so quite pointedly, others only hinted at them. The key dilemma undermining the reform, according to Frank Ryan and a few other observers, was the persistence of traditional instructional patterns focused on a textbooks and low-level questions, asking for recall of "facts," and comprising a "bland mixture of information to be swallowed unquestionably." To be sure, these were difficult patterns to change, and many critics of the reform thought it stood little chance of making a significant difference in the schools. But, at least a few educators were well aware, even before Hoetker and Ahlbrand's analysis of the persistence of recitation, that instructional change would be difficult. Moreover, the critics, it seems, were not well attuned to the historical origins of the reform, and few sought to place the movement in historical perspective. Perhaps, it was a reflection of the times. The attention of many Americans was undoubtedly diverted to the explosion of issues and tensions that seemed, quite literally, to be tearing the society apart.

CONCLUSION

In his 1967 book *The New Social Studies*, Ted Fenton reviewed the status of the reform movement to that point. He offered an overview of a "revolution" that would "shake the entire educational system." His overview survey and analysis offered a broad and somewhat critical perspective, discussing the reform movement's goals and objectives, its funding and support, the publishers, its efforts at improving teacher training, its work with local schools and teachers, and the reform's target audience. Fenton described a movement that, in his view, was still "a-borning" and that within a few years would lead to "coherent programs" that would "shake the entire educational system." Despite the general scholarly tone of the volume, parts of the work and the general upshot read as if written by a missionary, the prophet of the new social studies movement. The tone was forward-looking and hopeful, with aspects of uncertainty over details, but with a sense of assuredness that the reform would, in the long run, make a profound difference in the way social studies was taught in schools. To his credit, Fenton took pains to assess the needs for reform and to examine specific ways to enhance and extend the movement. The book's final paragraph captures the hopeful tone quite well:

> Observers can see the proof of their good fortune in an inquiry-centered class. In the short run, the act of discovery transforms a shy child into an eager participant waving his hand to try out his new idea on his teacher and classmates. In the long run, the knowledge that he can think for himself gives a child the courage to debate with fellow students and the desire to strike out intellectually on his own. Every child deserves the opportunity to discover his talents and to recognize his worth. The new

social studies, even in their present imperfect form, can help him reach his goal.[21]

Though Fenton offered a cogent assessment and suggestions, it seemed he failed to recognize or even acknowledge any of the critiques and dilemmas beginning to emerge, which ultimately had so much to do with the failure of the new social studies to reach the expectations of its creators.

A TIME OF HOPE, A TIME OF FEAR

THE NEW SOCIAL STUDIES WAS BORN in a time of hope, a time during which Americans were inspired by President John F. Kennedy to "bear any burden . . . to ensure the success of liberty." Citizens were encouraged to service by the remarkable phrase "Ask not what your country can do for you—ask what you can do for your country." They were called upon to turn back the threat of totalitarian communism, and asked to defeat "tyranny, poverty, disease, and war itself." Kennedy's meticulously crafted inaugural address in 1961 captured the zeitgeist of the time. During the postwar era, a time in which the United States emerged as one of the world's superpowers, leaders of the science and social studies reform movements operated under the belief, influenced by a vision of American omnipotence and rooted in hubris, that they could solve most any problem, if only they resolutely applied the techniques of science, research, and development.[1]

The new social studies was born in a time of fear. From the end of World War II and the beginning of the cold war, American society was riven with fears of nuclear war. Popular media portrayed the effects of a nuclear holocaust in graphic terms. Homeowners built fallout shelters in their backyards, and schools conducted duck and cover drills to ready children for the imminent possibility of a nuclear attack.[2] As a grade school child living in south Florida during the early 1960s, the time of the Cuban missile crisis and the height of the conflict, I participated in those drills. My parents and teachers warned us not to look at the flash because it could be blinding. When a rumor emerged that shots were fired between an American destroyer and a Soviet warship during the American blockade of Cuba, my fourth grade class erupted in cheers, only to be chastised by our teacher, who asked, "Do you realize what this means?" In every conceivable way, the new social studies was a product of its times.

ORIGINS

The reform had its origins in criticisms of progressive education that had been brewing for decades, but which reached full force during the postwar era with critiques from leading intellectuals such as Arthur Bestor and from red-baiting critics who revived and extended the arguments made against Rugg, Counts, and others. The reform gained its power from cold war manpower concerns, fears driven by CIA reports that suggested the Soviets were developing scientists and engineers at a rapid pace and would soon overtake U.S. technological leadership. It mattered little at the time that many of the government's closest advisors harbored deep misgivings over the true nature of what one later suggested was an exaggerated threat.[3] The reform also found sustenance in the reformer's faith in the redemptive power of reason and science and the desire of many scientists and social scientists to imbue a significant segment of schoolchildren and the nation with that power.

Following Woods Hole, Jerome Bruner argued that "any child" could learn the underlying and fundamental ideas of the disciplines at some appropriate level. In grand fashion, Jerrold Zacharias projected a new curriculum that would eventually span all of our educational endeavors and fully embody the scientific mantra of posing fundamental questions, followed by observation and reflection on beliefs.[4] The reform applied the wartime research model and systems analysis that had proven their mettle in creating American technological superiority. The problem of educating children was seen as a domestic variation of the techno-logical problem—hence the education system was conceived as a sort of weapons system to be used in an effort to strengthen the selection and preparation of scientists, engineers, and citizens who would inquire and who would come to the right conclusions in support of western capitalism and democracy. Thus, schools were conceptualized as a minor league extension of the research university in service of the nation's needs as defined in the context of cold war through the prism of the military-industrial-academic complex.[5]

Gradually, with the backing of big science and big government and through strong assistance from the National Academy of Sciences (NAS), National Science Foundation (NSF), United States Office of Education (USOE), and several key individuals whose influence reached to the highest levels, the curriculum reform that started in science and math morphed into a broader movement aimed at revolutionizing social studies instruction in schools. The meeting at Endicott House brought conflicting views among the interest groups present to a head, in reaction to Feldmesser's claim that we would make no progress until we "slaughter the sacred cow of history." The discussion that followed brought a general consensus around a shared realization that the problem wasn't so much history vs. social science as it was the way the subjects were typically taught in schools, with emphasis on a textbook and a pattern of recitation.[6] A short time later, Project Social Studies was officially launched.

THE PROJECTS

The projects and materials that emerged were pedagogically advanced. Without doubt, they were among the most intellectually stimulating and pedagogically engaging social studies materials ever created, the product of brilliant minds, millions of dollars, and countless hours of development. They enacted inquiry learning in ways that were applicable for many students. They were also deeply flawed. Project directors made core assumptions about student motivation and readiness, they ignored the pivotal contexts of culture and social class that seem to have such power over student readiness and what actually goes on in schools.

Moreover, the reformers knew little about the history of education and projected unrealistic hopes for change. Critics challenged the reform on a number of grounds: that it lacked a clear and thoughtful rationale; that it embodied a "scholacentric" reverence for the disciplines sited at universities; that it neglected normative and affective components of schooling; that it gave too little attention to the needs and interests of the child; that it was fragmented by articulation problems and lack of a coherent scope and sequence; that there was general confusion over key terms and concepts such as inquiry, discovery, inductive thinking, and structure; that it lacked a powerful model for dissemination; that many of the materials were "teacher proof" by design; and, last but not least, that the reformers failed to address the commonplace aspects of schooling that would limit implementation.

STRENGTHS

The new social studies had many strengths. It made social studies intellectually stimulating and engaging for many students and teachers via its application of the inquiry method. The concepts of inquiry, discovery, and similar strategies, while far from new, breathed new life and form into a field that suffered from harsh criticism and stagnation in the postwar years.

The movement reengaged many historians and social scientists in development work and dialogue on school curriculum and teaching strategies after years of neglect and disinterest. Many of the materials that were produced were first-rate and remain of interest, a treasure trove for those willing to mine it.[7] The social science inquiry approach and the emphasis on depth over superficial coverage made popular during the era remains a useful prototype for social studies instruction, still relevant and with continuing influence to this day. The approach and the materials created in the 1960s and later are of enduring value.

Despite the failure to realize the lofty expectations of some of its protagonists, the era of the new social studies can serve as an important foundation of knowledge about educational reform and as a source of building blocks for future reform efforts. The attention to curriculum development and research instigated by the period is one of its lasting legacies. It created a new language of social studies teaching and reform, rooted in the ideas of Bruner, Fenton, Oliver, and others, and in its aftermath, led to a number of meaningful analyses of the influence and prospects for reform. Moreover, the roots of several research areas within social studies and education can be found in the period, notably the cognitive revolution, the recent and substantial body of research on the teaching of history, and the continued interest in classroom constancy and the grammar of schooling.

WEAKNESSES AND FLAWS

The new social studies also had many weaknesses. As pointed out by numerous critics, the movement failed to develop a full and powerful framework and rationale. Its advocates never grappled successfully with issues of scope and sequence, fragmenting and limiting the reform's overall influence. Its leaders overemphasized disciplinary knowledge, overlooked the interests of the child, and consciously bypassed the education establishment, a choice ordained in part by the reform's origins. Moreover, they largely ignored the context and history of previous attempts to improve the school curriculum. Ironically, while its advocates espoused intellectual freedom, many of the materials they produced served to routinize and restrict student thought to a limited set of alternatives through "guided" forms of inquiry. Finally, the reform had a notable lack of impact on classroom practice.

A COMPARISON

The current accountability-oriented reform movement, focused on standards and testing, bears a few striking similarities to the curriculum reform movement of the 1960s, along with some profound differences.

ORIGINS

Both reforms originated outside the education establishment and shared similar assumptions on its generally poor quality. The new social studies was inspired by national security issues centered on the exaggerated fear that the Soviet Union was threatening to overtake the United States in science and engineering manpower development. It was led by federal government initiative combined with leadership from elite members of the Nation's academic community. Recent accountability reforms were inspired by a "manufactured crisis" centered on issues of international economic competition and the desire of those in business and government to develop human capital so that American business could maintain a position of global hegemony.[8] In both reforms, government played a key role. And, in both cases, the nature of the reform was shaped by a perceived external threat and fear rather than a fully developed notion of what is in the best, long-term interest of children and our society.

REFORM MODEL

Both movements share a top-down, technological model of school reform. In the era of the new social studies, the reform model was drawn from wartime research and development. In the accountability reforms, the model combined a similar approach with ideas drawn from business.[9] In each case, reformers are focused primarily on manipulation of one key component of the educational system, seeking to reform schools by modifying that key element. During the era of the new social studies, the reform focused on improvement of teaching materials, seeking to transform schools by creating more engaging, intellectually oriented materials to either replace or supplement the standard textbook. In the current reform, the emphasis is on the assessment component, with reformers seeking to improve schools via high stakes accountability measures. In both cases, the reform model is a reflection of a hierarchical, capitalist society and exemplifies the myriad ways in which the reigning social structure influences efforts to improve schools.

PEDAGOGY

In terms of pedagogy, the 1960s reform was theory-driven, with notions of inquiry and discovery learning fully embraced by reformers, and was led by scientists and social scientists from the academic community. It sought to extend the church of reason from the universities into the schools. We know from research on classroom practice and a series of status studies conducted in the 1970s and later that it made little headway on changing the standard instructional practices of schooling. The current reform is efficiency-oriented, with theories of educational improvement drawn from business models, and is led by business leaders and politicians, or by educational administrators who have borrowed approaches to management from business models. The reform has led to the reification of traditional methods of teaching, which are, ironically, more congruent with what might be called the "grammar" of social studies and the culture of the school.[10]

EDUCATION

Both reforms made negative assumptions about "educationists," blaming the education establishment for the perceived failures of the schools. The leaders of the new social studies, more often than not, chose to sidestep the educational establishment and appeal directly to teachers. In more recent years, accountability reformers have hijacked the educational establishment, seeking to control it through state legislatures and federal law. In both cases there was an arrogance among reformers, a tragic disrespect for teachers and scholars in education, a belief that reformers outside education know what is best and that scholars within the educational establishment have little to offer for the improvement of schools. Belief in the inadequacy of educators was established with certainty by critics who simply pointed to problems in schools as evidence for failure.

CURRICULUM

The era of the new social studies marked a revival of discipline-based learning in social studies, but with increased emphasis on the social sciences, including anthropology, history, geography, sociology, economics, and political science, along with increased attention to issues. Reformers stressed the structure of the disciplines, including a mode of inquiry and key concepts. The current reform emphasizes traditional history, geography, and civics, with less attention to other social sciences and issues. It has led, sadly, to a narrowing of the social studies curriculum, an increasing lack of flexibility, a reemphasis upon traditional methods of teaching, and a mad rush to coverage.[11]

CONCLUSION

Ultimately, the new social studies was inexorably tethered to its origins in the national security structure of the United States during the context of cold war. The reform sprang from the reengagement of scientists, social scientists, and historians with the schools after years of neglect. This evolved largely for political reasons linked to the integration of science into the national security structure of the nation during World War II, which led to tightly intertwined institutional arrangements that had previously not existed.[17] Key players in the reform served in overlapping positions on various government and scientific committees. While the fear of Soviet manpower development provided an opening, leading scientists and social scientists seized the opportunity to have a more accurate and inquiry-oriented version of their work imposed on schools. Ironically, while the reformers espoused the value of intellectual freedom, many of the materials they created sought to replace the textbook with the disciplinary expert's materials that were often "teacher proof," at least to some extent. In the final analysis, social studies reform became a handmaiden to American cold war foreign policy. Sputnik shock led to a dramatic expansion of the federal government's role in curriculum reform, which entailed backing a particular vision of social studies and bankrolling it with millions in tax dollars. In hindsight, the period demonstrates the truism that educational reform inescapably embodies social and political ends and strong influences from the context of the times. In the morality play that is social studies reform, this episode illustrates the ways that curriculum policy and governance can be shaped by power and context. It stands as a fascinating and important episode in the continuing parade in which competing curricular armies clash on the battlefield of curriculum development and dissemination only to have their reforms splintered, fragmented, or deflected over the anvil of classroom constancy.

The pedagogical theories, innovations, and materials of the era are of continuing educational relevance. Bruner's books and articles as well the work of Fenton, Oliver, and others (and, to a lesser extent, the classroom materials of the period) are read and discussed by educational theorists and practitioners and undoubtedly have some influence on their actions. In hindsight, Bruner's work might be seen, somewhat ironically, as an extension and refinement of Dewey's pedagogy, a "more contemporary and scientifically valid re-writing of Dewey's *Democracy and Education*." In long perspective, both Dewey and Bruner, and the school reform movements they helped spawn, have been shelved, largely set aside by the institutional constraints of schooling. They remain part of the background of education, continuing to influence ideas, never completely discarded. Their marginalization can be partially explained by the overarching influence of the managerial tradition of education for social efficiency; the emphasis on what can be tested and measured; and a tendency to focus on the certainties, not the doubts.[13] Inquiry fosters doubts while a strong segment of the public wants certainties—hence, curriculum politics intervene. "That was how it ended. How it always ended," Bruner later lamented. "American education is about what you know, what you can achieve, and what you can be tested on. It didn't fit."[14]

In closing, the era of the new social studies offers a stark contrast with curricular trends of the present, a strong reminder of what is possible, and a compelling vision of inquiry learning. Despite its flaws and failures, the era of the new social studies poses a continuing challenge to the field. Social studies reform toward meaningful learning in classrooms reached a high point during the Deweyan progressive era, especially through the work of Harold Rugg and other leading progressives. It reached another high point during the era of the new social studies through the work of Bruner, Fenton, Oliver, and other new social studies reformers. In each case, the reforms had a profound influence on a small but significant number of classrooms, teachers, and students. With sustained support and continued development, it is possible that inquiry teaching and learning could be popularized among a significant number of teachers and students again at some point in the future.

In judging any reform—its successes, its failures, its enduring worth—we return to questions of value, questions surrounding the purposes and functions of schooling in American society. If the troubled history of the new social studies stands for anything at all, it represents a vision of the hope for inquiry learning tempered by the difficulties of sustaining such a vision. Whether we read its history as a narrative of hope or as a cautionary tale may depend as much on who we are as on the particulars of the story itself. For my part, I prefer to view the episode in a positive light, emphasizing the continuing desire for social improvement and the quest for meaningful learning in social studies that the reform represents.

LIST OF ABBREVIATIONS

AP	Advanced Placement (Program)
ABE	Advisory Board on Education, National Academy of Sciences
ACLS	American Council of Learned Societies
ACSP	Anthropology Curriculum Study Project
AEC	Atomic Energy Commission
AHA	American Historical Association
CIA	Central Intelligence Agency
CBE	Council for Basic Education
CIN	Curriculum Information Network
EDC	Education Development Center, Inc.
ESI	Educational Services, Incorporated
FRASCO	The Foundation for Religious Action in the Social and Civil Order
HEW	Health, Education, and Welfare
HSGP	High School Geography Project
LAE	Life-Adjustment Education
LNS	Laboratory for Nuclear Sciences
MACOS	Man: A Course of Study
MIT	Massachusetts Institute of Technology
NAM	National Association of Manufacturers
NAS	National Academy of Sciences
NCSS	National Council for the Social Studies
NDEA	National Defense Education Act
NEA	National Education Association
NRC	National Research Council
NSF	National Science Foundation
ODM	Office of Defense Mobilization
ONR	Office of Naval Research
OWI	Office of War Intelligence
PEA	Progressive Education Association
POWs	prisoners of war
PSSC	Physical Science Study Committee
PSAC	President's Science Advisory Committee

SAC	Science Advisory Committee
SAC-ODM	Science Advisory Committee, Office of Defense Mobilization
SRA	Science Research Associates
SRSS	Sociological Resources for the Social Studies
SICTSE	Special Interdepartmental Committee on the Training of Scientists and Engineers
USOE	United States Office of Education
UICSM	University of Illinois Committee on School Mathematics

JOURNAL TITLES ABBREVIATED IN NOTES

HER	*Harvard Education Review*
NYT	*New York Times*
PDK	*Phi Delta Kappan*
PE	*Progressive Education*
SE	*Social Education*
SR	*Saturday Review*
TCR	*Teachers College Record*
TRSE	*Theory and Research in Social Education*
TSS	*The Social Studies*

LIST OF MANUSCRIPT COLLECTIONS ABBREVIATED IN NOTES

Carnegie Mellon University Archives

Edwin P. Fenton Papers: [Fenton Papers]

Dolph Briscoe Center for American History, University of Texas at Austin

National Council for the Social Studies Records, Manuscript Collection # 17*: [NCSS]

Harvard University Archives

Records of Educational Services Incorporated and Education Development Center, Inc.**: [EDC]

Jerome S. Bruner Papers: [Bruner Papers]

Kennedy Presidential Library

Kennedy Presidential Library: [JFK]

President's Office Files: [JFK/POF]

Francis Keppel, Commissioner of Education: [Keppel Papers]

Massachusetts Institute of Technology Institute Archives

Records of the Office of the President, AC4: [MIT/ROP]

James R. Killian Papers: [Killian Papers]

Jerrold R. Zacharias Papers: [Zacharias Papers]

National Academy of Sciences Archives

Advisory Board on Education: [NAS/ABE]

Central Policy Files

Woods Hole Papers: [WH]

National Archives II, College Park, Maryland

Records of the Office of Education, RG 12

Office Files of the Commissioner of Education: [USOE/OFCE]

National Intelligence Survey: [NIS]

Records of the Office of Science and Technology, RG 359: [OST]

President's Science Advisory Committee: [PSAC]

Records of the National Science

Foundation, RG 307 Office of the Director, Subject Files: [NSF/ODSF]

Historian File: [NSF/HF]

*At Milbank Memorial Library and Archives, Teachers College, Columbia University at the time research was conducted.

**In the personal library of Peter Dow at the time research was conducted.

NOTES

INTRODUCTION

1. See William Appleman Williams, *The Tragedy of American Diplomacy* (Cleveland, OH: World Publishing Company, 1959).
2. Geoff Scheurman, Ronald W. Evans, James E. Davis, and Keith Reynolds, eds., *Constructivism and the New Social Studies: A Collection of Classic Inquiry Lessons* (Charlotte, NC: Information Age, in preparation).
3. Ronald W. Evans, *The Social Studies Wars: What Should We Teach the Children?* (New York: Teachers College Press, 2004).
4. Walter Parker, "Introduction." In *Social Studies Today: Research and Practice*, ed. Walter Parker (New York: Routledge, 2009), 1.
5. Ronald W. Evans, *The Tragedy of American School Reform: How Curriculum Politics and Entrenched Dilemmas Have Diverted Us from Democracy* (New York: Palgrave Macmillan, 2011).

CHAPTER 1

1. Ronald W. Evans, *The Social Studies Wars: What Should We Teach the Children?* (New York: Teachers College Press, 2004).
2. Clarence Karier, *The Individual, Society, and Education* (Urbana: University of Illinois Press), 287.
3. Ibid., 287–289, 307–313.
4. Todd Gitlin, *The Sixties: Years of Hope, Days of Rage* (New York: Bantam, 1987), 20.
5. Editor, "Notes and News: Ten Major Educational Events of 1947," *SE* 12, no. 2 (February 1948): 82–83.
6. William L. O'Neill, *American High: The Years of Confidence, 1945–1960* (New York: Free Press, 1986), 33–35.
7. Harry S. Truman, quoted in Walter L. Hixson, *Parting the Curtain: Propaganda, Culture, and the Cold War, 1945–1961* (New York: St. Martins Press, 1997), 14.
8. John L. Rudolph in *Scientists in the Classroom: The Cold War Reconstruction of American Science Education* (New York: Palgrave Macmillan, 2002), 11–13; Articles in the NYT by Benjamin Fine played a key role in earlier controversies over social studies, notably the Rugg textbook controversy

and the controversy over the teaching of American history instigated by historian Allan Nevins.

9.   Rudolph, *Scientists in the Classroom*, 12–13.

10. Stephen J. Whitfield, *The Culture of the Cold War* (Baltimore, MD: Johns Hopkins Press, 1991); Rudolph, *Scientists in the Classroom*, 14–15.

11. Rudolph, *Scientists in the Classroom*, 16.

12. David C. Hulburd, *This Happened in Pasadena* (New York: Macmillan, 1951).

13. Irene C. Kuhn, "Your Child Is Their Target," *American Legion Magazine*, June 1952, 18–19, 54–56.

14. Arthur Zilversmit, *Changing Schools: Progressive Education Theory and Practice, 1930–1960* (Chicago: University of Chicago Press).

15. O'Neill, *American High*.

16. Mortimer Smith, *And Madly Teach: A Layman Looks at Public School Education* (Chicago: Henry Regnery, 1949).

17. Albert Lynd, *Quackery in the Public Schools* (New York: Grosset and Dunlap, 1953); Albert Lynd, "Quackery in the Public Schools," *Atlantic Monthly*, March 1950.

18. Arthur E. Bestor, *Educational Wastelands: The Retreat from Learning in Our Public Schools* (Urbana: University of Illinois Press, 1953), 90. See also, David Jenness, *Making Sense of Social Studies* (New York: Macmillan, 1990), 125. For a thorough and friendly treatment of Bestor, see Burton Weltman, "Reconsidering Arthur Bestor and the Cold War in Social Education," *TRSE* 28 (Winter 2000): 11–39.

19. Bestor, *Educational Wastelands*, 9–10.

20. Ibid., 18.

21. Ibid., 59.

22. Ibid., 55, as cited in Rudolph, *Scientists in the Classroom*, 29, n. 89; The notion of the "structure" of the disciplines would gain currency during the curriculum reform movement, especially after Woods Hole, almost as if Bestor had been present.

23. Ibid., 21.

24. Ibid., 22.

25. Ibid., 46.

26. Ibid., 46–47.

27. Ibid., 100.

28. Ibid., 56.

29. Harry J. Fuller, "The Emperor's New Clothes or *Prius Dementat*," *Scientific Monthly* 72 (1951): 38, as quoted in Rudolph, *Scientists in the Classroom*, 28, n. 88.

30. Bestor, *Educational Wastelands*, 102.

31. Ibid., 121, as quoted in Rudolph, *Scientists in the Classroom*, 30, n. 93.

32. William Clark Trow, "Academic Utopia?: An Evaluation of Educational Wastelands," *Educational Theory* 4, no. 1 (January 1954): 16–26.

33. Leo J. Alilunas, "Bestor and the 'Social Studies.'" *SE* 22 (May 1958): 238–240.

34. Hazel W. Hertzberg, *Social Studies Reform, 1880–1980* (Boulder, CO: Social Science Education Consortium), 86–87.

35. John Dixon, "What's Wrong with U.S. History?" *The American Legion Magazine*, May 1949, 15–16, 40–41.

36. Mrs. W. T. Wood, "How Well Are Our Schools Doing the Job?" *Vital Speeches of the Day*, March 1, 1952, 309; Robert Keohane, "The 'Unjustified Attack' on the Teaching of American History," *The School Review*, October 1951, 382–383; Verne P. Kaub, "A Critic," *The Saturday Review of Literature*, April 19, 1952, 16–17, 57. For a full description of the attacks on *Building America*, see Robert E. Newman, Jr., "History of a Civic Education Project Implementing the Social-Problems Technique of Instruction," Doctoral dissertation, Stanford University, 1960. Building America was the object of a sustained attack in California that resulted in the discontinuation of the series.

37. Clarence Karier, *The Individual, Society, and Education*, 307–310.

38. "Atomic Information Committee" folder, box 17, series 4C, NCSS.

39. Daniel Melcher to Merrill Hartshorn, January 24, 1946, "Atomic Information Committee" folder, box 17, series 4C, NCSS; "Your Last Chance," reprinted from *Look*, "Atomic Information Committee" folder, box 17, series 4C, NCSS.

40. *SE* (1946): 53, 63, 257; "Education or Annihilation," *SE* (1946): 363; "Sanity," *SE* (1954): 339.

41. John T. Flynn, "Who Owns Your Child's Mind?" *The Reader's Digest*, October 1951, 24.

42. Kitty Jones and Robert Olivier, *Progressive Education is REDucation* (Boston: Meador Publishing Company, 1956), 45–46, 98, 130, 136.

43. Mary L. Allen, *Education or Indoctrination* (Caldwell, OH: The Caxton Printers, 1956), 27–53.

44. Archibald W. Anderson, "The Cloak of Respectability: The Attackers and Their Methods," *PE* 29, no. 3 (January 1952): 68. Anderson lists seven national organizations, the most well-known being Allen Zoll's National Council for American Education.

45. Diane Ravitch, *The Troubled Crusade: American Education, 1945–1980* (New York: Basic Books, 1983), 105–113.

46. David Hulburd. *This Happened in Pasadena* (New York: Macmillan, 1951).

47. Newman, "History of a Civic Education Project."

48. Jenness, *Making Sense of Social Studies*, 118.

49. Hertzberg, *Social Studies Reform*, 87–88. See also, *The Past Before Us*, ed. Michael Kammen (Ithaca, NY: Cornell University Press, 1980).

50. Archibald W. Anderson, "The Charges Against American Education: What is the Evidence?" *PE* 29, no. 3 (January 1952): 91–105.

51. O. E. Melby, "American Education Under Fire: The Story of the 'Phony Three-R Fight" (New York: Anti-Defamation League of B'nai B'rith, 1951), 17, as cited in Anderson, "The Cloak of Respectability."

52. See Diane Ravitch, *The Troubled Crusade*, 81–113, and especially 91–105 of the chapter titled "Loyalty Investigations."

53. See the January 1952 number of *PE* 29, no. 3, and the June 1953 issue of *PDK* 34, no. 9; See also, Hollis Caswell, "The Great Reappraisal of Public Education," *TCR* 54, no. 1 (October 1952), 21–22.

54. C. Winfield Scott and Clyde M. Hill, eds. *Public Education Under Criticism* (New York: Prentice-Hall, 1954).

55. Robert L. Page, "Book Reviews: Public Education Under Criticism," *SE* 21, no. 4 (April 1957): 186–187.

56. Anderson, "The Charges Against American Education."

57. See, for example, Anderson, "The Charges Against American Education"; Anderson, "The Cloak of Respectability"; Special issue of *PDK*, June 1953; Hollis L. Caswell, "The Great Reappraisal of Public Education," *TCR* 54 (October 1952): 12–22; and Hollis L. Caswell, *Curriculum Improvement in the Public School Systems* (New York: Bureau of Publications, Teachers College, 1950). Ravitch reads Caswell's book as an accurate description of school practice. I don't.

58. Karier, *The Individual, Society, and Education*, 296.

59. William H. Cartwright, "The Social Studies—Scholarship and Pedagogy," November 1957, 5–6, "Cartwright Presidential Address" folder, box 4, Series IV B, NCSS.

60. Karier, *The Individual, Society, and Education*, 307–313.

61. Dale Greenawald, "Maturation and Change, 1947–1968," *SE* 59, no. 7 (1995): 416–428.

62. Notably, John Dewey held deeply anticommunist views going back to his second visit to the Soviet Union in the late 1920s and his concern that the second five-year plan made schools serve narrow ends and thus sliced away their potential intellectual and democratic vitality. Counts, Kilpatrick, Rugg, and others followed a similar path.

63. "Communism" folder (and others), box 3, Series IV D, NCSS; "Frasco-Communism" folder, box 1, Accession #850001, NCSS.

64. Karl E. Ettinger, Research Consultant, U.S. House of Representatives, to Editor, *SE*, January 14, 1954, "Reece Commission" folder, box 53, Series IV D, Executive Reference Files, NCSS Papers.

65. "DOD and HEW: POWs" folder, box 52, Series IV D, Executive Director Reference Files, NCSS.

66. Ibid., Hugh Milton, "The Prisoner of War Problem," 7.

67. Ibid., 10.

68. *The Nation*, October 27, 1951.

69. Joseph DiBona, "The Intellectual Repression of the Cold War," *Educational Forum* 46, no. 3 (Spring 1982), 343–355.

70. Sidney Hook, "Should Communists Be Permitted to Teach?" *NYT Magazine*, February 27, 1949; Alexander Meiklejohn, "Should Communists Be Allowed to Teach?" *NYT Magazine*, March 27, 1949.

CHAPTER 2

1. "National Intelligence Survey, U.S.S.R., Section 44, Manpower," February 1, 1953, National Intelligence Surveys, 1948–1965, Box 125, NIS.

2. "National Intelligence Survey, U.S.S.R., Section 44, Manpower," January 1, 1958, 13, 15; National Intelligence Surveys, 1948–1965, box 125, NIS.

3. "National Intelligence Survey, U.S.S.R., Section 44, Manpower," March 1, 1963, 1, 4; National Intelligence Surveys, 1948–1965, box 125, NIS.

4. Dwight D. Eisenhower to Arthur S. Fleming, August 1, 1953, "Subject files, M," box 11, NSF/ODSF.

5. Arthur S. Fleming, director, Office of Defense Mobilization, to Dwight D. Eisenhower, January 6, 1954, "Subject files, M," box 11, NSF/ODSF.

6. William L. O'Neill, *American High: The Years of Confidence, 1945–1960* (New York: Free Press, 1986), 33–35.

7. "Russian Science Threatens the West," *Nation's Business*, September 1954, pp. 42–54, in "Scientists and Engineers" folder, box 71, USOE/OFCE; Benjamin Fine, "Russia Is Overtaking U.S. in Training of Technicians," *NYT*, November 7, 1954, "Scientists and Engineers File," box 71, USOE/OFCE.

8. Walter A. McDougall, *The Heavens and the Earth: A Political History of the Space Age* (New York: Basic Books, 1985), 5.

9. Daniel J. Kevles, "K1S2: Korea, Science, and the State." In *Big Science: The Growth of Large-Scale Research*, ed. Peter Galison and Bruce Hevly (Stanford, CA: Stanford University Press, 1992), 325.

10. "Technical Questions," attached to Killian to Zacharias, December 21, 1949, folder 11 "Zacharias, Jerrold 1945–1957," box 242, MIT/ROP.

11. Daniel J. Kevles, *The Physicists: The History of a Scientific Community in Modern America* (Cambridge, MA: Harvard University Press, 1987).

12. John Rudolph, *Scientists in the Classroom*, 47–55.

13. Ibid., 57–59.

14. Ibid., 60–61.

15. Ibid., 62–63, Arthur S. Fleming to Alan T. Waterman, May 24, 1954, box 18, NSF/ODSF, cited in Rudolph, *Scientists in the Classroom*, 62–63, n. 23.

16. Rudolph, *Scientists in the Classroom*, 63–67.

17. House Committee on Appropriations, *Hearings before the Subcommittee on Independent Offices*, 84th Congress, 1st Session, February 9, 1955, 234–235, as cited in Rudolph, *Scientists in the Classroom*, 71, n. 60.

18. Eisenhower to Fleming, August 1, 1953, "Committee on Manpower Resources for National Security" folder, Subject file "M," box 11, 1951–1956, NSF/ODSF.

19. Attached to Lawrence A. Appley to Arthur S. Fleming, December 18, 1953, "Manpower Resources for National Security: A Report to the Director of the Office of Defense Mobilization, "Committee on Manpower Resources for National Security" folder, Subject file "M," box 11, 1951–1956, NSF/ODSF.

20. Henry H. Armsby, "Scientific and Professional Manpower: Organized Efforts to Improve Its Supply and Utilization," April 1954, "Scientists-Engineers" folder, box 71, NSF/ODSF.

21. M. H. Trytten, "Engineering Education in Russia," September 1954, and M. H. Trytten, "Russia and the United States: Engineering Graduates," November 24, 1954, "Scientists-Engineers" folder, box 71, NSF/ODSF.

22. Trytten, "Engineering Education in Russia," 5.

23. "Educational Factors Basic to Economic Growth," outline apparently authored by Waterman, "Scientists-Engineers" folder, box 71, NSF/ODSF.

24. Annotated Agenda, SICTSE, 1954, "Scientists and Engineers" folder, box 71, NSF/ODSF.

25. Benjamin Fine, "Russia Is Overtaking U.S. in Training of Technicians," *NYT*, November 7, 1954; Rudolph, *Scientists in the Classroom*, 71.

26. "Building Tomorrow's Scientist," *Business Week*, October 30, 1954.

27. "The Red Challenger," *Newsweek*, November 1, 1954, 83–84.

28. Press release, January 9, 1955, Grass Roots Educational League of Texas, "Scientists and Engineers" folder, box 71, NSF/ODSF.

29. Nicholas DeWitt, *Soviet Professional Manpower* (Washington, D.C.: National Science Foundation, 1955).

30. Rudolph, *Scientists in the Classroom*, 72–73.

31. House Committee on Appropriations, *Hearings before the Subcommittee on Independent Offices*, 84th Congress, 2nd Session, January 30, 1956, 522, as cited in Rudolph, *Scientists in the Classroom*, 75, n. 80.

32. "Policy Recommendations of the National Science Foundation, Maintenance of Technological Superiority." Presentation before the National Security Council, May 31, 1956 (Confidential), "ATW Special Papers" folder, box 81, NSF/ODSF.

33. James R. Killian, *Sputnik, Scientists and Eisenhower: A Memoir of the First Special Assistant to the President for Science and Technology* (Cambridge, MA: MIT Press, 1977), 192.

34. ATW diary note, July 8, 1957, box 25, NSF/ODSF; Waterman to Byron T. Shaw, July 18, 1957, "Diary Notes-1957," "C-E" folder, 1957–1959, box 25, NSF/ODSF; David M. Blank and George F. Stigler, *The Demand and Supply of Scientific Personnel* (New York: National Bureau of Economic Research, 1957).

35. ATW, "Diary Notes-1957," "C-E," folder, 1957–1959, box 25, NSF/ODSF. This file contains a flurry of letters expressing concern over the Blank and Stigler findings.

36. NSF internal memo, June 20, 1956, box 21, Records of the Presidents Committee on Scientists and Engineers, Eisenhower Presidential Library, as cited in Rudolph, *Scientists in the Classroom*, 80, n. 99.

37. Phillip S. Jones and Arthur F. Coxford, Jr., "Mathematics in the Evolving School," in *A History of Mathematics Education in the United States and Canada* (Washington, D.C.: National Council for the Teachers of Mathematics, 1970), 69–70.

38. Ibid., 69–70.
39. Beberman, as quoted in Peter B. Dow, *Schoolhouse Politics: Lessons from the Sputnik Era* (Cambridge, MA: Harvard University Press, 1991), 20, n. 20.
40. Ibid., 22.
41. Zacharias to Killian, memo, March 15, 1956, "13-18 ESI Correspondence A-Z" folder, box 31, Killian Papers.
42. Jack S. Goldstein, *A Different Sort of Time: The Life of Jerrold R. Zacharias, Scientist, Engineer, Educator* (Cambridge, MA: MIT Press), 154; from the MIT/Oral History Collection.
43. As of February 21, 1957, PSSC steering committee members included Paul Brandwein, science editor, Harcourt, Brace & Co.; Vannevar Bush, chairman of the Corporation, MIT; Frank Capra, film producer; Robert Carleton, executive secretary, National Science Teachers Association; Henry Chauncey, president, Educational Testing Services, Inc.; Bradley Dewey, member, MIT Corporation; Nathaniel Frank, chairman, MIT Physics Department; Francis Friedman, associate professor of Physics, MIT; Mervin Kelly, president, Bell Telephone Laboratories; James Killian, president, MIT; Edwin Land, president, Polaroid Corporation; Elbert Little, executive director, PSSC; Morris Meister, principal, Bronx High School of Science; Walter Michels, chairman, Physics Department, Bryn Mawr; Edward Purcell, Professor of Physics, Harvard University; I. I. Rabi, institute professor (Visiting), MIT; and Jerrold Zacharias, Professor of Physics, MIT and Chairman of the Committee.
44. Biographical sketch, Dr. Jerrold Reinach Zacharias, "Biogr. Info." folder, box 42, Zacharias Papers.
45. Goldstein, *A Different Sort of Time*, 93.
46. Ibid., 151.
47. Rudolph, *Scientists in the Classroom*, 121.
48. Goldstein, *A Different Sort of Time*, 164–165; MIT/Oral History Collection. Zacharias always capitalized them because they were of fundamental importance.
49. Statement by the President's Science Advisory Committee, *Education for the Age of Science*, issued at the White House, May 24, 1959, attached to Killian to DuBridge, March 10, 1960, "19-6 PSAC folder," box 37a, Killian Papers.
50. PSAC, *Education for the Age of Science*.
51. Ibid., 12.
52. Zacharias interview, PSSC/Oral History Collection, as quoted in Rudolph, *Scientists in the Classroom*, 136, n. 110.
53. Bruner interview conducted by the author in Bruner's study, May 12, 2008.
54. John D. Haas, *The Era of the New Social Studies* (Boulder, CO: Social Science Education Consortium, 1977), 14–15.
55. John L. Rudolph, "From World War to Woods Hole: The Use of Wartime Research Models for Curriculum Reform," *TCR* 104, no. 2 (March 2002): 212–241.

56. PSAC, "Government Research and Development," October 4, 1960, "18-25 PSAC Correspondence" folder 4, box 36, Killian Papers.

57. James R. Killian, "The Return to Learning: The Curse of Obsolescence in the Schools Can Be Mitigated by the Scholars in the Universities," Correspondence, A-Z, 1962–1966, folder 2, box 31, ESI, Killian Papers; Jerome S. Bruner, *In Search of Mind: Essays in Autobiography* (New York: Harper and Row, 1983), 179–180.

58. Gerald Gutek, *Education in the United States: A Historical Perspective* (Englewood Cliffs, NJ: Prentice-Hall, 1986).

59. Zacharias interview, Physical Science Study Committee, Oral History Collection, MIT Archives, as cited in Rudolph, *Scientists in the Classroom*, 102, n. 87.

60. Transcript of interview regarding science advising to President Eisenhower, 1957–1959, Folder 1, re: Columbia University Oral History Project, box 30, Killian Papers.

61. Hyman G. Rickover, *Education and Freedom* (New York: E. P. Dutton and Co., 1959).

62. Ibid., 59.

63. E. Merrill Root, *Brainwashing in the High Schools* (New York: Devin-Adair, 1958), 3, 11, 18, 55, 136, 137, 119–149; "A Reply to the Charges Made in the 13 Chapters of *Brainwashing in the High Schools*," "Attacks on Texts" folder, box 12A, Series IV D, Executive Reference Files, NCSS.

64. Pamphlet, "Progress Report, 'Operation Textbook,'" "Attacks on Textbooks" folder, box 12A, Series IV D, Executive Director Reference Files, NCSS.

65. Kermit Lansner, ed. *Second Rate Brains* (New York: Doubleday News Books, 1958).

66. "New Cabinet Post Eisenhower Ideal," *NYT*, March 11, 1959.

67. "President to Aid Drive for Science," *NYT*, October 31, 1957; Waterman to Eisenhower, November 20, 1957, box 4, Records of the President's Science Advisory Committee, Eisenhower Presidential Library, as cited by Rudolph, *Scientists in the Classroom*, 109, n. 137.

68. Press Release, text of the address on "Our Future Security," delivered by the president, November 13, 1957, "S-1946 to Science and Engineering" folder, box 17, Scientists, NSF/ODSF.

69. Clyde C. Hall, public information officer to the senior staff, January 2, 1958, office memorandum, White House Releases on Proposed Programs for Increased Aid to Education and Education in the Sciences, "C-E" folder, Subject Files 1957–1959, box 25, NSF/ODSF.

70. Idaho Task Force Conference, "Educational Implications of Sputnik," January 20, 1958, "S-1946 to Science and Engineering," box 17, Scientists, NSF/ODSF.

71. State Action to Improve Educational Programs, New York State Board of Regents; "Ike Praises Huron's Program, *The Megaphone*, "S-1946 to Science and Engineering," box 17, Scientists, NSF/ODSF.

72. Alan T. Waterman, "General Considerations Concerning United States Progress in Science and Education," July 31, 1958, "1963 W" folder,

ATW Special Papers, NSF/ODSF; published as, Alan T. Waterman, "U.S. Progress in Science and Education," *Technology Review* 61, no. 1 (November 1958): 33–34.

73. See Barbara Barksdale Clowse, *Brainpower for the Cold War: The Sputnik Crisis and the National Defense Education Act of 1958* (Westport, CT: Greenwood Press, 1981).

74. Ibid.; Pamela E. Flattau, *The National Defense Education Act of 1958: Selected Outcomes* (Washington, D.C.: Institute for Defense Analysis, 2006).

75. Edward Purcell interview, PSSC Oral History Collection, MIT Institute Archives, as cited by Rudolph, *Scientists in the Classroom*, 111, n. 148; Bruner, *In Search of Mind.*

76. Minutes of board of directors, 1958, 32–33, Series II B, NCSS.

77. Dale Greenawald, "Maturation and Change, 1947–1968, *Social Education* 59, no. 7 (1995), 421; note the similarity to the 1990s reform movement in the non-social studies definition of the field, focusing on history, geography, and civics.

78. Karl Shapiro, "Why Out-Russia Russia?" *New Republic*, June 9, 1958, 10.

79. Thomas N. Bonner, "Sputniks and the Educational Crisis in America," *The Journal of Higher Education* 29, no. 4 (April, 1958): 181–183.

80. John Hershey, *The Child Buyer* (New York: Knopf, 1960).

81. Carl F. Hansen, "Educator vs. Educationist," *New Republic*, October 10, 1960, 23.

82. Craig Nelson, *Rocket Men: The Epic Story of the First Men on the Moon* (New York: Viking, 2009); Nelson characterizes the space race as "The one noble proxy" for direct armed conflict between the United States and USSR.

83. "Proposed Conference on Psychological Research in Education," 1958, memo from ABE, NAS, to Lanier et al., March 5, 1958, enclosure, "Proposed conf." folder, NAS/ABE.

84. R. M. Whaley notes, National Academy of Sciences—National Research Council Governing Board, Advisory Board on Education, Meeting re: PSSC, April 22, 1958, "Coordination with MIT PSSC/Formation of ESI" folder, Governing Board, 1958, NAS/ABE.

85. Bruner, *In Search of Mind,* 180.

86. Zacharias memo, "Role of Federal Government in Education," January 2, 1957, "PSSC 1957" folder, box 41, Zacharias Papers.

87. Ibid.

CHAPTER 3

1. R. M. Whaley, executive director, Advisory Board on Education, "For Agenda, NAS-NRC Governing Board Meeting—9 February 1958," January 27, 1958, "Proposed Conference on Psychological Research in Education" folder, NAS/ABE.

2. "Proposed Conference on Psychological Research in Education," 1958, memo from ABE, NAS, to Lanier et al., March 5, 1958, enclosure, "Proposed conf." folder, NAS/ABE.

3. National Academy of Sciences—National Research Council, *Psychological Research in Education* (Washington, D.C.: National Academy of Sciences—National Research Council, 1958), 6–7, 10, in "Conference on Psychological Research in Education, 1958 April" folder, NAS/ABE.

4. Ibid., 12–17. Underlined for emphasis in original, perhaps reflecting the psychologists and the popular disdain for a focus on "methods," per se.

5. Randall M. Whaley to Detlev W. Bronk, July 2, 1959, "Tentative Schedule" attached, "General" file, WH Papers. The executive committee that coordinated the work of the conference included Edward G. Begle, John Blum, Henry Chauncey, Lee J. Cronbach, Francis L. Friedman, Arnold Grobman, Randall M. Whaley, and Jerome S. Bruner, chair.

6. Jerome S. Bruner, *In Search of Mind: Essays in Autobiography* (New York: Harper and Row, 1983), 182.

7. Members of the Woods Hole Conference included Carl Allendoerfer, University of Washington, mathematics; Richard Alpert, Harvard, psychology; Edward Begle Yale, mathematics; John Blum, Yale, History; Jerome S. Bruner, Harvard, psychology; C. Ray Carpenter, Pennsylvania State University, psychology; John B. Carroll, Harvard University, education; Henry Chauncey, Educational Testing Service, education; Donald Cole, Phillips Exeter Academy, history; Lee Cronbach, University of Illinois, psychology; Gilbert Finlay, University of Illinois, physics; John H. Fischer, dean of Teachers College, Columbia University, education; John Flory, Eastman Kodak Company, cinematography; Francis L. Friedman, MIT, physics; Robert M. Gagne, Princeton, psychology; Ralph Gerard, University of Michigan, biology; H. Bentley Glass, Johns Hopkins University, biology; Arnold Grobman, American Institute of Biological Sciences, biology; Thomas S. Hall, Washington University, biology; Barbel Inhelder, Institut Rousseau, Geneva, psychology; John F. Latimer, George Washington University, classics; George A. Miller, Harvard, psychology; Robert S. Morison, Rockefeller Foundation, medicine; David L. Page, University of Illinois, mathematics; Richard Pieters, Phillips Academy, Andover, mathematics; William C. H. Prentice, Swarthmore College, psychology; Paul C. Rosenbloom, University of Minnesota, mathematics; Kenneth W. Spence, State University of Iowa, psychology; H. Burr Steinbach, University of Chicago, biology; Donald Taylor, Yale, psychology; Herbert E. Vaughn, University of Illinois, mathematics; Randall M. Whaley, Purdue University, physics; Don Williams, University of Kansas City, cinematography; Jerrold Zacharias, MIT, physics. See Jerome S. Bruner, *The Process of Education* (Cambridge, MA: Harvard University Press, 1960), vi.

8. Bruner, *Process of Education*, x.

9. Statement on NAS-NRC contained at back of the Report of the Easton Conference, NAS—NRC, *Psychological Research in Education*.

10. Bruner later attributed his selection as director to Francis Friedman. See Bruner, *In Search of Mind*, 181.

11. Bruner interview.

12. Bruner, notes for the Woods Hole Conference, July 22, 1959, NAS, WH.

13. Whaley, "Proposal for a Summer Study on Fundamental Processes in Education," April 29, 1959, WH.

14. Tentative schedule, Summer Study on Educational Processes, attached to Whaley to Bronk, July 2, 1959, and Bruner to Dear Colleague, June 16, 1959, "General" folder, WH.

15. "Apparatus of Teaching" report, September 16, 1959, 1, 4, 5, WH.

16. Arthur W. Melton, Report of the NAS—NRC Symposium on Education and Training Media, August 18–19, 1959; Bently Glass Papers, American Philosophical Society, Philadelphia, as cited in Rudolph, *Scientists in the Classroom*, 99, n. 77.

17. Zacharias interview, PSSC, Oral History Collection, as cited in Rudolph, *Scientists in the Classroom*, 100, n. 79.

18. Bruner interview.

19. Bruner, *Process of Education*, 2–3.

20. Ibid., 11–12.

21. Ibid., 32.

22. Ibid., 17–18.

23. Ibid., 20.

24. Ibid., 20–22.

25. Ibid., 33.

26. Ibid., 39.

27. Ibid., 43–45. Italics in original.

28. Ibid., 52.

29. Ibid., 13–14, 58–59.

30. Ibid., 14.

31. Ibid., 72.

32. Ibid., 77.

33. Ibid., 77.

34. Jerome Bruner, "Motivational Factors in Curriculum Planning," September 12, 1959, Memorandum to the Panel on Motivation, 2–3, "General" folder, WH.

35. Jerrold Zacharias, November 15, 1974, interview with Peter Dow, EDC Papers; Jerrold Zacharias, "Woods Hole Revisited," 1965, EDC Papers, as cited in Peter B. Dow, *Schoolhouse Politics: Lessons from the Sputnik Era* (Cambridge, MA: Harvard University Press, 1991), 35.

36. "Apparatus of Teaching" Report, September 16, 1959, 1, 4, 5, WH. For panel membership, see Bruner, *Process of Education*, xi.

37. Ibid., 10, 14.

38. "Panel on Sequence" report, September 14, 1959, 12, WH.

39. Ibid.

40. Bruner to Mr. Conant, March 3, 1960, "Bruner" folder, box 13, Zacharias Papers.

41. Dow, *Schoolhouse Politics*, 39–41; Bruner, *Process of Education*, 77.
42. Bruner to J. Myron Atkin, March 11, 1960, box 1, "A" folder, Correspondence, Topical, 1956–1961, Bruner Papers; Bruner to Mr. Conant, March 3, 1960, "Bruner" folder, box 13, Zacharias Papers.
43. Interview with Peter Dow, May 19, 2008, Buffalo, New York.
44. Jerome Bruner to Bob Creegan, April 11, 1958, and Creegan to Bruner, April, 27, 1958, box 3, "C folder," Accession # HUG 4242.9, Bruner Papers.
45. Lee Cronbach to Jerome Bruner, October 5, 1960, and Bruner to Cronbach, October 10, 1960, box 3, "C folder," Accession # HUG 4242.9, Bruner Papers.
46. Jerome Bruner to Bob Creegan, November 16, 1960, box 3, "C folder," Accession # HUG 4242.9, Bruner Papers.
47. Interview with Peter Dow.
48. David F. Labaree, *The Trouble with Ed Schools* (New Haven, CT: Yale University Press, 2004).
49. Bruner, *In Search of Mind*, 184–185.
50. Ibid., 185–186.
51. Panel Reports, WH.
52. Bruner interview.
53. Minutes of board of directors, 1958, 32–33, Series II B, NCSS.
54. Ibid., 10.
55. Ibid., 74–76.
56. Jerome Bruner, memo to Working Group on the Apparatus of Teaching, Woods Hole, September 1959 WH.
57. Allan A. Needell, "Project Troy and the Cold War Annexation of the Social Sciences," in *Universities and Empire: Money and Politics in the Social Sciences during the Cold War*, ed. Christopher Simpson (New York: New Press, 1998), 3–38.
58. Jack S. Goldstein, *A Different Sort of Time: The Life of Jerrold R. Zacharias, Scientist, Engineer, Educator* (Cambridge, MA: MIT Press).
59. Bruner, *In Search of Mind*, 210.
60. Charles R. Keller, "Needed: Revolution in the Social Studies," *SR*, 16 September 1961, 60.
61. Ibid., 61–62.
62. Edwin P. Fenton, *32 Problems in World History* (Glenview, IL: Scott, Foresman, 1964).
63. John Haas, *The Era of the New Social Studies* (Boulder, CO: Social Science Education Consortium, 1977), 21–22.
64. Robert N. Kreidler, technical assistant, PSAC to the Panel on Educational Research and Development, "Subject: Organizational Meeting," February 21–22, 1962, Box 138, "Education—Title Folder 1962," PSAC.
65. J. Boyer Jarvis, special assistant to the U.S. Commissioner of Education, "The Role of the United States Office of Education in Curriculum Experimentation," September 27, 1961, 4–6, "Instruction (Curriculum)" folder, box 111, USOE/OFCE.

66. "New Directions in Office of Education Programs," 1962, "Four Year Progress Report in Health, Education and Welfare, 1961–1964" folder, box 134, USOE/OFCE.

67. Jarvis, "The Role of USOE," 10.

68. Ibid., 9.

69. Ibid., 12.

70. USOE, "New Directions in Office of Education Programs," 34, undated document, appears to be from 1962, "Four Year Progress Report in Health, Education, and Welfare, 1961–64" folder, box 134, USOE/OFCE.

71. Sterling M. McMurrin to Arthur Bestor, May 14, 1962, "Reading file," box 140, USOE/OFCE.

72. John F. Kennedy to Jerome B. Wiesner, January 23, 1961, "PSAC 1/61–3/61" folder, Departments and Agencies, JFK/POF.

73. Robert N. Kreidler to Wiesner, Waterman, and McMurrin, November 22, 1961, "Education-Title Folder 1961," box 83, OST.

74. Robert N. Kreidler to Marin Mayer, January 26, 1962, Roll 38, Education, OST, Records of Government Agencies, JFK.

75. Full membership of the Panel on Educational Research and Development included Jerrold Zacharias, chairman, James E. Allen, Jr., B. Frank Brown, Jerome S. Bruner, Frederick Burkhardt, Bowen C. Dees, Charles A. Ferguson, John H. Fischer, Ralph C. M. Flynt, Francis L. Friedman, Francis Keppel, Martin Mayer, Alfred C. Neal, Ralph W. Tyler, Benjamin C. Willis, and O. Meredith Wilson. See participant list from earlier meeting for details. Agenda, April 20–21, 1962, "Education-Title Folder 1962," box 138 PSAC.

76. Robert N. Kreidler, memorandum for The Panel on Educational Research and Development, March 1, 1962, "Education-Title Folder 1962" folder, box 138, PSAC.

77. Agenda, April 20–21, 1962, Panel on Educational Research and Development, "Education-Title Folder 1962," box 138, PSAC.

78. Robert N. Kreidler, memorandum for the Panel on Educational Research and Development, May 29, 1962, 2–3, "Education—Title Folder 1962," box 138, PSAC.

79. Ibid., 4–5.

CHAPTER 4

1. Jerome S. Bruner, *In Search of Mind: Essays in Autobiography* (New York: Harper and Row, 1983), 188.

2. The steering committee was composed of a number of well-known scholars, several of whom had been previously involved in the curriculum reform movement. The membership included Henry Bradgon, history, Philips Exeter, John H. Fischer, Teachers College, Columbia; Francis Keppel, Harvard Graduate School of Education; Harry Levy, classics, Hunter College; Elting Morison, history, MIT; Stephen White, ESI; and ex officio

members James R. Killian, President of MIT and Chairman of the Board, ESI; Carroll V. Newsom, President, ESI; and Frederick Burkhardt, President, ACLS, and Jerrold Zacaharias, MIT, who served as cochairs.

3. Stephen White to Donald Oliver, March 5, 1962, "Spring 1962—Endicott House" folder, "Early Development" drawer, EDC; Peter B. Dow, *Schoolhouse Politics: Lessons from the Sputnik Era* (Cambridge, MA: Harvard University Press, 1991).

4. ACLS-ESI Social Studies and Humanities Curriculum Program, undated, "Instruction (Curriculum)" folder, box 111, USOE/OFCE.

5. Bruner, *In Search of Mind*, 187.

6. "June Conference," attached to letter from Stephen White to Donald Oliver, March 5, 1962, "Spring 1962—Endicott House" folder, "Early Development" drawer, EDC.

7. "Report: Conference of Social Studies and Humanities Curriculum Program," 1962, "Endicott House" folder, "Early Development" drawer, EDC; Appendix II, "Advance Reading Material Sent to Conference Participants, 23 April, 1962," "Report," box 1, Correspondence, miscellaneous, Bruner Papers.

8. For a complete list of participants, see Appendix I, "List of Participants and Observers, June Meeting—Humanities and Social Studies Program," "Spring 1962—Endicott House" folder, Early Development Drawer, EDC.

9. Ibid., 3.

10. Report, 3–4.

11. Ibid.

12. Dow, *Schoolhouse Politics*, 43.

13. Interview with Edwin Fenton, May 18, 2008, South Wellfleet, MA; interview with Peter Dow, May 19 and 21, 2008, Buffalo, NY.

14. Interview with Elting Morison, October 11, 1974, conducted by Peter Dow, EDC.

15. Report, 5.

16. Ibid., 6–11.

17. Ibid., 11–12.

18. Ibid., 12–14.

19. Ibid., 14–15.

20. Ibid., 21.

21. Ibid., 21.

22. Zacharias, interview by Peter Dow, October 11, 1974, EDC; Dow, *Schoolhouse Politics*, 45.

23. Ibid., 22–23.

24. Dow, *Schoolhouse Politics*, 44; Morison, interview by Peter Dow, 1974, EDC.

25. Report, 5–6.

26. Ibid., 6.

27. Ibid., 23–24.

28. Ibid., 24.

29. A ripple tank is a shallow glass tank of water used in schools and colleges to demonstrate the basic properties of waves. It is used in physics and engineering, hence Zacharias was the most likely source for this definition.

30. Appendix III, Report, 1–2.

31. Appendix VIIa, notes 1–4.

32. Martin Mayer, *Social Studies in American Schools* (New York: Harper & Row, 1963), 57–58, as quoted in Dow, *Schoolhouse Politics*, 50, n. 26.

33. Clinchy interview by Dow, October 15, 1974, EDC.

34. Jones, Appendix VIIb, Report, 2–4.

35. Ibid., emphasis in original.

36. Dow, *Schoolhouse Politics*, 51.

37. Brief report of a two-week conference held at Endicott House by the ACLS and ESI, 1962, 2, "Endicott House" folder, "Early Development" drawer, EDC.

38. Ibid., 3.

39. Ibid., 4, 5–6.

40. Ibid., 5–6.

41. Dow interview; Fenton interview.

42. Jack S. Goldstein, *A Different Sort of Time: The Life of Jerrold R. Zacharias, Scientist, Engineer, Educator* (Cambridge, MA: MIT Press); Fenton interview with Peter Dow, October 15, 1974, EDC.

43. Altree interview with Peter Dow, December 4, 1974, EDC papers.

44. Bruner, *In Search of Mind*, 190–191.

45. Evans Clinchy, "Description and Results of a First Experiment," August 24, 1962, "ESI pre-1965" folder, box 1, "Correspondence miscellaneous," Bruner Papers.

46. State Curriculum Commission, *Social Studies Framework for the Public Schools of California* (Sacramento, CA: California State Department of Education, 1962).

47. Joseph Turner to Ralph Tyler, September 18, 1962, attached to Turner to Jerome B. Wiesner, "Statement for President re: Education Panel," "Education-Title Folder, 1962," box 138, PSAC.

48. Jerome B. Wiesner to John F. Kennedy, September 19, 1962, "PSAC 1962" folder, box 86A, Department and Agencies, JFK/POF.

49. Jerome B. Wiesner, Untitled note, September 28, 1962, OST Microfilm Roll 38, Records of Government Agencies, Education, JFK.

50. "Social Sciences," attached to "Plans for Winter Conferences," Panel on Educational Research and Development, PSAC, "Education, Vol. 2" file, box 138, PSAC.

51. Joseph Turner to Malcolm Collier, November 8, 1962, "Education, Vol. 2" file, box 138, PSAC.

52. Ibid., "History."

53. Jerome B. Wiesner to John F. Kennedy, November 9, 1962, attached report, "Meeting Manpower Needs in Science and Technology: Report Number One: Graduate Training in Engineering, Mathematics, and

Physical Sciences," PSAC, December 12, 1962, "PSAC- Panel on Science and Technical Manpower (Gilliland) March & April, 1962" folder, box 78, NSF/ODSF.

54. Supplement to "Meeting Manpower Needs in Science and Technology," PSAC, November 19, 1962, Privileged, "Meeting Manpower Needs in Science and Technology" folder, box 86A, PSAC, Departments and Agencies, JFK/POF.

55. "National Intelligence Survey, USSR, Section 44, Manpower," 01 March, 1963, NIS Surveys, 1948–1965, box 125, NIS.

56. Staff memorandum, "Suggested Approach for Administration Education Proposals," December 5, 1962, "National Education Act of 1963" folder 1, box 2, Keppel Papers.

57. "'Don't Expect Fast Reform' Keppel Says," *Milwaukee Journal*, December 21, 1962, "Clippings" folder, box 2, Keppel Papers.

58. "Will It Be Education or Indoctrination," *The National Observer*, December 10, 1962, "Clippings" folder, box 2, Keppel Papers.

59. "New Push for Federal Aid," *Miles City Star*, December 14, 1962 (Montana), "Clippings" folder, box 2, Keppel Papers.

60. The White House Message on Education, January 29, 1963, 1–2, "P" folder, box 78, NSF/ODSF.

61. Ibid., 2–3.

62. Ibid., 8–10.

63. Ibid., 13.

64. Jerrold R. Zacharias to John E. Fogarty, Chairman, Subcommittee on Appropriations, "Statement of Jerrold R. Zacharias, Professor of Physics, MIT," March 14, 1963, "RS 2–4 Support of Cooperative Research" folder, box 108, USOE/OFCE.

65. Steve Hoenisch, "Education Policy of the Democratic Party," Encyclopedia of the Democratic and Republican Parties. (Accessed online at: http://www.criticisim.com/policy/democrats-education-policy.php.); Lyndon B. Johnson, "Remarks upon Signing the Higher Education Facilities Act," December 16, 1963, in John T. Woolley and Gerhard Peters, The American Presidency Project [online]. Santa Barbara, CA. (Accessed online at: http://www.presidency.ucsb.edu/ws/?pid=26387.)

66. Barbara Barksdale Clowse, *Brainpower for the Cold War: The Sputnik Crisis and the National Defense Education Act of 1958* (Westport, CT: Greenwood Press, 1981).

67. Gerald R. Smith, "Project Social Studies—A Report," *School Life* (reprint), July 19, 1963, "R S 2–3 Research Contracts," box 108, USOE/OFCE.

68. Ibid., 2–3. The conference included papers from Peter Odegard, Paul R. Hanna, I. James Quillen, Arno Bellack, and Ralph Tyler.

69. Ibid., 3.

70. Joseph J. Schwab, "The Concept of the Structure of a Discipline," *Educational Record* 43, no. 3 (July 1962): 197–205; Earl S. Johnson,

"The Concept of Structure in the Social Sciences," *Educational Record* 43, no. 3 (July 1962): 206–209.

71. See G. W. Ford and Lawrence Pugno, eds. *The Structure of Knowledge and the Curriculum* (Chicago: Rand McNally & Company, 1964).

CHAPTER 5

1. "Announcement for Project Social Studies," *SE* 26 (October 1962): 300.

2. Van R. Halsey, Jr. "American History: A New High School Course," *SE* 27, no. 5 (May 1963): 249–252.

3. Gerald R. Smith, "Project Social Studies—A Report," *SE* 27, no. 7 (November 1963): 257–259; also appeared in USOE's *School Life*, 42, no. 9 (July 1963): 25–27.

4. Edwin Fenton and John M. Good, "Project Social Studies: A Progress Report," *SE* 29, no. 4 (April 1965): 206–208.

5. John D. Haas, *Era of the New Social Studies* (Boulder, CO: Social Science Education Consortium, 1977).

6. Ibid., 55–57; Edwin Fenton, *The New Social Studies* (New York: Holt, Rinehart, and Winston, 1967); *Teaching the New Social Studies: An Inductive Approach,* ed. Edwin Fenton (New York: Holt, Rinehart, and Winston, 1966); Donald W. Oliver and James P. Shaver, *Teaching Public Issues in the High School* (Boston, MA: Houghton Mifflin, 1966); Byron G. Massialas and C. Benjamin Cox, *Inquiry in Social Studies* (New York: McGraw-Hill, 1966); Millard H. Clements, William R. Fielder, and Robert Tabachnick, *Social Study: Inquiry in Elementary Classrooms* (Indianapolis, IN: Bobbs-Merrill, 1966).

7. Haas, *Era of the New Social Studies*, 57–58. The USOE approved funding for 132 NDEA Institutes for the summer of 1968 to accommodate 5,200 participants. See "NDEA 1968 Institutes," *SE* 32, no. 2 (February 1968): 153–156.

8. Haas, *Era of the New Social Studies*, 64–66.

9. Ibid., 67.

10. Ibid., 69.

11. Norris M. Sanders and Marlin L. Tanck, "A Critical Appraisal of Twenty-Six National Social Studies Projects," *SE* 34, no. 4 (April, 1970): 383–388.

12. Ibid., 388, citing Edmund Traverso, materials supervisor for the Committee on the Study of History, and Jean Grambs, writing for the Education Development Corporation.

13. For an in-depth look at the projects and materials, along with selected lessons, see Scheurman and Evans, *Constructivism and the New Social Studies*.

14. Edwin P. Fenton, "Learning to Teach: The Brimmer and May School," unpublished memoir acquired from the author in May 2008.

15. Edwin P. Fenton, "Organizing a Project: The Advanced Placement Program," unpublished memoir, 2008, acquired from the author in May 2008.

16. Fenton, "Learning to Teach," 8.

17. Edwin Fenton, "Notes on a Proposed Sequence in History and the Social Sciences for the Program of Directed Studies," undated, folder 54, box 3, Fenton Papers.

18. Edwin Fenton, John Good, and Mitchell P. Lichtenberg, *Final Report: A High School Social Studies Curriculum for Able Students* (Washington: USOE Bureau of Research, 1969), 1–3. See also, Georgia P. Schneider, *Teachers Guide for an Experimental Unit: Selected Readings from Comparative Economic Systems* (New York: Holt, Rinehart, and Winston, 1967).

19. Fenton, *Final Report*.

20. Interview with Ted Fenton conducted by the author, May 18, 2008, South Wellfleet, MA.

21. Stanley Kleiman, "Carnegie-Mellon University Slow Learner Project," *SE* 36, no. 7 (November, 1972): 733–734. Fenton told me that *The Americans* sold better than the Holt series; Fenton interview.

22. Edwin Fenton, "The New Social Studies Reconsidered," in *The New Social Studies: Analysis of Theory and Materials,* ed. Mark M. Krug, John B. Poster, and William B. Gillies III (Itasca, IL: F. E. Peacock Publishers, 1970), 177.

23. Bruner, *In Search of Mind*, 191; Dow later commented that Bruner's book was the only thing he read that "made sense," and he "invited" himself to join the project; interview with Peter Dow conducted by the author, May 19, 2008.

24. Sanders and Tanck, "A Critical Appraisal," 389.

25. Charles Laird, *Through These Eyes* (Watertown, MA: Documentary Educational Resources, 2003), DVD. See also, Jay Ruby, "Anthropology as Subversive Art: A Review of *Through These Eyes*," *American Anthropologist* 107, no. 4 (2005): 684–693.

26. Curriculum Development Associates, *MAN: A COURSE OF STUDY* (Washington, D.C.: Curriculum Development Associates, 1971), 2, EDC Papers. For a thorough and engaging insiders account of the MACOS story, see Dow, *Schoolhouse Politics*.

27. Curriculum Development Associates, *Man: A Course of Study*, 2–3; Jerome Bruner interview in Laird, *Through These Eyes*. Bruner quotes in the publication cited above derive from *The Process of Education*; interview with Peter Dow, May 18, 2008.

28. Asen Balikci interview in Laird, *Through These Eyes*.

29. Peter Dow interview in Laird, *Through These Eyes*.

30. Jerome S. Bruner, *In Search of Mind: Essays in Autobiography* (New York: Harper and Row, 1983), 193.

31. Irving Morrissett, "Curriculum Information Network (CIN) First Report: Evaluation of Curriculum Materials" *SE* 37, no. 7 (November 1973): 665–668; Irving Morrissett, "CIN Third Report: Ratings of

24 Social Studies Materials," *SE* 39, no. 2 (February 1975): 96–99. The materials were rated somewhat lower in the 1975 Report, perhaps because controversy and criticism of MACOS had reached a high point and was beginning to have some influence on survey results. See Irving Morrissett, "CIN Fifth Report: Ratings of 21 Social Studies Materials," *SE* 39, no. 7 (November-December 1975): 510–513. Survey respondents included teachers, department chairs, administrators, and university personnel.

32. Robert B. Pratt, "Educational Development Center, Inc., Man: A Course of Study," *SE* 36, no. 7 (November 1972): 744.

33. Laird, *Through These Eyes.*

34. Donald W. Oliver, "The Selection of Content in the Social Studies," *HER* 27, no. 4 (Fall 1957): 291–292.

35. Ibid., 292–299.

36. Fred M. Newmann, "The Analysis of Public Controversy: New Focus for Social Studies," *School Review* 73, no. 4 (1965) as reprinted in Krug, *The New Social Studies*, 221–222.

37. Oliver and Shaver, *Teaching Public Issues in the High School* (Boston: Houghton Mifflin, 1966); Krug, *The New Social Studies*, 228–229; Gunnar Myrdal, *An American Dilemma* (New York: Harper & Row, 1944).

38. Donald W. Oliver and James P. Shaver, *Teaching Public Issues in the High School* (Boston, MA: Houghton Mifflin), 239.

39. Malcolm Levin, Fred M. Newmann, and Donald W. Oliver, *Final Report: A Law and Social Science Curriculum Based on the Analysis of Public Issues* (Washington, D.C.: Bureau of Research, U.S. Office of Education, 1969), 40–41.

40. Ibid.; Oliver and Shaver, *Teaching Public Issues*, 115.

41. Levin, Newmann, and Oliver, *Final Report*, 45–46.

42. Ibid., 41–49.

43. Donald W. Oliver, Fred M. Newmann, and Mary Jo Bane, *Guide to Teaching* (Middletown, CT: Xerox Publishing Company, 1967), 3.

44. Donald W. Oliver and Fred M. Newmann, *The New Deal: Free Enterprise and Public Planning* (Public Issues Series/Harvard Social Studies Project) (Middletown, CT: Xerox Publishing, 1968).

45. Morrissett, "CIN Reports."

46. Telephone interview with Fred M. Newmann by Geoff Scheurman and Ronald W. Evans, 2007.

47. Thomas J. Switzer, Malcolm A. Lowther, William M. Hanna, and Ralph D. Kidder, "Dissemination and Implementation of Social Studies Project Materials," Paper presented at the Annual Meeting of the National Council for the Social Studies (Chicago, IL: November, 1974).

48. See High School Geography Project and Sociological Resources for the Social Studies, *Experiences in Inquiry: HSGP and SRSS* (Boston, MA: Allyn and Bacon, 1974). This compilation was used as a textual source in the social studies methods course I took as a preservice teacher from

Daniel Selakovich at Oklahoma State University in the spring semester of 1976. My team taught a sample lesson from the book titled "The Eye of Childhood." I knew something was up when my peers gave us a spontaneous ovation following the lesson. I have copies of at least two editions of the Fenton textbook for high school American history purchased at used bookstores, a sign that they were widely distributed.

49. Morrissett, "CIN Reports."
50. Switzer et al. "Dissemination and Implementation of Project Social Studies Materials."
51. Barbara Barksdale Clowse, *Brainpower for the Cold War: The Sputnik Crisis and the National Defense Education Act of 1958* (Westport, CT: Greenwood Press, 1981), 159.
52. See Rudolph, *Scientists in the Classroom*; Haas, *The Era of the New Social Studies*; Hertzberg, *Social Studies Reform*; and John Rossi, "Uniformity, Diversity, and the 'New Social Studies,'" *The Social Studies* 83 (1: 1992): 41.
53. Paulo Freire, *Pedagogy of the Oppressed* (New York: Continuum, 1970).
54. Stephen J. Thornton, "Teacher as Curricular Instructional Gatekeeper in Social Studies," in *Handbook of Research on Social Studies Teaching and Learning*, ed. James P. Shaver (New York: Macmillan, 1991).
55. Henry Giroux, *Teachers as Intellectuals: Toward a Critical Pedagogy of Learning* (Granby, MA: Bergin and Garvey, 1988).
56. See especially, Oliver and Shaver, *Teaching Public Issues in the High School.*
57. Mark M. Krug, John B. Poster, and William B. Gillies III, *The New Social Studies: Analysis of Theory and Practice* (Itasca, IL: F. E. Peacock Publishers, 1970).
58. Dorothy McClure Fraser, ed., "Reviewing Curricular Materials," *SE* 31 (April 1967: 307–312, 325–332.

CHAPTER 6

1. Donald W. Robinson, "Ferment in the Social Studies," *SE* 27, no. 7 (November 1963): 360–364, 410.
2. James M. Becker, "Prospect for Change in the Social Studies," *SE* 29, no. 1 (January 1965): 20–22.
3. These comments are based on an impressionistic review of the contents of *SE* and other sources. The early to middle 1970s were probably the peak for such innovation.
4. Lewis Paul Todd, "The Seamless Web," *SE* 27, no. 4 (April 1963): 181, 204.
5. Shirley H. Engle, "Decision Making: The Heart of Social Studies Instruction," *SE* 24, no. 7 (November 1960): 301–306.
6. Shirley H. Engle, "Thoughts in Regard to Revision," *SE* 27, no. 4 (April, 1963): 182.

7. Ibid., 184.

8. Byron G. Massialas, "Revising the Social Studies: An Inquiry-Centered Approach," *SE* 27, no. 4 (April 1963): 185–189.

9. Lawrence E. Metcalf, "Some Guidelines for Changing Social Studies Education," *SE* 27, no. 4 (April 1963): 197–201.

10. Paul R. Hanna, "Revising the Social Studies: What Is Needed?" *SE* 27, no. 4 (April 1963): 190–196.

11. Samuel P. McCutchen, "A Discipline for the Social Studies," *SE* 27, no. 2 (February 1963): 61–65.

12. William Cartwright to Samuel McCutchen, June 17, 1962, folder 8, box 4, Curriculum Committee Records, Series VII, NCSS.

13. Samuel McCutchen to Jack Allen, July 9, 1962, folder 8, box 4, Committee Records, Series VII, NCSS.

14. Erling M. Hunt, "Criterial For As (*sic*) Adequate Social Studies Curriculum," 1962, folder 8, box 4, Curriculum Committee Records, Series VII, NCSS.

15. "Reactions to the Reports on Project Social Studies," *SE* 29, no. 6 (October 1965): 356–360.

16. Krug cites Fred M. Newmann, "The Analysis of Public Controversy—New Focus on Social Studies," *The School Review* 73, no. 4 (Winter 1965): 413.

17. Mark M. Krug, "Bruner's New Social Studies: A Critique," *SE* 30 (October 1966): 400–406. At least one educational psychologist, David Ausubel, probably would have supported Krug's critique. While he believed that discovery was important, he viewed Bruner's emphasis on it as "unrealistic" because it left too little room for reception learning and assimilation of subject matter via direct instruction. See David Olson, *Jerome Bruner: The Cognitive Revolution in Educational Theory* (New York: Continuum, 2007), 65.

18. Mark F. Emerson, "Letters: Krug's Critique," *SE* 31, no. 2 (February 1967): 124.

19. Richard H. Brown, "History and the New Social Studies," *SR*, October 1966, 3–5. Another historian, Mary Alice White, expressed enthusiasm but harbored doubts that students could really "think as historians unless they have the training of historians." See Olson, *Jerome Bruner*, 65.

20. Gerald Leinwand, "Queries on Inquiry in the Social Studies," *SE* 30, no. 6 (October 1966): 412–414.

21. Robert E. Jewett and Robert B. Ribble, "Curriculum Improvement and Teacher Status," *SE* 31, no. 1 (January 1967): 20–22.

22. Jack Allen, "Assessing Recent Developments in the Social Studies," *SE* 31, no. 2 (February 1967): 99–103; Stephanie G. Edgerton, "'Learning' by Induction," *SE* 31, no. 5 (May, 1967): 376.

23. James P. Shaver, "Social Studies: The Need for Redefinition," *SE* 31, no. 7 (November 1967): 588–592, 596.

24. Fred M. Newmann, "Questioning the Place of Social Science Disciplines in Education," *SE* 31, no. 7 (November 1967): 593–596.

25. Newmann, "The Analysis of Public Controversy," 215–216 in Krug.

26. Ibid., 218–219.

27. Ibid., 219–220.

28. Ibid., 220–221.

29. Donald W. Oliver and James P. Shaver, *Teaching Public Issues in the High School* (Boston, MA: Houghton Mifflin), 230–232.

30. Ibid., 233.

31. Marion Brady, "The Key Concept," *SE* 31, no. 7 (November 1967): 601–604; Ivor Kraft, "Social Studies: The Search for Meaning," *SE* 31, no. 7 (November, 1967), 597–600.

32. Albert S. Anthony, "The Role of Objectives in the 'New History'," *SE* 31, no. 7 (November 1967): 574–580.

33. Leonard S. Kenworthy, "Changing the Social Studies Curriculum: Some Guidelines and a Proposal," *SE* 32, no. 5 (May 1968): 481–486.

34. William W. Goetz, "The 'New' Social Studies: Boon or Bust?" *Clearing House* 44, no. 7 (1970): 404–405.

35. Ibid., 405–406.

36. Martin LaForse, "The New Social Studies Mania: Pause for Thought," *TSS* 61, no. 7 (December 1970): 325–328.

37. Jules Henry, "Docility, of Giving Teacher What She Wants," *The Journal of Social Issues* 11, no. 2 (1955): 33–41.

38. LaForse, "The New Social Studies Mania."

39. Jerome Bruner, "The Process of Education Revisited," *PDK* 53, no. 1 (September 1971): 19.

40. Ibid., 21.

41. Joseph V. Ellis, "A Philosophical Analysis of the 'New' Social Studies," *TSS* 62, no. 5 (October 1971): 195–203.

42. Terry Northrup, "Philosophical Analysis of the "New" Social Studies—A Response," *TSS* 63, no. 7 (December 1972): 315–317. Nortrup's analysis was drawn from Terry Northrup, "Structure-Discovery and Reflective Inquiry: An Exploration of Two Positions in Social Studies" (Doctoral dissertation, Purdue University, 1971).

43. Robert D. Barr, James L. Barth, and S. Samuel Shermis, *Defining Social Studies* (Washington, D.C.: National Council for the Social Studies, 1977).

44. June R. Chapin and Richard E. Gross, "Making Sense out of the Terminology of the New Social Studies," *TSS* 63, no. 4 (April 1972): 147–148.

45. Ibid., 149–151.

46. Ibid., 151–154.

47. Richard F. Newton, "Induction in the New Social Studies," *TRSE* 1, no. 1 (1973): 30, 41. See also, Richard F. Newton, "An Epistemological Critique of the New Social Studies" (Doctoral dissertation, Michigan State University, 1970).

48. Ibid., 42–44.

49. Ibid., 44–45.

50. Ibid., 46–48.

51. Ibid., 48–54.

52. Richard F. Newton, "What's New About the New Social Studies," *TSS* 63, no. 4 (April 1972): 161–162.

CHAPTER 7

1. Thomas S. Popkewitz, "Latent Values in Discipline-centered Curriculum," Paper presented at the annual meeting of the National Council for the Social Studies, Atlanta, GA, November, 1975, 1; later published as Thomas S. Popkewitz, "The Latent Values of the Discipline Centered Curriculum," *TRSE* 5, no. 1 (April 1977): 41–60.

2. Ibid., 4–10.

3. Ibid., 10–16.

4. Ibid., 16–19.

5. Ibid., 19–20.

6. Ibid., 20; Paulo Freire, *Pedagogy of the Oppressed* (New York: Continuum, 1970), 60.

7. Michael W. Apple, "The Hidden Curriculum and the Nature of Conflict," *Interchange* 2, no. 4 (1971): 27–33.

8. Ibid., 34.

9. Ibid., 35.

10. Ibid., 35.

11. Ibid., 37–38.

12. Jonathan Kozol, *The Night Is Dark and I Am Far from Home* (Boston: Houghton Mifflin, 1975), 7, 13.

13. Ibid., 95–96, 123, 125–130.

14. Ibid., 139.

15. Ibid., 146, 149, 158–159, 168.

16. Ibid., 185.

17. Ibid., 168.

18. Frank L. Ryan, "Implementing the Hidden Curriculum of the Social Studies," *SE* 37, no. 7 (November 1973): 679–680.

19. Ibid., 680–681.

20. James Hoetker and William P. Ahlbrand, Jr., "The Persistence of the Recitation," *American Educational Research Journal* 6, no. 2 (1969): 145–167.

21. Edwin P. Fenton, *The New Social Studies* (New York: Holt, Rinehart, and Winston, 1967), 134.

CONCLUSION

1. Stacey Bredhoff, *American Originals* (Seattle: University of Washington Press, 2001), 108–109; Williams, *The Tragedy of American Diplomacy* (Cleveland, OH: World Publishing Company, 1959).

2. See, for example, "The Challenge of the Atomic Bomb," "Sovereignty in the Atomic Age," and "I'm a Frightened Man," in Atomic Information Committee folder, 1946, box 17, Series 4C, Director's Files, NCSS.

3. James R. Killian, *Sputnik, Scientists, and Eisenhower: A Memoir of the First Special Assistant to the President for Science and Technology* (Cambridge, MA: MIT Press, 1977).

4. Jerome S. Bruner, *The Process of Education;* Jack S. Goldstein, *A Different Sort of Time: The Life of Jerrold R. Zacharias, Scientist, Engineer, Educator* (Cambridge, MA: MIT Press).

5. Bruner memo to Working Group on the Apparatus of Teaching, Woods Hole, September 1959, WH; John L. Rudolph, *Scientists in the Classroom: The Cold War Reconstruction of American Science Education* (New York: Palgrave, 2002); Simpson, *Universities and Empire: Money and Politics in the Social Sciences during the Cold War*, ed. Christopher Simpson (New York: New Press, 1998).

6. "Report: Conference of Social Studies and Humanities Curriculum Program," 1962, "Endicott House" folder, "Early Development" drawer, EDC.

7. Scheurman and Evans, *Constructivism and the New Social Studies.*

8. David Berliner and Bruce J. Biddle, *The Manufactured Crisis: Myths, Fraud, and the Attack on America's Public Schooling* (Reading, MA: Addison Wesley, 1995).

9. Larry Cuban, *The Blackboard and the Bottom Line: Why Schools Can't Be Businesses* (Cambridge, MA: Harvard University Press, 2004).

10. David Tyack and Larry Cuban, *Tinkering Toward Utopia: A Century of Public School Reform* (Cambridge, MA: Harvard University Press, 1995); Christopher R. Leahey, *Whitewashing War: Historical Myth, Corporate Textbooks, and Possibilities for Democratic Education* (New York: Teachers College Press, 2010); Diana Hess, *Controversy in the Classroom: The Democratic Power of Discussion* (New York: Routledge, 2009).

11. See, for example, David Hicks, Stephanie van Hover, Jeremy Stoddard, and Milissa Lisanti, "From a Roar to a Murmur: Virginia's History and Social Science Standards, 1995 to 2009," *TRSE* 38, no. 1 (Winter 2010): 82–115.

12. Rudolph, *Scientists in the Classroom;* Needell, "Project Troy and the Cold War Annexation of the Social Sciences," in *Universities and Empire.*

13. David Olson, *Jerome Bruner: The Cognitive Revolution in Educational Theory* (New York: Continuum, 2007).

14. Jerome S. Bruner, *In Search of Mind: Essays in Autobiography* (New York: Harper and Row, 1983), 195; Bruner interview.

INDEX